3 9082 12730 9253

W9-AQS-923

JS/16

THE FURNITURE BIBLE

THE FURNITURE BIBLE

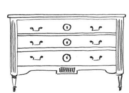

CHRISTOPHE POURNY

with JEN RENZI

foreword by MARTHA STEWART

photographs by JAMES WADE
illustrations by CHRISTOPHE POURNY

ARTISAN

684.104
P

ROYAL OAK
DEC 1 1 2014
PUBLIC LIBRARY

To my mother, Arlette Pourny

Copyright © 2014 by Christophe Pourny and Jen Renzi
Photographs copyright © 2014 by James Wade, except for photographs
on pages 52, courtesy of Edelman Leather; 59, courtesy of Maison Gerard;
and 89, courtesy of Sotheby's Inc. © 2013
Illustrations copyright © 2014 by Christophe Pourny
Foreword copyright © 2014 by Martha Stewart

All rights reserved. No portion of this book may be reproduced—
mechanically, electronically, or by any other means, including
photocopying—without written permission of the publisher.

Artisan books are available at special discounts when purchased in bulk for premiums
and sales promotions as well as for fund-raising or educational use. Special editions or
book excerpts also can be created to specification. For details, contact the Special Sales
Director at the address below, or send an e-mail to specialmarkets@workman.com.

Published by Artisan
A division of Workman Publishing Company, Inc.
225 Varick Street
New York, NY 10014-4381
artisanbooks.com

Published simultaneously in Canada by Thomas Allen & Son, Limited.

Library of Congress Cataloging-in-Publication Data
Pourny, Christophe, author.
 The furniture bible / Christophe Pourny with Jen Renzi ;
 foreword by Martha Stewart.
  pages cm
 Includes bibliographical references and index.
 ISBN 978-1-57965-535-8
 1. Furniture finishing—Amateurs' manuals. I. Renzi, Jen. II. Title.
 TT199.4.P68 2014
 684.1'043—dc23   2014004628

Design by Bloom & Co. Design

Printed in Singapore
First printing, September 2014
10 9 8 7 6 5 4 3 2 1

3 9082 12730 9253

CONTENTS

FOREWORD

Christophe Pourny restores, transforms, fixes, preserves, and teaches in this, his first book, *The Furniture Bible*. He also encourages us, the homeowner, the decorator, the collector, the furniture buyer, to appreciate, to discriminate, to determine, and to choose furniture that might have a place in our life, a spot in our home, a future as a collectible or as an investment.

This is a very useful and important book for anyone who owns furniture—antique, modern, or new—or anyone who plans to fix or restore it. It is encyclopedic in its scope, and unusual in its clear, straightforward, and understandable approach to all aspects of a very large subject matter. Christophe is extremely knowledgeable, and with extreme clarity he has demystified a subject heretofore covered only in part in many instructional manuals or much simpler DIY books. I, personally, welcome this book into my library, and I know it will be used not only by me, but by anyone who dusts and polishes, repairs, or restores.

Chapter by chapter, the history of furniture—its construction, its components, its finishes, and its decoration—is written about and illustrated with photographs and charming drawings. The chapter on how furniture is made teaches us how and why certain woods are used for the bottoms of drawers, for the fronts of chests, and for the legs of chairs. The Finishing School chapter is extremely valuable in helping us understand the materials and the methods by which furniture makers have evolved the various surfaces we lay our hands upon or dust with a soft rag. The chapter on techniques is illuminating in its references and step-by-step instructions, not just about the woods employed in a piece of furniture, but also for the metals and other materials used in the beautification of certain pieces, or for practical utilitarian reasons.

Congratulations, Christophe Pourny! You have created for all of us, laymen, artisans, and collectors alike, a compelling reason to look at our own furniture in a new way, to appreciate fine craftsmanship and understand what is good, what is better, and what is best. And, above all, you have given us the impetus to repair, restore, and preserve the legacy of past makers so that those in the future will have great examples with which they can be inspired.

—Martha Stewart, 2014

"Every artisan has in his brush, his pencil, his tool, not only what links his task to his mind but also to his memory. A move that may appear spontaneous is actually ten years in the making, thirty maybe. In art, everything is knowledge, labor, patience and what comes in an instant has taken years to blossom."

—French architect Fernand Pouillon (1912–1986)

INTRODUCTION

Coming from a long line of artisans, I was weaned on the antiques business. When I was five, my parents opened their first antiques store, in the Var region of the South of France. At that time, it was still possible to buy and resell the contents of an entire castle. Growing up in the village of Fayence, my sisters and I performed puppet shows amid the giant carved armoires residing in the courtyard of our father's atelier. His studio was in an 18th-century stone barn built to house sheep on their annual pilgrimage to higher feeding grounds, up in the Alps. Where livestock once snoozed, furniture pieces of every style and period were piled atop one another, arranged in pyramids of wood, dark and glowing like an amber fire. The interior was very dark, the windows small—natural protection against the Provençal sun— but the space was also beautiful and magical, perfumed with beeswax and the musk of centuries of use.

My father in the garden of his Var-region atelier

I trained under my father from an early age, first fetching tools and stains for his artisans and finally learning to use these items to cut, join, sand, and so on. More than once I swore I'd never touch another piece of furniture! (Using slivers of glass to strip off old varnish will do that to a person.) But I eventually succumbed to my father's love of wood. I discovered how various species responded differently to our care. I learned to evaluate trueness, texture, and grain even as I climbed the olive trees around our house. In a language passed down through the generations, my father taught me that oak was good for certain applications and elm for others, that Cuban mahogany was very rare and French walnut very versatile. I came to understand that wood is the craftsman's medium, like canvas for an artist or paper for a writer, and that one piece can be coaxed into an endless variety of colors, textures, and shapes. Eventually, I discovered how these finishes interacted with the lines of furniture to create beauty—and how this beauty informs the way we feel about a table, a room, or even a house.

After university, I moved to Paris to apprentice with my uncle, Pierre Madel, who had a shop on rue Jacob. He was a legend, and his loyal clientele extended from Saint-Tropez to San Francisco. There I met all the artisans and art dealers who made Paris the heart of the antiques world. It was easy to get swept up in the glamour and romance of it all. Nevertheless, I became restless, and I felt New York calling my name. I moved to Manhattan in my late twenties, eventually opening my own studio in Brooklyn. My days are now spent regilding Louis XVI bergères, refreshing the French polish of 18th-century dining tables, or working magic on timeworn straw marquetry surfaces. Restoring rare antiques to their original condition in the same manner that my father instructed me back in Fayence became my life in New York. Just as important, I also transform less distinguished pieces into stunners via a completely new and often unexpected finish. My passion for and deep understanding of historical methods have taught me how to take creative license when a piece merits it.

Me and my sisters. Our "playground" included old cars and motorbikes.

Sadly, these techniques that are my lifeblood are also a dying art these days, in the era of spray-on one-coat varnishes. What happened to traditional methods of wood finishing, the techniques of my father and grandfather and other highly specialized ateliers? What used to be common knowledge is now the purview of a few aging artisans, surrounded in their studios by bottles labeled with names as exotic as Persian perfumes. Even experienced woodworkers may not know the secret behind the perfect wax finish unless their library is filled with dusty early-19th-century French guides. So little of this old-world knowledge ever crossed the pond in the first place, and scholastic programs that teach refinishing are an endangered breed. One of the last and best, at New York's Fashion Institute of Technology, was recently canceled.

Ironically, this body of knowledge is also being threatened by a misguided fetishization of the old at the expense of all else. Cultural phenomena like *Antiques Roadshow* may have opened viewers' eyes to the potential value of quirky heirlooms, but they've also done a disservice by making people unjustifiably fearful of having pieces refinished and compromising their worth. But "original finish" is not always synonymous with charm, and what many people *mistake* for the original may actually be a more recent (and shoddy) redo. Do not be a slave to history: I promise you that Grandma's blah, dark-stained oak credenza will look so much sexier with a high-contrast ceruse finish! As long as you embrace traditional, natural mediums and methods, you won't damage the piece—and your work will be reversible.

Don't let intimidation keep you from educating yourself. Take a cue from foodie culture. Not being a professional chef—or even adept in the kitchen—doesn't stop most of us from buying shelves full of cookbooks for edification, guidance, or pure inspiration. More to the point: Today's hottest chefs are renowned not for being tied to revered cooking techniques, but for modernizing them. Caffeine enthusiasts, too, are reviving and tweaking old-school methods. Those who have no intention of buying a Chemex still like being well-versed enough to ask their barista for a cold pour-over.

In writing this book, I hope to make people as passionate about traditional wood finishing as they are about cooking, or drinking artisanal whiskey, or buying

My first on-site project—all by myself!

furniture. I set out to demystify this sometimes-esoteric material, to pull the veil of obscurity from these historical wood-finishing techniques and explain them in everyday terms. To understand furniture finishing, you first need to understand furniture: how it's constructed, how to recognize wood varieties and design styles, how veneers and ormolu are affixed. You will learn how to tell a Louis XIV chair from a Louis XV one, identify assorted chaises longues, distinguish between different woods, reupholster a stool, set up a workshop, fix a cracked table leg, and even care for vintage leather surfaces. If you are a woodworker, I will teach you the full spectrum of finishing techniques and how to execute a flawless French polish, refine your skills, apply new finishes, and better organize your atelier. (I also divulge shortcuts; I mean, how could I not?) Whether you want to uncover the history of ceruse or execute it yourself, you'll come away inspired and informed.

Of course, everyone loves a good transformation. Thus the heart of the book is an accessible primer on my favorite effects—ceruse, *ciré rempli*, and water gilding among them—with step-by-step how-tos. Even if you have no intention of ever refinishing a piece yourself, you can use this as a reference book to figure out possible colors, textures, coverings, special accents, and decorative effects you can hire a refinisher to execute on your behalf (and ask for using the insider lingo).

Once you see how easy some of these techniques are, you just might be inspired to give them a try after all! However obscure and specialized they have become, these methods require neither expensive power tools nor the concoctive ability of an industrial chemist. Instead, traditional restoration and refinishing techniques rely on three mediums—oil, wax, and alcohol—and all are worked by hand. Moreover, you don't even need a studio or workshop: Many can be done in your kitchen, with just a drop cloth below.

My father—ever the buffoon—on Saint-Tropez's antiques row

There are myriad benefits of these techniques besides period appropriateness. They are better for your furniture—and for the earth. That's no small consideration at a time when we value recycling, material longevity, and ecological choices. Since World War II, the development of chemicals and mass-marketed consumer products has made toxic machine-sprayed wood finishes the norm. Offered in light, medium, or dark, these industrial finishes have been touted as the most protective and economical option. But they are a fickle fix, at best, and usually irreversible. In contrast, traditional finishes are thinner and slower to dry, but they penetrate the wood to become *part* of the piece—transforming it rather than simply coating it—and the act of hand application polishes the wood during the finishing process. Multiple thin coats allow adjustments, combinations, the addition of colors, and evolving effects that age into the rich look of true artisan furniture. Inevitably, every finish wears off. But while the modern mass-produced versions crack, peel, and become cloudy, and then have to be completely removed, old-world finishes tend to fade more gently and encourage your older self, your children, or your children's children to buff and sand them down or to reapply oil, wax, or lacquer to reinvigorate the piece for another generation.

Read on for my comprehensive guide to restoring, transforming, fixing, preserving, and learning about your favorite possessions—whether family heirlooms or funky flea-market finds. In each piece I refinish in my studio, I see the grain, the lines, and its potential beauty. This book will teach you to find that beauty on your own and to draw it out via the clean, simple techniques established over hundreds of years in the studios of the great French ateliers. Read the book from start to finish, or dip into sections on particular topics or techniques that interest you. Whether you're a hobby woodworker or a DIY crafter, a furniture enthusiast or a neophyte, you'll find plenty of inspiration and readable, practical advice.

Christophe Pourny

PART 1

MEET YOUR FURNITURE

Before diving into the minutiae and methodology of finishing techniques, it's important to get acquainted with your furniture: Connoisseurship is the foundation of good technique! First, I'll walk you through a history of furniture styles that you're likely to come across in your collecting and refinishing efforts. Then, I'll show you how furniture is constructed, from cutting tree trunks to slipping on casters. Also explained are some of the materials besides wood you may encounter on your antiques, with tips on how to rejuvenate and restore them (hint: call the pros). Last, I'll take you for a tour of my favorite deal-hunting haunts, and divulge what I respond to in a piece. So you'll know how to score, too.

AN ABBREVIATED HISTORY *of* FURNITURE

Although furniture dates back to at least the Neolithic period, for our purposes, it makes sense to start with the Middle Ages. That's because anything that predates the medieval period is considered an antiquity and belongs to museums, whereas some simple medieval furnishings are still available on the market today—and not always outrageously priced. (Nevertheless, everything important you need to know about Greek, Roman, or Egyptian furniture design is discussed in the context of later revivals.) In addition, culture in the Western world decayed drastically during the so-called Dark Ages, the unstable feudal era following the fall of the Roman Empire; art and literacy were kept alive only by the monasteries. From this tabula rasa, furniture evolved from simple, archetypal forms addressing only the most bare-bones needs to increasingly decorative pieces that reflected shifting political powers and the domestication—and eventual democratization—of society.

Renaissance Cassone

The focus of the brief history that follows is on identifying various period styles and movements. Note that the further back in time you go, the more likely it is that any well-built pieces of furniture that have survived into the 21st century were made for royalty, the highest levels of the clergy, or the richest nobility, so the discussion and samples here obviously don't represent all social strata. Let's start at the beginning, shall we?

BACK TO BASICS: EARLY MEDIEVAL PERIOD
Roughly 5th to Early 12th Centuries

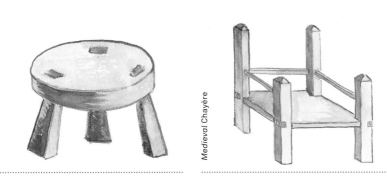

Medieval Stool

Medieval Chayère

Medieval society was one of dominators and the dominated—a few warlords, their military, and a sea of serfs. Furniture was very limited and made on the spot with local resources, since there was little trade or commerce to speak of. Accordingly, everything was elemental. Furniture-making techniques were primitive: wood boards assembled with coarse nails, rough mortises and tenons, the use of animal hides, woven marsh grasses, and crude iron structures. Spartan lifestyles meant few furnishings were needed—a bench, some stools, trestles and boards that could be reconfigured for multiple uses (tables, cooking surfaces). Beds were usually no more than a pile of hay on the floor or horsehair covered in coarse fabric and set on an arrangement of boards and low trestles. The main piece was the chest or coffer for securing one's few possessions.

THE LOOK: Boxy and purely functional; very limited ornamentation.

WHAT YOU'LL FIND: Trunks, mainly. Also practical trestles and benches.

THE SPACE: People lived in one big room where gathering, eating, and sleeping took place, so all furnishings had to multitask—and be knocked down or pushed up against the walls when not in use.

A RETURN TO STABILITY: FROM ROMANESQUE TO GOTHIC

Late 12th Century to 1500

Cathedral Chair

Gothic Stool

As civilization began to flourish again, furniture became more functional and permanent. Legs were used to lift pieces off the ground, chests boasted feet and more elaborate iron hardware, curtains enfolded beds to block drafts, benches and stools sprouted backs and arms. Designs also grew more decorative. Simple ornamentation appeared, starting with geometric carvings—details that endured on rustic furniture in the countryside until almost the 19th century. By the late 1400s, furniture had diversified even more; every piece had a precise function, and embellishments had become more sophisticated.

THE LOOK: As Romanesque shifts to Gothic, pieces are characterized by dark, glowing wood; arched forms; architectural ornamentation; grotesque figures.

WHAT YOU'LL FIND: High-backed cathedral chairs; two-part dressers; heavily carved beds and chests.

THE SPACE: With cultural advancement and social evolution came the great divide: in homes of the nobility, a wall to separate living and sleeping areas— more separation between the master and the entourage! The bed, no longer needing to be stowed away during the daytime, became more permanent and solid.

16th Century

Renaissance Chaise à Bras

Renaissance Scabelle

As the Renaissance thrived, relative peace and comfort allowed for a revival of art and education; at the same time, a growing bourgeoisie was developing. Ancient Rome and Greece once again became objects of study and inspiration, and classical motifs were incorporated into Renaissance architecture, visual arts, and furniture. Popular adornments included fluted columns, capitals, balusters, floral carvings, finials, profiles, and moldings. High-relief carvings brought about a softer, three-dimensional feel, and paint and veneer flourished. Drawers replaced the coffer's lift-up top; this innovation allowed the chest to evolve into a full-blown dresser.

Meanwhile, among the aristocracy, status and style played an increasingly important role. The Renaissance prince had more leisure time, and his function was more social. Noblemen became patrons of the arts (formerly the purview of the church) and beauty no longer had to serve a purely sacred function. The mercantile class prospered and aspired to luxury while, especially in northern Europe, becoming patrons of the arts, too.

During this period, every European king developed a style reflective of his sensibility. Prosperity and commerce created more porous frontiers, allowing design influences to travel from kingdom to kingdom.

THE LOOK: Lighter and more comfortable furniture. Aesthetics became as important as function.

WHERE IT'S FROM: Italy was the birthplace of the Renaissance, but other countries initiated their own designs and spread them across Europe. Furniture styles in different countries evolved in parallel.

WHAT YOU'LL FIND: Sophisticated ornamentation including floral motifs, Roman and Greek patterns, and architectural details.

THE SPACE: While medieval castles were basically fortified military compounds, and thus dark and closed in, Renaissance versions were luxurious residences of a nobility who wanted to enjoy space, light, and volume.

IN TRANSITION: LOUIS XIII
Early 17th Century

Louis XIII Armchair

Louis XIII Chair

This transitional aesthetic was still quite Italianate, but Flemish and Dutch baroque influences also spread across France, Germany, and England, as well as to America, via the pilgrims.

In the 16th century, Francis I lured the best Italian and European artists to France, but styles took time to meld and gel before synthesizing into the unique national style of French classicism (which later reached full flower under the aegis of Louis XIV). Under Louis XIII, the look was austere with simple lines, and furnishings became larger and darker. For the richest *demeures*, pieces were typically crafted of oak or ebony; the word *ébéniste* (French for *cabinetmaker*) was coined at this time. And the armoire was born!

THE LOOK: Austere, simple, and chunky, with architectural detailing. Balusters, turned wood, and diamond patterns were common.

WHERE IT'S FROM: France, the Netherlands, and Spain.

WHAT YOU'LL FIND: Large cabinets; armoires; Cordoba-leather-upholstered seats.

THE SPACE: Larger (and darker) classic and formal rooms; increasing use of upholstered walls, tapestry, fabric, and leather to match the furniture.

ABSOLUTE POWER: LOUIS XIV
1643–1715

Louis XIV Formal Armchair

Louis XIV Pliant (Folding Stool)

In contrast to many of its neighbors, 17th-century France was a relatively stable and centralized regime. There were only two rulers in this century, Louis XIII and his long-reigning son, Louis XIV. These monarchs were the first to systematically use furniture design as a political statement, an instrument of protocol and social presentation. Working with his court of artisans, each of these kings developed and propagated his style. Meanwhile, social and professional rules allowed a concerted and rigorous evolution of style and techniques.

From the mid-17th century, Louis XIV, the Sun King, imposed his grand and solemn aesthetic, replete with architecturally inspired ornamentation and luxurious decorations, including veneers, rich fabrics, and precious materials like gold, exotic woods, and stone. The aesthetic of the courts became so rich and formal that it distinguished itself from that of the other social classes and even the provinces, where royal style was interpreted in a more pared-back, simplified form.

THE LOOK: Massive and heavy, with baroque lines—very masculine. Imposing and architectural; think chair and table legs in the form of balusters.

WHERE IT'S FROM: France. The 17th century was a coveting culture, and other courts realized there was political profit in copying France, although creative liberties were taken by each court to assert its originality.

WHAT YOU'LL FIND: Regal armchairs; rich three-drawer chests; canopy beds; heavy curtains and upholstery; gold and silver ornament.

THE SPACE: The palace or noble residence became a succession of rooms designed to uphold protocol and support official life, separated from another suite of rooms for private use.

Get to know your Louis, one (chair and pant) leg at a time.

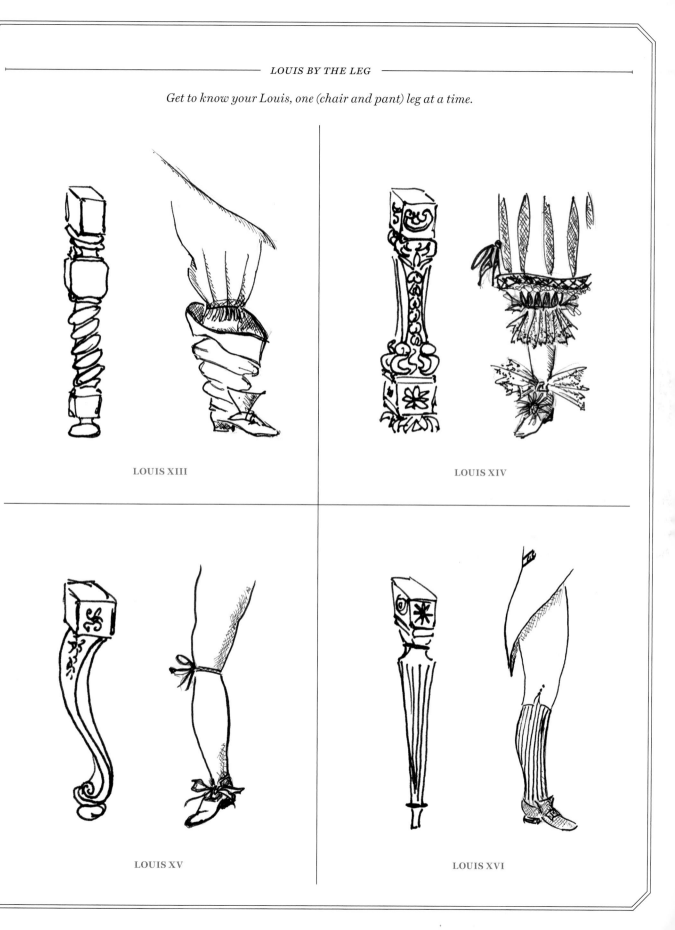

LOUIS XIII

LOUIS XIV

LOUIS XV

LOUIS XVI

Early to Mid-18th Century

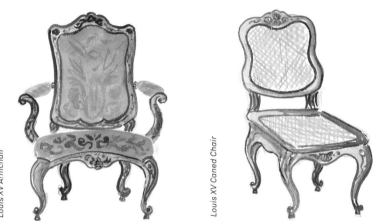

Louis XV Armchair

Louis XV Caned Chair

The 18th century was very much a reaction to what preceded it. Absolutist monarchs still ruled over Europe, but they were enlightened. As rules of protocol and etiquette softened, formality and grandeur were swept away and everything from furniture to rooms became smaller, lighter, and more livable. Ornament followed natural inspirations and took on more fluid forms: Consider the curved cabriole legs, floral motifs, and curvaceous lines of the Rococo age.

The function of furniture changed, too. Pieces were designed with ease and comfort in mind—a reflection of a more leisurely lifestyle based on intimate socializing. Instead of owning just one kind of chair, the middle and upper classes had a little stool for perching, dining chairs, side chairs, a comfy armchair, a low armchair by the fire, big and small sofas, the reception sofa, etc.

Being au courant was paramount, too. Among the upper classes, furniture was treated more like a consumer good, and people frequently overhauled their decor to suit shifting trends.

THE LOOK: Rococo forms, curved lines, floral decoration, and a general overabundance of ornamentation for purely aesthetic purposes.

WHERE IT'S FROM: All over Europe—from Queen Anne and George III in England to Frederick II in Prussia—but France was still the trendsetter.

WHAT YOU'LL FIND: This style of furniture has been very popular and was reproduced until the beginning of the 20th century; you can still find simple, provincial pieces everywhere and more sophisticated ones at auctions.

THE SPACE: Rooms continued to multiply. More intimate rooms equaled smaller furniture—with more specialized functions and more personal use. Louis XV famously repaired to his formal stateroom—the official sleeping chamber—every night, before sneaking off to his smaller private bedroom.

A GLOSSARY OF CHAISES LONGUES

The seat reflects how you socialize; leave it to the French to develop a full-blown taxonomy of different seating styles in the 18th century—one for every activity and every time of day.

CAUSEUSE
(2 SEATS)

CANAPÉ
(3 SEATS)

BANQUETTE

DIVAN

LIT DE JOUR

RÉCAMIÈRE

CHAISE LONGUE

SULTANE

OTTOMANE

PAPHOSE

VEILLEUSE

DORMEUSE

TURQUOISE

MÉRIDIENNE

DUCHESSE

DUCHESSE EN BATEAU

DUCHESSE BRISÉE

Late 18th Century

Louis XVI Armchair

Louis XVI Chaise Volante ("Flying Chair")

For every action, a reaction: A more sober sensibility rooted in the classical order contrasted with the previous period's Rococo frippery. The neoclassical Louis XVI style lasted all the way through the French Revolution by being adapted and adjusted. The latter part of the 18th century shed the overornamentation of previous decades. Furniture became lighter and more mobile; chairs and tables were brought to the service of people.

THE LOOK: Pure neoclassical architectural lines and stylized ornamentation; lighter finishes and upholstery.

WHERE IT'S FROM: France still led the pack; the inspiration was neoclassical and spurred by renewed interest in classical Greece and Rome— thanks largely to the rediscovery of Pompeii and the resulting vogue for archaeology.

RELATED MOVEMENTS OF NOTE: Federal in America; Hepplewhite, Sheraton, and Adam in England; Gustavian in Sweden.

THE SPACE: Sobriety and straight lines ruled, as did architectural elements, lighter colors, ornamentation, and upholstery. Think comfort paired with simplicity.

RETURN TO ORDER: THE FIRST EMPIRE
Early 19th Century

Empire Retour d'Egypte

Empire Court Stool

After the chaos of the French Revolution, the First Empire emerged with Napoléon I at the helm, ready to restore order. The heavy, ponderous style of furniture reflected a regime trying to impose a new legitimacy. The wars Napoléon initiated all over Europe ensured that this style was well diffused.

THE LOOK: Heavy, straight lines with ornamentation still inspired by classicism; the introduction of ancient Egyptian details; a preponderance of mahogany and dark, rich colors.

WHERE IT'S FROM: France.

WHAT YOU'LL FIND: More official and imposing pieces like sideboards, heavy seats, bigger dressers, and armoires.

THE SPACE: Still very geometrical lines but with heavier ornamentation inspired by Rome and Egypt. Heavy fabric like velvet, and the use of dark greens and reds.

THE MIDDLE (CLASS) AGES: THE INDUSTRIAL REVOLUTION AND THE SECOND EMPIRE

19th Century

Fauteuil Voltaire

Charles X Romantique Chair

This was an age of political revolutions, which spread all over Europe, coupled with the continuing changes effected by the Industrial Revolution, which had started in Great Britain in the 18th century. Furniture was more likely to be made in a factory than handcrafted; as a result, it became less expensive and more accessible. A rapidly growing middle class—the bourgeoisie—with disposable income and dreams of upward mobility began to exert its buying power. The response to this trend was Biedermeier, a design movement inspired by Empire's sober lines but shedding its heaviness in tone and ornamentation, and translating to more comfortable, cozier profiles and simpler designs.

The faster cycle of fashion and the inability to continually create innovative new styles also impelled historical cribbing. Thus the various revivals of earlier eras—Romanesque, Gothic, Renaissance, Louis XV, etc.—that loosely interpreted previous centuries. That culminated in the more ornate, heavier designs of the Victorian age and its French equivalent, the Second Empire of Napoléon III, both of which reflected the taste for opulence of the new moneyed elite. In America, this was the Gilded Age period.

THE LOOK: Hybrid, redundant, and overdesigned—yet generally comfortable.

WHERE IT'S FROM: From the Second French Empire to Austrian Biedermeier, from Louis-Philippe to Victorian, the cross-influences were numerous and reflected the conformity of the emergent 19th-century bourgeoisie.

WHAT YOU'LL FIND: Bold and ornamented furniture; ponderous hardware and upholstery. This was the century of mahogany par excellence.

THE SPACE: Rooms became encumbered with all signs of opulence and the availability of goods, thanks to the mechanization of production.

This could have been a textbook case for Darwin: a design evolution that mirrors its environment—more so than any other piece of furniture. (My next publication will be an ethnographic essay called "Off My Chest"!)

COFFER

The chest, also called a coffer, was originally no more than a box without a lid, constructed from planks and nails or simple mortise-and-tenon joinery—all methods and tools readily available in medieval times. A chest held the household's prized possessions (closets being a modern invention) and doubled as a seat, a bed, a table, etc., as needed, since any proper, dedicated piece of furniture was a luxury. In insecure times, coffers were also easy to transport, courtesy of heavy iron handles on both sides.

MEDIEVAL CHEST

Over time, feet were added to lift the chest off the ground and better protect its contents from dampness, rodents, and the like. Construction now included a frame, floating panels, and joined parts. From the 12th century onward, carvings and iron hardware slowly started to appear.

ONE-DRAWER CHEST

During the Renaissance, one of the lower framed panels became a box (or rudimentary drawer) that could move in and out—a more practical way to retrieve items and organize the contents. Elaborate carvings including architectural elements, grotesque figures, and acanthus leaves were common.

JACOBEAN CHEST

With dovetail construction replacing nails and slides (and the coarse frame), drawers multiplied. With no need for a lid—and no longer used as a seat—the chest grew to waist height and now held and displayed lights, mirrors, and other status pieces. It was in the 17th century that the chest of drawers became what it is today in terms of shape and refinement: a symbol of status, as it reflected design trends and received ornamental details and attention.

A BREAK FROM THE PAST: MODERN MOVEMENTS

20th Century

Furniture design was no longer associated with sovereigns. From the beginning of the 20th century, successive styles reflected a multiplicity of influences, innovations, new lifestyles, and aspirations. World War I ushered in modernity, and subsequent movements were less cohesive trends than they were searches, inquiries, and trials. Those movements included the following:

Arts and Crafts Armchair

Frank Lloyd Wright Chair

Art Nouveau Chair

ARTS AND CRAFTS, which originated in Britain, was distinguished by a natural, honest aesthetic rooted in traditional handicrafts. The movement was one of the first organized reactions to increasingly harsh industrialization. Accordingly, it championed a return to more traditional methods and styles inspired by artisans from previous eras—Romantique, Gothic, Renaissance—but in a highly innovative and original way (in contrast to the Victorian-era ethos of overdecorated neo-everything copies).

MISSION OR CRAFTSMAN STYLE, another reaction to Victorian excesses, was distinguished by a sober look. It was the American answer to the concurrent British Arts and Crafts movement and featured the same return to elemental roots and reaction to over-industrialization. The movement also found a more rational and socially minded outlet as a model for middle-class architecture and furniture.

ART NOUVEAU AND JUGENDSTIL likewise sought a simple, natural aesthetic that reflected the budding 20th-century faith in progress and technology. Although rooted in the Arts and Crafts style and philosophy, Art Nouveau and its German counterpart, Jugendstil, were more forward-looking in that they embraced new techniques and materials—sometimes very sophisticated and expensive ones. That made the movement quite elitist, especially in comparison to its democratic American counterpart. The look was more continental than the British Arts and Crafts.

Art Deco Armchair

Bauhaus Chair

Eames Midcentury Chair

MODERNISM, an evolution of Art Nouveau, adopted all-new techniques with simpler and more geometric lines.

ART DECO AND BAUHAUS pushed industrial aesthetics and Modernist techniques to a new level of innovation. Both movements arose after World War I: the more luxurious Art Deco from war-victor France, and the starker Bauhaus from war-torn Weimar-era Germany. (Many German designers actually immigrated to France at the time.) Though their combined influence was worldwide, the movements were relatively short-lived. The Bauhaus school was shut down by the National Socialist government in 1933, and many of its best-known instructors left Germany or were forced to keep a low profile. And the difficulty of procuring exotic materials during World War II hastened the demise of Art Deco.

MIDCENTURY MODERNISM put forth a simple, natural, function-first aesthetic that countered Art Deco excess. Although the movement was established prior to the advent of World War II, postwar austerity spurred its rise—the movement's minimalism, sober finishes, and clean lines largely the consequence of designers' creatively making do with limited resources. (Hence so many chairs made of teak with papercord seats.)

Chairs Across the Eras

Seats are a perfect way to illustrate different periods and styles.
The chair is a witness to the evolution of interiors, functionality,
technical progress, ornamentation, and materials and therefore
a perfect way to explicate the history of design and show you how
global movements have overlapped.

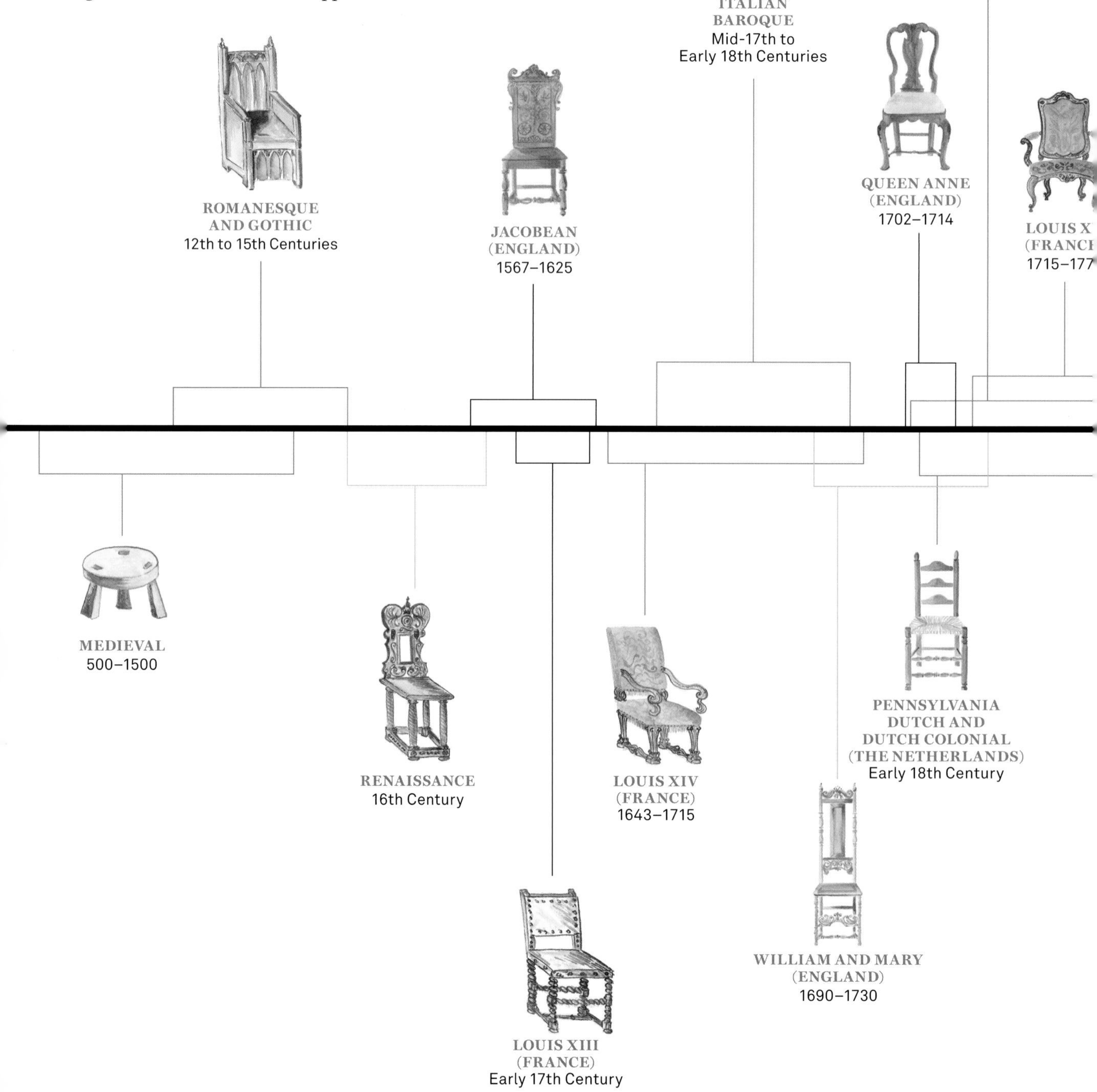

**ROMANESQUE
AND GOTHIC**
12th to 15th Centuries

**JACOBEAN
(ENGLAND)**
1567–1625

**ITALIAN
BAROQUE**
Mid-17th to
Early 18th Centuries

**VENETIAN
ROCOCO
(ITALY)**
1700–1760

**QUEEN ANNE
(ENGLAND)**
1702–1714

**LOUIS X
(FRANC
1715–177

MEDIEVAL
500–1500

RENAISSANCE
16th Century

**LOUIS XIV
(FRANCE)**
1643–1715

**LOUIS XIII
(FRANCE)**
Early 17th Century

**WILLIAM AND MARY
(ENGLAND)**
1690–1730

**PENNSYLVANIA
DUTCH AND
DUTCH COLONIAL
(THE NETHERLANDS)**
Early 18th Century

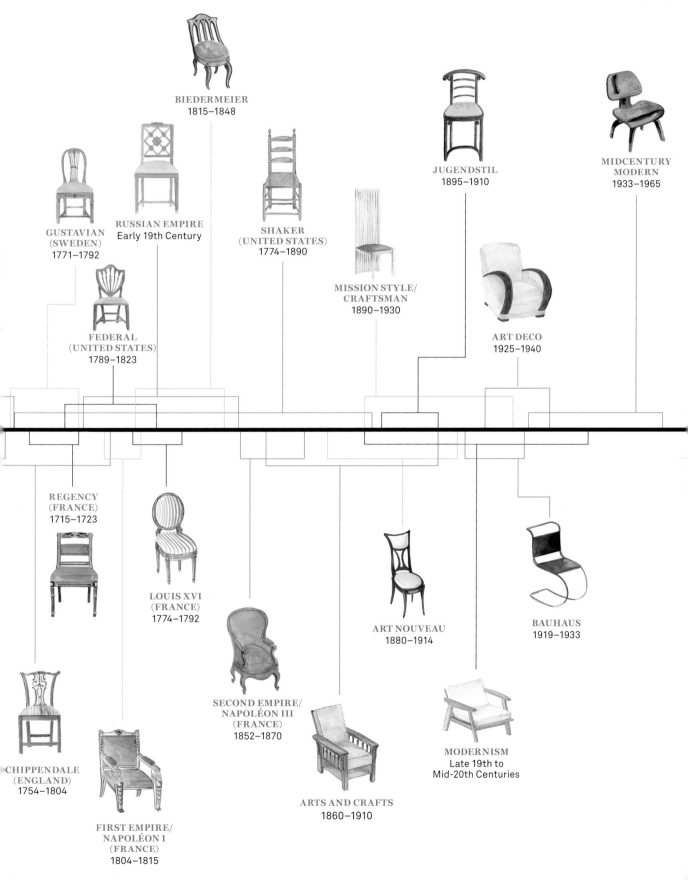

BIEDERMEIER
1815–1848

JUGENDSTIL
1895–1910

**MIDCENTURY
MODERN**
1933–1965

**GUSTAVIAN
(SWEDEN)**
1771–1792

RUSSIAN EMPIRE
Early 19th Century

**SHAKER
(UNITED STATES)**
1774–1890

**MISSION STYLE/
CRAFTSMAN**
1890–1930

ART DECO
1925–1940

**FEDERAL
(UNITED STATES)**
1789–1823

**REGENCY
(FRANCE)**
1715–1723

**LOUIS XVI
(FRANCE)**
1774–1792

ART NOUVEAU
1880–1914

BAUHAUS
1919–1933

**CHIPPENDALE
(ENGLAND)**
1754–1804

**SECOND EMPIRE/
NAPOLÉON III
(FRANCE)**
1852–1870

MODERNISM
Late 19th to
Mid-20th Centuries

**FIRST EMPIRE/
NAPOLÉON I
(FRANCE)**
1804–1815

ARTS AND CRAFTS
1860–1910

HOW FURNITURE IS MADE

How does a plank of wood get transformed from a tree trunk into an armoire frame? Read on to acquaint yourself with the most common wood species that furniture is built from, the defining features of their grain, and how logs get sliced into slabs and assembled into structurally sound tables and chairs via pegs, mortise-and-tenon joints, or dovetails. Embellishments like veneer and parquetry are decoded, too, as is the full taxonomy of hardware, both functional and decorative. Also explained are the precious materials you're likely to find cladding your piece—some common (leather, cane), others less so (shagreen, tortoiseshell)—and a primer on how to handle them. An understanding of the building blocks of fine-furniture making will help you identify, care for, and respect what you own—and the artisan who made it.

18th-Century French Provençal Armoire

COMMON WOOD SPECIES

How to identify them, where you'll find them—and how to (re)finish them.

WOOD	COLOR	CHARACTERISTICS
almond	Rich reddish blond	Fine grain
applewood	Pinkish blond	Sinuous grain
ash	White to pale brown	Sinuous, open grain
beech	Blond	Fine, linear grain
birch	Pale blond with reddish streaks	Hardwood with a fine, sinuous grain
boxwood	Blond	Very dense; no grain
burls	Walnut burl: contrasted browns; Elm and Circassian walnut burl: blond	Highly figured (burls are knots and roots)
cedar and cypress	Light reddish brown	Lightweight and resinous; insect-repellent
cherry	Rich reddish brown	Uniform, straight, fine grain with a smooth texture; darkens with age
chestnut	Warm brown with a hint of red	Rustic texture and grain
ebony	Traditionally black, but huge variations exist	Hard, brittle wood with a closed, figured grain
elm	Light blond	Hard, dense wood with a medium grain
hickory	Blond to light brown	Dense hardwood
holly	White	Fine, uniform grain
kingwood	Rich, violet brown	Straight, intense grain

SEEN ON	USED FOR	RECOMMENDED TREATMENTS
Louis XIV	Rare cabinetry	Fine finishes; polishes
American Colonial; William and Mary	Rich inlay; marquetry	Polishes; oil
American Colonial; Biedermeier	Rustic furniture	Wax; ceruse
Louis XV; Gustavian; Biedermeier	Frames	Paint; bleaching; staining; oil
Gustavian; Shaker; Biedermeier	Almost all furniture	Staining; oil rub and wax
Louis XIV; Second Empire	Precious carvings; turning; inlay	Clear wax; oil rub
Louis XIV; Art Deco	Precious veneer	High-gloss finishes; French polish
"Syrian" furniture; Spanish Colonial; American Colonial	Trunks and wardrobes	Avoid finishing!
American Colonial; Queen Anne; Louis XV; Chippendale; Shaker; Federal; Biedermeier	Large furniture such as armoires, tables, and buffets	Oil and wax; shellac
Rustic French	Large furniture such as armoires, hutches, tables, and buffets	Rustic finishes; wax; tung oil
Louis XIV, XV, and XVI; First Empire; Second Empire; Victorian; Art Deco	Support for precious marquetry	Tung oil; wax
American Colonial; Gustavian; Biedermeier	Traditional support for veneer	Wax; staining; paint
American Colonial	Solid, massive furniture; rustic furniture; trunks	Wax; oil rub
Renaissance; Louis XIV; Second Empire	Inlay and marquetry	Ebonizing; fine polishes
Louis XIV, XV, and XVI	Precious inlay; fine veneer	Fine polishes

WOOD	COLOR	CHARACTERISTICS
lime	White	Fine, uniform grain
macassar	Reddish brown with black stripes	Tight grain
mahogany	Reddish brown	Hardwood with a close grain, straight grain (ribbon), or figured grain (cathedral)
maple	Straw blond	Hardwood with a fine grain
oak	Red or white	Very hard wood with an open grain. Flat-cut oak has a figured grain; quartersawn oak has a straight grain.
pear	Yellowish brown	No grain
pine	Blond to light brown	Soft wood with a straight grain and knots
poplar	White	Inconsistent color and pattern
rosewood	Red and black	Hardwood with a close, straight grain
satinwood	Rich blond	Fine-grained hardwood with beautiful streaks
sycamore	White with flecks	Tight grain
teak	Rich brown and red	Heavy, dense, and oily
walnut	Rich brown	Hardwood with a fine grain, straight or figured
willow	White	Fine, uniform grain
zebrawood	Yellowish brown with dark stripes	Hardwood with a nice streaky figure— very decorative

SEEN ON	USED FOR	RECOMMENDED TREATMENTS
Renaissance-era and 18th-century Venetian furniture	Inlay and marquetry	Ebonizing; fine polishes
18th-century French furniture; Art Deco	Formal furniture and veneer	The most formal or the simplest finish: French polish or wax polish
Queen Anne; Georgian; Louis XVI; Federal; Empire; Victorian; Second Empire	Limited to very expensive furniture until the 19th century	Perfect for all refined finishes, such as French polish
American Colonial; William and Mary; Queen Anne; Chippendale; Shaker; Federal	Almost all types of furniture	Natural wax and oil; ebonizing
Tudor; Jacobean; Dutch and Flemish; Louis XIV; William and Mary; Victorian	Massive furniture	Oil and wax; rustic finishes; decorative effects
Louis XIV; Second Empire; Art Deco; Modernist	Inlays and precious furnishings during Louis XIV's time; ebonized Second Empire furniture; Art Deco and Modernist furniture	Ebonizing; natural-colored finishes (clear wax or tung oil)
William and Mary; Dutch Colonial; Pennsylvania Dutch; Alpine and rustic European furniture; English *pitchpin*	Cheaper support for veneering	Paint; wax; oil
Ubiquitous	Backs and insides of furniture and other paint-grade parts	Paint; primers
Sheraton; Regency; Victorian	Precious furniture and veneer; inlay and marquetry	French polish; shellac and clear wax
Adam; Hepplewhite; Sheraton; 18th-century Irish; Federal	Precious veneer; refined furniture	French polish; shellac and clear wax; clear-oil rub
William and Mary; Venetian furniture; Colonial; nice early-American country furniture	Marquetry in Europe	Oil; wax
Indo-Portuguese furniture; Anglo-Indian; Chinese export; midcentury modern; Modernist	Outdoor furniture; nice carvings; trunks and wardrobes	Unfinished is okay; tung oil; teak oil
Ubiquitous	Carvings; prized furniture	Great for French polish; wax; oil
Renaissance; Venetian	Inlay and marquetry	Clear wax; oil rub
Regency; Art Deco	Precious veneers and furniture	French polish; shellac and clear wax

CUTS OF WOOD

Can't quite visualize how a tree trunk gets transformed into planks suitable for building furnishings? There are three methods used to slice it up. Exactly where the tree is cut affects the plank's overall stability—and thus what applications it's best for—as well as the presentation of the grain pattern. (Plain-sawn inner boards offer the heaviest figuration.)

PLAIN-SAWN is the fastest, cheapest method, utilizing the entire tree with minimum waste. Trees are cut in cross section, resulting in a varied appearance that's not to everybody's taste (nevertheless, the cut does produce the beautiful cathedral pattern). Plain-sawn planks are subject to lateral shrinking, making them less sturdy for frames and joints.

QUARTERSAWN planks are more stable and moisture-resistant than plain-sawn and will shrink only in thickness, so there's no gapping or cupping between them once they're assembled. The resulting pattern is also fairly regular. (It's most noticeable in oak, evidenced by a play of light specks across the grain.) Although widely used for furniture, quartersawn wood is also suitable for paneling and floors.

RIFT-SAWN is preferred for furniture and fine cabinetry. It's the costliest to produce, wasting the most wood during the cutting process, but it is also the most stable cut, with the densest and most regular vertical pattern. A piece of furniture crafted entirely of rift-sawn stock will have perfect uniformity.

Trunk Cross Section

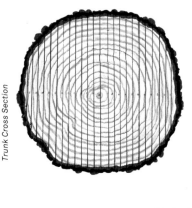

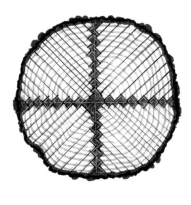

Board Cross Section

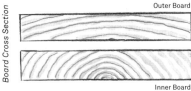

Outer Board

Inner Board

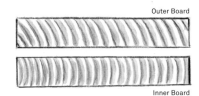

Outer Board

Inner Board

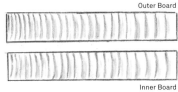

Outer Board

Inner Board

Board from Above

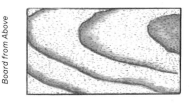

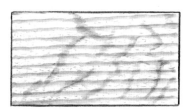

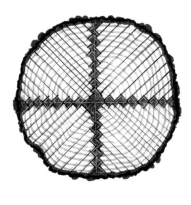

TYPES OF JOINERY

The three main joinery styles—peg or nail, mortise and tenon, and dovetail—all date back many centuries. Simple peg or nail construction was favored during the medieval era, as were through-wedge tenons. But as cabinetry evolved, more refined mortise-and-tenon joints and sophisticated interlocking dovetail systems became increasingly ubiquitous.

PEG OR NAIL: The earliest form of joinery, this technique involved sticking one piece of wood into the socket of another and locking it in place with a large peg or hand-forged nail. The method was practiced until the Renaissance (and continued much later in the countryside).

MORTISE AND TENON: From through-wedge tenons to refined mortise-and-tenon techniques, this joint type has existed since antiquity and is still employed today—it is the favored method for constructing furniture frames, from seats to armoires. (Nails, meanwhile, are relegated to lower-quality, rustic, or construction woodworking.)

DOVETAIL: The intricate pattern of interlocking pins and tail cuts makes this style easy to identify. That said, the genre is surprisingly broad in scope, including open, semi-blind, full-blind, and secret dovetails—each involving a different level of detailing and craftsmanship. You can date a piece by the size of the keys. The advent of machinery in the 19th century enabled much smaller cuts.

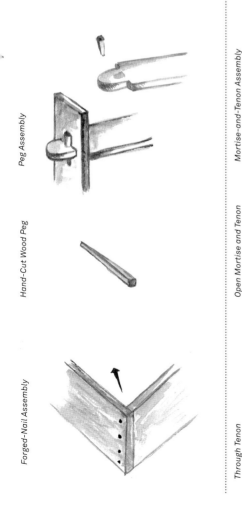

Peg Assembly

Hand-Cut Wood Peg

Forged-Nail Assembly

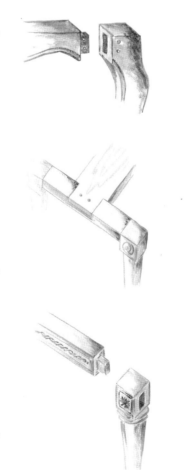

Mortise-and-Tenon Assembly

Open Mortise and Tenon

Through Tenon

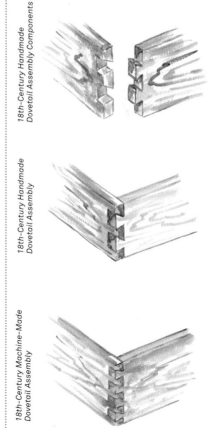

18th-Century Handmade Dovetail Assembly Components

18th-Century Handmade Dovetail Assembly

18th-Century Machine-Made Dovetail Assembly

FURNITURE CONSTRUCTION

Rather than subject you to a long-winded dissertation on how chairs, tables, and armoires are constructed, I thought it would be more fun—and edifying—to *show* you how they're made!

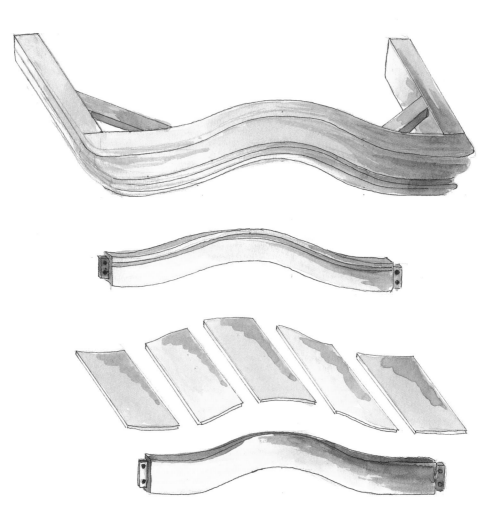

The top, dismantled: This includes the formal cornice as well as the roof, which—like all unexposed parts of European furniture—was roughly cut and joined and left unfinished.

The front, dismantled: Construction is all mortise-and-tenon, with wood pegs that allow pieces to expand and contract in response to weather and environmental conditions.

The side, assembled   *The back, assembled*

The side, dismantled: The design is as formal and refined as the armoire's front. All elements have floating panels to allow expansion and contraction of the wood.

The back, dismantled: Also roughly cut and unfinished. The rough hand-sawn pattern imprinted on the wood helps date the piece to the preindustrial era before mechanization.

VENEER

Veneer often gets a bad rap, calling to mind images of cheap factory-made furniture with an overlay of wood masking shoddy particleboard construction. But with respect to antiques and finely built contemporary pieces, veneer is considered a sign of quality. Far from being a cheat, it is actually an ancient craft used to achieve refinement and to showcase the most beautiful cut of the tree. And, of course, to enable ornamentation, such as inlay and marquetry. Any intricate motif or patterning that embellishes an antique is usually the result of veneer. The fabrication method also provides a way to craft furnishings in exotic species that are prohibitively expensive or hard to get in large pieces—and thus unsuitable for building a piece top to bottom.

HOW DOES IT WORK? A thin layer of decorative wood is applied to the armature, or frame. Today's machinery is capable of slicing millimeter-thin sheets, but veneer was originally cut by hand, meaning that it was heftier (about ⅛ inch thick) and thus sturdier than contemporary versions. For this reason, professional restorers keep old scraps of veneer in their workshop: They're the ideal thickness for repairing period pieces, whereas patching with contemporary veneer may require layering two or three pieces (alternating the grain direction for stability).

WHAT'S IT MADE OF? Mahogany, ebony, macassar, rosewood, and tulipwood were among the most frequently used species in the 18th century—the high point of embellishment. The veneer's top layer was traditionally glued to an armature built from solid pine (common to the provinces) or oak (the mark of Parisian cabinetmakers), species that have very plain figuration but are ideal for structural purposes given their sturdiness and/or ability to expand and contract.

MARQUETRY, PARQUETRY, AND INLAY

The famous 18th-century French cabinetmaker/scholar André Jacob Roubo described the art of marquetry as "painting in wood." While veneering is the application of a full sheet of wood onto a lesser substrate, marquetry's intricate designs are formed by a puzzle-like mosaic of small veneer pieces, encompassing many species. The technique is used to create geometric motifs (called *parquetry*), landscapes, or even scenes (*saynètes* in French).

After hand-cutting the wood pieces to size and gluing them to the substrate, the artisan levels the surface. The delicacy of the design is furthered by staining as well as a chiaroscuro effect: shading created by burning the wood slightly with heated sand. For added depth, calligraphic outlines are often hand-chased into the design and then filled with a dark compound. A high-shine finish—often French polish—shows off the motif even more. Over the centuries, marquetry became more elaborate and luxurious with the introduction of semiprecious stones, metals, mother-of-pearl, tortoiseshell, and ivory. The combination of other materials with wood is known as *inlay* or *incrustation*.

MARQUETRY: An application of wood veneer on a wood substrate to create decorative patterns, pictorial scenes, floral arrangements, etc. Over the years, it has become the blanket term to describe any veneer work. Called *l'art de la marqueterie* in French.

PARQUETRY: A wood inlay, usually slightly thicker than veneer, that creates geometric patterns on a wood substrate. Commonly found on furniture, floors, paneling, and more. (The term comes from the French word *parquet*, for "wood floor.")

INLAY: The inclusion of wood, metal, or precious material into a groove or channel carved into the wood, often creating a contrasting pattern with the substrate. The inserted piece is thicker than veneer and (unlike parquetry) does not cover the entire surface.

HARDWARE

Technological progress had great impact on hardware design's evolution. Materials became more workable and construction more sophisticated—from the wood pegs used to lock medieval coffers to the intricate 18th-century gilded masterpiece locks with secret mechanisms and decoys as well as the streamlined 19th-century forms. Although the aesthetic shifted from functional to ornamental and back again over the centuries, hardware's utilitarian aspect was always coupled with its decorative purpose. For instance, the inside of a lock, never to be seen after being installed, could still be decorated with chiseled figures, dated and signed by a master. Ornamentation enhanced the quality of the piece, and always followed the current style. A Louis XV chest of drawers cannot have Louis XVI hardware!

PRE-18TH CENTURY: Hardware was mainly iron, forged, and filed—an exceedingly difficult and time-consuming art. Yes, *art*! Locksmiths were members of a guild with strict rules; no one was considered a professional locksmith until he had produced a masterpiece. But while forging required a high level of craftsmanship, there was a blacksmith in every community—making iron hardware locally available. Sometimes called *soft steel*, iron is mainly found on these older pieces or on rustic, provincial-style furniture of later centuries.

18TH CENTURY: The introduction of brass and bronze—which was either polished or gilt—allowed casting and chiseling, and thus even more ornamentation. During this period, lock mechanisms got boxed in the manner that prevails today. English artisans also perfected techniques for working with steel, a harder and more resistant metal better suited to precision cutting.

19TH CENTURY: Industrialization sparked technical progress and performance while inspiring the simplification—sometimes to the point of eradication—of ornament, except on high-end luxury items.

20TH CENTURY: Starting with the Art Deco period, hardware was frequently plated with chrome or nickel. Porcelain and glass knobs are often seen on later pieces, used to replace earlier hardware.

types of hardware

ORMOLU

Gilt bronze—common on high-quality pieces—is called *ormolu* (from *ormoulu*, French for "melted gold"). In addition to simple utilitarian pulls and handles, you'll find antiques embellished with ornamental elements such as hooves, inlays, and macaroons. Until the mid-19th century, gilding bronze was achieved via a highly toxic technique: A mixture of mercury and gold was applied to brass and then heated, which burned off the mercury and left behind a thin plating of pure gold (this method is now illegal). Since then, metal plating has been achieved by electrolysis. It's easy to distinguish between 18th- and 19th-century gilt ormolu by looking at the back side of the hardware. Electroplating coats every surface of the hardware, so the back will look the same as the front, only unpolished. By contrast, in the older technique, gilt was applied just to the front, so the back side is raw bronze or brass, probably patinated to a dull green, and bordered with an uneven brushed line of gilt finish.

HANDLES, KNOBS, AND ESCUTCHEONS

These parts are generally the most decorative and varied. Their style is very important since they usually dictate how you treat a piece—that is, whether you refinish it to match, enhance, or be deliberately anachronistic to the existing hardware. The decorative plate encircling keyholes and handles is called an *escutcheon* (deriving from the French word for "coat of arms"). Designed to match the surrounding hardware, its role is to protect the wood surface.

HINGES

Hinges are veritable workhorses, keeping door operation smooth and sound. A wide variety exists, each with a different mechanism: lift-off hinges (such as *fiche*), flat-back hinges, and pivot (also called *knife*) hinges. There are also specialty hinges for specific uses, such as on pianos and screens.

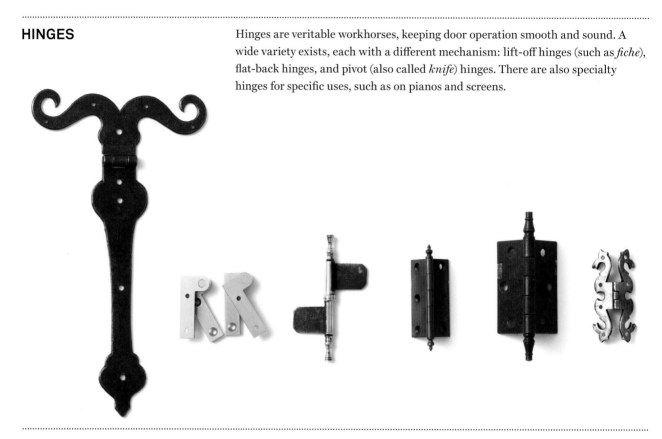

TOE CAPS

Originally designed for a purely functional purpose—to protect the ends of table and chair legs—toe caps evolved over the centuries into a more decorative feature. Some are square, others round, and many are quite ornate, with architectural details or foliage. Made primarily of brass or bronze, they are kept in place via tiny brass nails—which should never be allowed to loosen, as they could tear the wood apart or scratch floors.

CASTERS

Designed to easily move tables and upholstered seats, casters are mainly found on 19th-century furniture. Brass wheels are the norm. Plate casters have a rod or a screw that projects into the end of the leg, while cup casters receive the end of the leg and screw onto it. They can be pretty decorative, incorporating claw feet or architectural details. Broken casters must be replaced immediately, as damage will extend to the leg and the rest of the piece.

SPECIALTY HARDWARE

These usually have a specific function—drop-front desk arms, for instance—and get a lot of abuse. As with all aspects of fine antiques, the design of these elements (whether hidden or exposed) was a marriage of utility and ornament.

CANING

Weaving is almost as old as the wheel. Rush and wild grasses have always been readily available, even in times of scarcity, and were easy to work with in an era of limited craft techniques. Grasses were woven to make baskets, used to build huts and form shields for battle, and eventually employed to create furniture—from entire chairs to huge, basket-like chests. (Medieval England was particularly famous for its woven furniture and sophisticated weave patterns.) As furniture making evolved, weaving was used for more decorative purposes.

WHAT IT IS: Different plants were used, but for wickerwork and caning—two of the most important craft techniques—the primary material is rattan, the outer bark of a long, flexible vine.

WHERE YOU'LL FIND IT: On chairs and furniture from the Victorian era and the turn of the century, when winter gardens and greenhouses were popular.

COMMON PROBLEMS: The material may look fragile, but the woven structure keeps seat joinery—always prone to looseness—tight and safe. Accordingly, a broken or stretched weave will jeopardize the frame's integrity, necessitating recaning.

WHAT TO ASK FOR: You can choose between hand and mechanical caning, but, as always, I strongly recommend old-school handiwork. Yes, it's slower to execute (almost a day, versus thirty minutes for the mechanized version), and thus more expensive. But in a side-by-side comparison, the difference is obvious: The delicacy of hand caning, with its thin individual strips, spaced by hand, is instantly recognizable—and covetable.

types of caning

Your piece will tell you what it needs: Existing holes and grooves will reveal what type of caning was in place previously. There are several options.

HAND CANING

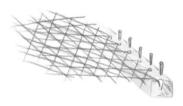

There are two varieties of hand caning. In *French caning*, strips are woven onto the frame one by one, then glued individually and secured with cut-reed pegs. This technique is most artful, as the back of the frame is left untouched: The strips of cane do not extend through it.

In the *English* method, the cane strips go all the way through the wood frame, and are then woven back to the front. This allows one long strip to be used for several back-and-forths.

In both methods, the edges of the caning can be left exposed or covered neatly with a strip that encircles the frame.

MACHINE CANING

In machine caning, developed in the late 19th century, ready-made sheets of woven material are used. The edges of the cut-to-size sheets are glued into a groove that's been routed around the frame. A strip of hard reed forced into the groove afterward sets everything tightly.

RUSH

Rush is another material found on simple, rustic chairs as well as fine French provincial furniture. Rush is soaked in water for fifteen minutes to make it pliable, and then woven around (rather than through) the frame. Cardboard or straw padding packed inside gives the cushion a nice shape.

finishing options

Caning or rush can be finished to your liking. Because caning does not take color easily, it is often tinted via spray-lacquering. Insist instead on linseed or tung oil, either natural or colored. The best choice for rush is natural or colored wax; wait at least a week for the rush to dry before finishing. In both cases, I prefer seats to get patinated by use—versus faux aging—so their newness fades naturally, without artifice.

LEATHER

Leather has always been closely associated with the evolution of furniture. It was first used for utilitarian purposes: to waterproof trunks, as seat straps, and even as rustic hardware like hinges, pulls, and handles. Once fabric became the material of choice for upholstery and metal for technical functions, leather came into its own as a decorative element, subject to elaborate craftsmanship and designs.

WHAT IT IS: Cowhide, mainly.

WHERE YOU'LL FIND IT: On upholstered seats dating as far back as the 15th century. Reeds and hides were used long before fabric, since these raw materials were more readily available than looms. On club chairs and sofas dating from the 19th century onward. On desktops. And on furnishings used for military campaigns and exploration expeditions. Leather always had a rough, masculine connotation.

COMMON PROBLEMS: Cracking, peeling, tearing, dryness, general wear and tear . . . all require expert help.

WHAT TO ASK FOR: An artisan will custom-dye leather upholstery to your taste or to match your existing piece. You can see the difference between a hide that's been dyed in the grain during the industrial tanning process versus custom-dyed, which gives it a deeper color and feel, more nuances in tone, and more character. In a custom upholstery job, the artisan will patina the leather *after* it's been stretched over the chair frame, in order to mimic natural wear spots. You can also choose among a wide variety of nail head designs. As for tabletops, desktops, and blotters, many of my clients don't want their leather tops restored, just cleaned lightly or spots removed. They tend to have a lot of character and patina as is, but sometimes the leather is so far gone that it has to be replaced. Although it could be a DIY job, consider hiring a professional.

TOOLS OF THE TRADE

The mark of an established artisan? Someone who has a lot of tools: rolling tools, medallion-stamping tools, double-line-engraving irons. Michele and Victor from MHG Studio, who demonstrate their leather-tooling handiwork on the next page, have spent years collecting theirs, from antique shops to auction houses. These specialty tools were originally made of bronze, which heats slowly and evenly (much more so than brass, which subpar contemporary versions are made of), thus making them resistant to wear and tear. Artisans will often add to their repertoire by having old motifs sent to an engraver for reproduction.

NEW LEATHER TOP

I am demonstrating this very dramatic process to make a case for connecting with good artisans: Look at the beauty they can bring to your life! I enlisted my favorite leather artisans, MHG Studio in Queens, New York, to showcase their tooling handiwork.

1

COMPLETELY REMOVE THE OLD LEATHER, scraping off any remnants as well as old glue and dirt.

2

PREP THE WOOD BELOW, which may have warped or split. Use wood filler to correct any surface asperity.

6

DO A DRY RUN to establish the exact placement of decorative elements and to test the tools. The artisan measures the leather (in this case also folding it lightly) to determine where the central medallion should go.

7

WARM YOUR TOOLS over a hot plate.

9

ENJOY THE RESULT. Immediately after, burnish the gilt to a shine with a bone knife.

3

CUT THE NEW LEATHER TOP to the exact size and glue in place. Although you may find some decent made-to-measure leather tops from woodworking catalogs—some already embossed with very nice tooling—an artisan will give you the custom color that suits your taste and your piece of furniture. He will also execute the gluing, tooling, and finishing of the leather.

4

ADD NEW EMBELLISHMENTS to enhance the piece's form, if you like. Typical designs include borders (usually several complementary parallel lines—some gilt, some blind), ornaments detailing the corners, and a central motif. You will be able to choose the motifs.

5

EXECUTE TOOLING once the leather is affixed to the furniture (though for the purposes of this tutorial, the process is being demonstrated on a small loose sample).

8

PLACE THE LEAF—which comes backed by ribbon—gold down, ribbon up on the leather, and roll or stamp over it. This style of leaf is available in myriad metals: silver, 10-karat gold, palladium, etc

10

DO OPTIONAL BLIND TOOLING—an embossed motif with no gold leaf—for a nice addition. Alternate with the gilding to enhance the overall design.

11

SEAL THE LEATHER lightly with shellac.

SHAGREEN

The rough skins of stingrays were initially used for sanding and to make shoe soles. Shagreen became very popular with 18th-century nobility as a covering for precious objects, boxes, and tools—applications for which softer leather is less resistant. The Art Deco period brought the material back in fashion.

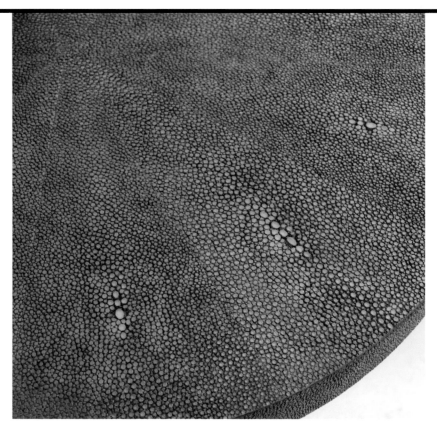

WHAT IT IS: Shagreen—or *galuchat*, as we call it in the antiques industry—encompasses sharkskin and, more commonly nowadays, stingray.

WHERE YOU'LL FIND IT: Covering Art Deco tables and consoles, as well as 18th-century boxes and cases.

CARE AND HANDLING: Consult a professional whenever repairs or restorations are required. Shagreen is complex to work with, involving numerous preparation steps. For maintenance, use a soft, natural-hair clothing brush to remove dust and dirt that accumulates between the grains of the skin. Use a damp soft rag once or twice a year to eliminate grime.

PARCHMENT

Parchment has a long history. It was first used as a precursor to paper and as a protective wrapping, and later to waterproof trunks and chests. Parchment and shagreen both evolved into rarefied coverings, since the materials are expensive and hard to handle and the process labor-intensive.

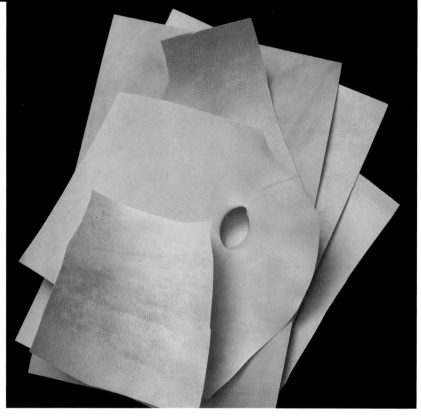

WHAT IT IS: Called *parchemin* in French, the category includes goat and lambskin. Lamb, the more expensive variety, has a uniform white appearance, whereas goat looks more like yellowed manuscript parchment—which is my preference.

WHERE YOU'LL FIND IT: Parchment was used only occasionally before its revival in the Art Deco period, when designers clad clean-lined furnishings—including elegant little side tables—with sheets and sheets of white *parchemin*.

CARE AND HANDLING: Use no product whatsoever, neither water- nor oil-based. At most, apply a light coat of virgin white beeswax, with the utmost delicacy, after having tested it on a hidden spot to make sure the product does not darken or "wet" the dry, white look of the skin. (Nevertheless, I strongly dissuade you from doing this unless you have a lot of experience.)

WHAT TO ASK FOR: Call a professional for any repairs. If you are commissioning a piece anew or replacing parchment wholesale, it can be dyed to take on varying tones.

TORTOISE-SHELL

The exploration of new continents introduced Europeans to exotic animals, plants, and materials—tortoiseshell among them—which were then used to enhance precious furniture and objects. On Baroque pieces created for the Sun King, 17th-century French furniture designer André-Charles Boulle deployed tortoiseshell ad nauseam. The material's stained pattern, transparency, and shine were further enhanced via gold- or silver-leaf backing. As with ivory, the use of tortoiseshell brought the species to near extinction, and selling it was banned in 1973.

WHAT IT IS: The shell from the hawksbill turtle. It was used like plastic is today: cut into pieces to make small objects like combs, snuffboxes, or glasses frames, and to veneer panels and mirror frames.

WHERE YOU'LL FIND IT: On mirror frames and decorative boxes.

COMMON PROBLEMS: Peeling and dryness.

WHAT TO ASK FOR: Restoration must be done by a professional accredited to own and deal with fair-trade tortoiseshell. A good and traditional finish is padded shellac, but it should be applied only on really clean material by an expert. A pro should also oversee the regluing of loose material, which will probably require removal and readhesion—a tricky process that involves softening the piece in saltwater to loosen it, lightly heating it to restore its shape, and then resetting it in place.

CARE AND HANDLING: Do not clean with water or polish; only a light dusting, please. If the shine needs reviving, the safest treatment is amber paste wax, rubbed on delicately with a rag or a finger. This may loosen some dirt and restore transparency.

MOTHER-OF-PEARL

Mother-of-pearl has been used to decorate precious furniture since antiquity, often inlaid into wood. Although regulated to avoid overfishing, the material can still be purchased to replace missing pieces.

WHAT IT IS: The shell lining of pearl oysters, freshwater pearl mussels, and, to a lesser extent, abalone.

WHERE YOU'LL FIND IT: Nowadays, you find mother-of-pearl mainly on Anglo-Indian pieces and what is called Syrian furniture (but which is actually made all over the southern Mediterranean shores).

COMMON PROBLEMS: Chips and dings.

WHAT TO ASK FOR: Any restoration requires a professional, who will shape the patch with fine files and sandpaper and give it a final polish. Since mother-of-pearl is usually paired with wood or other materials, avoid any refinishing, or sanding, as each surface will react differently to treatment. Cleaning should be all the care it requires, according to the needs of the wood around it.

STRAW MARQUETRY

The use of straw marquetry began in the European countryside, where rye straw was abundant. The flattened stems were typically applied to small boxes and objects in a manner that imitated the intricate patterns of exotic-wood veneers. It became fashionable for aristocrats to own sewing boxes, vanity cases, or precious boxes covered with straw marquetry. The 18th century was the height of the material's popularity, but this treatment fell out of favor in the industrially minded 19th century.

WHAT IT IS: Made of rye straw woven in geometric patterns, this lovely material was often referred to as "the veneer of the poor." (Now, of course, it's quite expensive.)

WHERE YOU'LL FIND IT: On Art Deco pieces. Jean-Michel Frank revived straw marquetry as a covering for furniture and even entire walls, which—as you can imagine—was astronomically expensive. (Jean Cocteau referred to Frank's putting his clients "on the straw," a double entendre in French that meant bankrupting them!)

COMMON PROBLEMS: If a segment becomes unglued, clean the wound delicately with a damp rag. Reattach with white glue only. Run your fingernail gently over the straw, like a burnisher, to ensure full adhesion, and let it dry.

CARE AND HANDLING: Silica in the sheathing gives straw natural protection; no finish or polish should be applied, at the risk of damaging the material. Use only a feather duster, never a rag; fabric may pull off some straw. Wax is the only product you can safely use to remove grime: rub delicately with a finger or soft cloth dipped in the purest beeswax.

ANTIQUE GLASS

Mirrors were originally made by backing glass with a coating of mercury and silver or tin, a highly toxic process that is now banned (and is today reproduced chemically, with acids). The coating is quite fragile and tends to corrode with time and humidity, resulting in a dramatic, distressed effect: the look of old mirror panes, with their ghostly silver patinated pattern. Antique glass is more art piece than functional object, as the reflection is obscured.

HISTORY: Artisans based on the famous Venetian glassmaking island of Murano perfected the process in the 16th century. It evolved until the middle of the 19th century, when modern techniques rendered the mercury process obsolete.

WHERE YOU'LL FIND IT: On antique mirrors, mirrored walls, furniture, or small objects like boxes.

COMMON PROBLEMS: Peeling and cracking.

CARE AND HANDLING: Do not touch the mercury backing of the mirror: You could damage it, and, worse, the coating is toxic. The glass itself is safe to own, but any loose material should be vacuumed and discarded. Old mercury glass is very fragile, so avoid taking it off its frame. And minimize exposure to humidity, as it speeds degradation.

WHAT TO ASK FOR: The process is now artificially reproduced on new mirrors. It comes in several levels of antiquing—I suggest a light-handed version, as the heaviest ones can look fake and a bit tacky.

ANOTHER THOUGHT

I advise selling any mercury glass furnishings you choose to deaccession. It would be a sin to throw away this endangered species, and antique dealers are very interested in using old mirror panes to replace broken ones.

TRADITIONAL HORSEHAIR UPHOLSTERY

Most people are awed to discover the exquisite handiwork and fine materials that make up traditional upholstery. This is especially true of those familiar with the guts of a contemporary piece, padded with synthetic foam and affixed to a wood-composite frame via staples. Historical furniture, in contrast, was crafted on a much more refined level, with myriad support layers designed to cosset the sitter and uphold the seat shape over time. Acquainting yourself with the ingredients of period upholstery will help you identify pieces of value— and know what to ask for when getting a seat reupholstered. Luckily, it is still possible to find devoted practitioners of these old-school methods.

the anatomy of upholstery

I dismantled an 1850s English Victorian chair to expose its underpinnings and then had it reupholstered in a custom-dyed deerskin with button tufting.

TOP FABRIC
Fabric will cover the top and bottom of the piece. Oftentimes, you'll find antiques half-undressed, in their muslin dishabille.

TRIMS
The edge of the fabric is often studded with decorative brass nail heads and/ or accentuated with passementerie: elaborate braided trimmings or edgings like tape, cords, and embroideries.

MUSLIN
This fabric underlayer, usually white, served to contain the padding below and keep dust from penetrating the seat. It also acted as a foundation garment of sorts, ensuring that the fabric cover smoothly on top.

TACKS
The fabric layers are sutured to the frame with tacks. Tacks hold the fabric firmly in place, yet are easy to remove when needed—and impart minimal damage to the wood structure. Nail heads abutting one another keep the fabric from pulling or wrinkling.

HORSEHAIR
You'll typically find many layers of horsehair, in increasing degrees of coarseness from top to bottom, held together with hand stitching.

SHREDDED HUSKS
Coarse palm or softer coconut fibers were often used to enhance the cushioning.

JUTE OR BURLAP
This layer lends structure to the padding and anchors it in place. Details like this are the earmark of a job carefully done! A tight corner—see, it looks like a little sausage—helps preserve a crisp seat shape.

MORE OF THE SAME
There are generally numerous layers, from rough to finer material: Rough burlap, coarse stuffing, finer burlap, finer stuffing, horsehair (wrapped in jute or muslin), then muslin—all held together with tacks and stitches.

SPRINGS
Metal coils, secured by hand with rope.

WEBBING
Heavy straps were woven across the frame, pulled tightly, and secured with tacks. In a traditional upholstery job, springs are hand-tied firmly in place atop the straps.

FRAME
This armature is crafted of beech, a stable wood that's both workable and light. Look how rough the wood surface is inside, where it's unfinished: This is where you can really see how the finishing process enhances the wood.

CABINETMAKER'S MARKS
The artisan would always sign the inside of the piece. An 18th-century Parisian *ébéniste* would have his mark ink-stamped or fire-branded, like so:

JACOB·FRERES
RUE MESLEE

Famous Parisian ébéniste

Official furniture of Marie Antoinette

FABRIC BOTTOM
This hides the innards and mitigates dust penetration. The mark of a historical piece (or a superior contemporary one) is a layer of cotton in a very fine, light weave. Although sometimes brown, it's usually pale blue to reflect light bouncing off the floor.

THE PROCESS OF REUPHOLSTERY

I am demonstrating the process on a Louis XVI stool that had been re-covered with cheap fabric, egregiously stapled to the frame. Although a period reupholstery job is best left to experts, you may want to execute some prep work—such as repairing or rebuilding your frame—before sending a seat off to the workshop.

DENUDING

1

REMOVE NAIL HEADS. Don't bother saving them, unless it's a museum-quality 18th-century piece. They can't be reused.

HORSEHAIR: SAVE OR TOSS?

Save! Especially if you are reupholstering only one of a pair of chairs: You'll want the two to look exactly the same. For that to happen, the chairs need to have identical innards. (Not to mention, horsehair is expensive.)

5

REMOVE *ALL* THE STAPLES! I pry them out with a screwdriver-like tool that has a notched end. Be sure to remove every last staple from the frame. If you miss one and then try to put a tack there later, you're out of luck.

9

THEN SPRINGS.

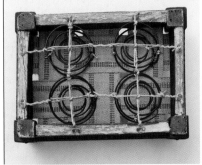

10

THEN BURLAP, FOLLOWED BY STUFFING.

11

THEN MORE BURLAP.

2

REMOVE TRIM.
Accents like piping
and tape are always
glued to the fabric.
Removing the trim
will expose more tacks
or staples.

3

REMOVE THE FABRIC. Undress the
underside of the piece first, then the
main upholstery. If the fabric was
tacked on, you're in luck; tacks pop
out cleanly and leave behind rows of
evenly spaced holes that are easily
filled. Staples, in contrast, leave a
barrage of microscopic holes that
shred (and often destroy) the wood—
and are excruciating to fill.

4

**REMOVE THE
PADDING,**
typically horsehair.

PREPPING THE FRAME

6

**REPAIR THE WOOD
STRUCTURE** as
needed, tightening
loose joints and fixing
any breaks.

7

**USE FILLER OR WOOD
PASTE TO PLUG THE
HOLES** left behind by
the tacks or staples
to prepare a sound
base for your new
upholstery job. (See
"Filling Holes and
Cracks," page 000; and
"Making Your Own
Fillers," page 000.)

REUPHOLSTERING

8

WEBBING FIRST.

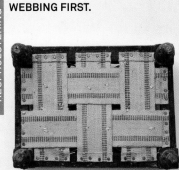

12

THEN MORE STUFFING.

13

THEN MUSLIN.

14

THEN FABRIC and trims,
(cords, nail heads, etc.).

THE HUNT: WHERE TO FIND GREAT PIECES— AND WHAT TO LOOK FOR

There are many places to find great antique and vintage items, from junk shops and flea markets to prestigious auction houses like Sotheby's. And don't forget your attic and even the curb: I've majorly scored during impromptu Dumpster-diving sessions!

The antiques business is a veritable ecosystem. Pickers buy objects in bulk from estate sales and tag sales, reselling them at places like giant flea markets, where precious antiques sit cheek by jowl with junkier castoffs. The good stuff is snapped up by dealers, who flip it to higher-end specialists. A piece may cycle through two or three dealers before it arrives at the top. Surmounting the food chain are upmarket dealers, who offer the most rarefied furniture and the best service and information— but at a price. Among other things, you are paying for them to vet and curate the product for you; they have more money plus a network of subdealers and pickers who sell to them.

If you are a neophyte or an aspiring collector, a good strategy is to educate yourself and cultivate your eye at the top: Attend auction-house previews, pore over websites like 1stDibs.com, visit dealers who focus on an era that intrigues you. But start buying toward the bottom, where the risk is low and the potential reward great. Work your way up until you hit your sweet spot vis-à-vis the amount of time and money you have to invest. Have a slim budget but a few free weekends? The best deals are had at estate sales and flea markets, but they require getting up early, sifting through a lot of dross, and going it alone without an expert to guide you. Can't bear the thought of waking up at 5:00 a.m. on a Saturday but have a little money to burn? A midrange antiques shop may be more your speed. And don't forget to check out local haunts whenever you travel.

Following are some of the venues to peruse, each addictive and adrenaline-pumping in its own way.

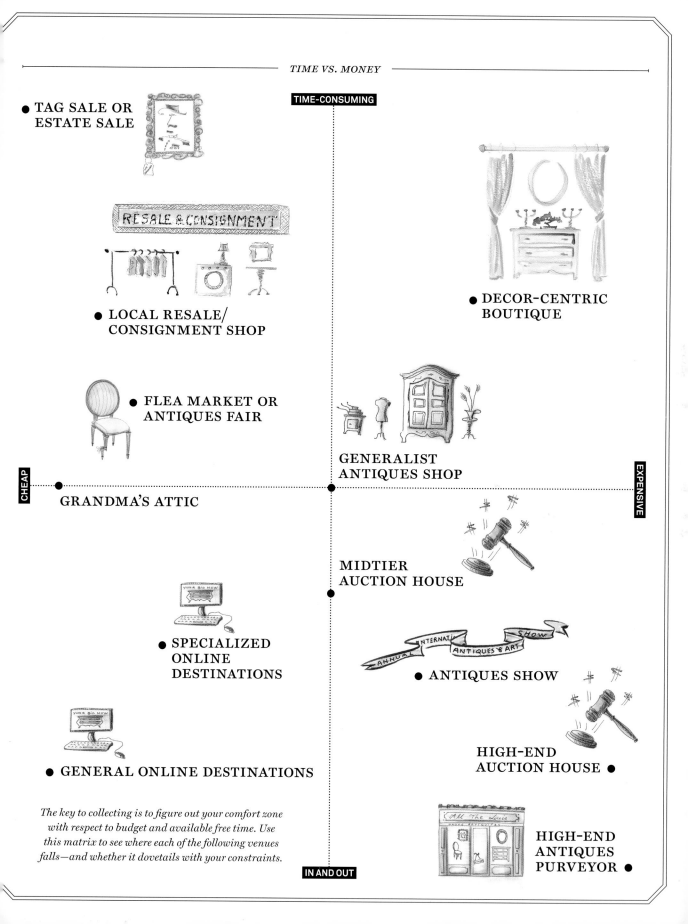

TIME-CONSUMING

● TAG SALE OR
ESTATE SALE

RESALE & CONSIGNMENT

DECOR-CENTRIC
BOUTIQUE

● LOCAL RESALE/
CONSIGNMENT SHOP

● FLEA MARKET OR
ANTIQUES FAIR

GENERALIST
ANTIQUES SHOP

CHEAP

EXPENSIVE

GRANDMA'S ATTIC

MIDTIER
AUCTION HOUSE

● SPECIALIZED
ONLINE
DESTINATIONS

ANTIQUES SHOW

● ANTIQUES SHOW

HIGH-END
AUCTION HOUSE ●

● GENERAL ONLINE DESTINATIONS

*The key to collecting is to figure out your comfort zone
with respect to budget and available free time. Use
this matrix to see where each of the following venues
falls—and whether it dovetails with your constraints.*

HIGH-END
ANTIQUES
PURVEYOR ●

IN AND OUT

THE HIGH-END ANTIQUES PURVEYOR

WHAT IT IS: From Madison Avenue shops to gallery-like settings, these purveyors generally specialize in a certain country, period, or type of item—sometimes a combination of the three (for instance, French 18th-century porcelain). In New York, Maison Gerard is one of my favorites for Art Deco and midcentury pieces; L'Antiquaire & the Connoisseur is a treasure trove as well.

WHAT YOU'LL FIND: Prices that are likely very high, since you pay for quality (and the reputation of the dealer). Because these shops have a devoted clientele, many pieces are accounted for before they even hit the sales floor.

HOW TO WORK IT: It's okay to browse—and to let the proprietor know you are just browsing. Start a conversation, asking about particular pieces that strike your fancy, a specific detail you've never seen before, or just about the history. This is an old-fashioned, relationship-driven business: Go back again and again, and they'll see that you're interested in educating yourself.

GO FOR: Advice. Some of the wares may be out of your price range, but an antique dealer's inventory is never all on the floor. And your genuine interest in a piece makes it easier to ask about a better price and start a relationship. Also, knowledge is free, and dealers are happy to share. Maybe you need an upholsterer or to have a marble tabletop repolished—dealers are almost always delighted to divulge their trade resources (it makes them look good and keeps their suppliers in business).

ANTIQUES SHOP ETIQUETTE: No reason to be intimidated, but show respect. The dealer may be busy with a regular client and have less time for you. Avoid asking the price of an item as your first question.

DO:

+ Be civilized.
+ Touch. (But it's nice to ask first.)
+ Say hello, good-bye, and thank you. So many people come, look around, and leave without saying anything!
+ Ask before entering with strollers, kids, dogs, or beverages.
+ Ask if you're curious about pricing, but in a polite way: "I wonder what sort of price that piece goes for?"

DON'T:

– Ask the price of everything; you'll seem flippant and amateurish.
– Roll your eyes or say "Yikes!" if the price is high.
– Say: "My grandmother had the exact same table/chest/chair—and we threw it away!" It implies that the dealer's merchandise is crap and that he is a thief.

THE ANTIQUES SHOW

WHAT IT IS: The hierarchy of venues ranges from populist markets and well-appointed, good-quality shows with a design-y twist to tony, high-end events like New York's Winter Antiques Show. These shows are a great way to spend a weekend afternoon and get tempted.

WHAT YOU'LL FIND: Regular antiques show: designers, antique dealers, and collectors. High-end venues: an international roster of top-notch dealers who've carefully curated their booth to satisfy a demanding clientele of collectors, museum curators, and the robber barons of today (with their interior designers in tow).

HOW TO WORK IT: These venues are ideal for browsing anonymously, learning the prices of museum-quality items, or—at the more accessible shows—checking things against your budget. The booth format puts you on a more equal level with the dealer, who is there specifically to network, so personal contact can be pretty easy. But shows are still a place of business, and your time with the proprietor will be limited. Asking for prices more directly is accepted.

REALITY CHECK: Keep in mind that at the highest-end venues, many items are sold during the invitation-only preview or on opening night, attended by seasoned collectors and regular clients.

THE GENERALIST ANTIQUES SHOP

WHAT IT IS: A more accessible version of the high-end purveyor. Antiques shops are usually grouped together on a particular street or in a certain neighborhood or village, so you can visit a bunch in a row. (The town of New Hope, Pennsylvania, is one such place.) Each shop will be a bit different, with a unique specialty or point of view. Balzac Antiques in New Orleans is a superior example of the genre.

WHAT YOU'LL FIND: A more diverse but still focused product mix. More affordable pieces in need of rejuvenation intermingled with items in pristine condition.

HOW TO WORK IT: It's always okay to bargain, but don't be crass and say, "I'll give you so many dollars for it." Ask politely if a price is their best. Don't expect a discount; it's not obligatory. Also, have some perspective: This is a cash business, proprietors cannot put pieces on sale or return them, and their inventory has to change all the time to keep their clientele interested. If you're polite and they can afford to swing you a deal, they usually will. And if they don't, now you understand why. Respect! Another tip: Shops tend to keep additional inventory in a warehouse, so it's worth asking if they have a certain item you're looking for—and that you don't see on the sales floor.

THE MIDTIER AUCTION HOUSE

WHAT IT IS: There is a huge middle ground between the likes of Sotheby's and the small local auctions that sell furnishings next to salvage items like old appliances. Sales, often held frequently, are well stocked, and a great introduction to the bidding process. Capo Auction and Beaux-Arts Auction are fine examples.

WHAT YOU'LL FIND: At secondary or local auction houses, you'll find a little bit of everything under one roof, from frames to fauteuils. The prices are accessible; many pieces start at low estimates. (And if a piece doesn't sell, you can sometimes call the next day and make an offer.)

HOW TO WORK IT: Attending a preview is a great way to learn about antiques and other decorative arts. You can see a lot, and there will be people on hand to answer your questions about a piece or about decorative-arts history. They'll even help you with measurements and answer queries about condition. You can also review catalogs online. Bid in person (show up and raise your paddle), by phone (not recommended; sometimes you'll miss the call), over the Internet, or through a proxy (a rep of the house who bids on your behalf, up to an agreed-upon amount). You'll get an adrenaline rush, so set your limits in advance, and remember to factor in the commission—about 20 percent—that's added to the sell price as well as delivery costs (you are responsible for arrangements). There are generally hundreds of lots, and the process can be quite slow; estimate sixty to a hundred per hour and time your arrival accordingly. Don't show up at 10:00 a.m. for Lot #450.

GO FOR: Free advice and expertise and to cultivate your eye. These auctions are best if you know exactly what you're looking for, or if you just want to absorb a lot of stuff or buy in a low-risk, unintimidating, and super-fun environment.

HELPFUL HINT: You can often sell things back easily, and also use them to auction off your own decent-quality deaccessions.

ALSO . . .

DON'T BE A SNOB ABOUT LOWER-QUALITY VENUES; they often have exactly what you need—or didn't even know you were looking for—at a price that cannot be beat. This is where the deals are.

DON'T BE INTIMIDATED BY HIGH-END VENUES! Dealers are a font of knowledge, and they love to educate.

DON'T UNDERESTIMATE THE POWER OF CONTEXT: The piece you said no to on a dirty field one rainy Saturday morning may enchant you once you see it on a pretty carpet, styled with lamps in a vignette. The key is to save yourself the trouble of the early-morning Saturday wake-up and wait for stuff at stores— or train your eye well enough to see a piece's promise in the dark of predawn.

THE DECOR-CENTRIC BOUTIQUE

WHAT IT IS: This new breed of antiques shop is becoming increasingly popular. The value of the pieces is more about style than provenance and period; the proprietor is selling his or her taste level and point of view. That's a mentality that meshes well with popular taste today, when few people aspire to an all-period look. The erstwhile Amy Perlin Antiques, where I worked when I first moved to New York, is the progenitor of the genre. Privet House in New Preston, Connecticut, is another delightful emporium.

WHAT YOU'LL FIND: Funky, inexpensive *objets* and books mixed with pricier furnishings, often from different eras. Antiques that have been beautifully refinished to create a particular look.

HOW TO WORK IT: Take notes! Observe how the proprietors juxtapose like items, and how they've reinvented pieces with new finishes or upholstery to suit their aesthetic. They don't necessarily care if a piece is 20th- or 18th-century, but they will care to create a unity or logic of look.

GO FOR: Decorating advice and inspiration.

THE LOCAL RESALE/ CONSIGNMENT SHOP

WHAT IT IS: Everything from slightly curated boutiques to glorified Salvation Army–type spots. My favorite around-the-corner emporium is the Chelsea location of Housing Works in New York City, which—like many stores of this genre—serves a great charity cause.

WHAT YOU'LL FIND: A wide variety of goods, with furniture and home accessories sprinkled in. While you may get helpful staff and good customer service, you will rarely encounter antiques experts.

HOW TO WORK IT: Pick one that's convenient to your home or work, because the key to scoring great finds is to drop by often—especially if you're looking for something specific. Find out if there's a particular day or hour they put out new merchandise, and plan your visit to coincide. Nine times out of ten you won't find anything interesting, and then—success!

GO FOR: Either something very specific—say, a tall bureau—or be open to whatever looks cool.

MARK OF A GOOD ONE: Merchandise turns over frequently.

This midtier auction house, which has monthly sales in Queens, New York, is a favorite. The thrill of discovery is irresistible! The lots are inevitably diverse: from pieces with flat, dried-up French polish and midcentury items begging for oil to buckets of silverware and oddball collections. The strategy is to focus on beautiful things that you know you can restore or reinvent, or something that just speaks to you—or cries out for a specific finish. A recent preview turned up these cool possibilities.

THE FIND **Drop-leaf Table**	THE FIND **19th-Century American Solid-Mahogany Table**	THE FIND **Early-20th-Century Chinese Export Furniture**

Drop-leaf Table

ESTIMATE
$100; sold for $200.

WHY IT'S GREAT
Drop-leafs are very practical pieces because you can use them anywhere, in any kind of space, for dining, working, serving, or display. And this is an easy refinishing job.

WHAT I'D DO
A quick coat of wax or shellac.

19th-Century American Solid-Mahogany Table

ESTIMATE
$500; sold for $250—so inexpensive!

WHY IT'S GREAT
It has a beautiful solid-mahogany top, probably Cuban, crafted from boards that are two feet wide—which you cannot find anymore.

WHAT I'D DO
French polish. You'll end up with a glittering wood: Cuban mahogany reflects light beautifully.

Early-20th-Century Chinese Export Furniture

ESTIMATE
$300 to $400; sold for $225.

WHY IT'S GREAT
Low-end Chinese export furniture is a fixture of these auctions; however, this is a quality version, beautifully crafted of nice wood. The hardwood is usually found in a very dry state like this, but the finish is easy to revive.

WHAT I'D DO
Refinish with oil and wax. Sometimes you get an unbelievable surprise: What looks like weathered and stained *zamu* (a softwood, like elm or pine) might turn out to be a beautiful *yungmu* (hardwood).

Set of 19th-Century Neoclassical-Style Side Chairs

ESTIMATE
$300 to $400; sold for $150. Forget about a real 18th-century set; even a decorative one would cost a couple thousand dollars!

WHY IT'S GREAT
The chairs have a versatile style with clean, straight lines that work well in all interiors. Two things make this an appealing purchase: It's a set, which you don't find often, and the chairs have beautiful faded needlepoint upholstery, almost like tapestries.

WHAT I'D DO
Great rid of the green. Whitewash the painted frames for a slightly shabby-chic, Gustavian feel or a more Provençal vibe. Or strip and paint them in a new color; since they're not real Louises, you can do anything you want. A great project!

Set of Thirty Violin Bows

ESTIMATE
$300; sold for $150.

WHY IT'S GREAT
I could see this quirky collection hung en masse on the wall behind a sofa as a statement.

WHAT TO DO
Clean 'em and hang 'em!

Cabriole-Leg Burl Table

ESTIMATE
$150. I scored it for $180!

WHY IT'S GREAT
Burl wood is very rare today. And the proportions are so pleasing. Side tables are also versatile.

WHAT I DID
I wanted to use the piece to illustrate the grain-filling process (see pages 136–137), but I got so carried away that I ended up doing an English-varnish-type finish (see page 88). Unbelievable result!

THE FLEA MARKET OR ANTIQUES FAIR

WHAT IT IS: A category that encompasses everything from small neighborhood weekend fleas to bigger venues like the Brimfield Antiques Show, mounted three times a year in a giant field in Massachusetts. The mother of them all is the famous Marché aux Puces de Saint-Ouen, in Paris.

WHO GOES: A lot of dealers, and a lot of pickers who are buying things on behalf of dealers; the giant shows are a major source for their goods. Some buy entire containers of furniture at Brimfield—enough to sustain their inventory for months.

WHAT YOU'LL FIND: A wide range of products, from junky goods to fine antiques, architectural fragments, decorative items, even folksy handmade items. Virgin stuff that has not been seen anywhere. Pieces are sold as is, and you have to inspect carefully; you can't return a piece if you notice later that the leg is broken.

HOW TO WORK IT: To get your pick of the best stuff, come very early (many markets open at dawn) armed with good shoes, warm clothes, a flashlight, and cash. The best stuff goes quickly, and the vibe can be frenetic. As long as you have your hand on a piece, you have first dibs—but lift your hand up, and it's fair game for others. Ask once for a better price, and be ready to take it or leave it—the dealers are here to sell, and fast!

HOW TO GET A BARGAIN: At the end of the day, proprietors are exhausted and desperate. They will be more than happy to dump their merchandise rather than take it back home, and you can often score major deals. This is the moment to wheel and deal: It's totally fine to make a lowball offer with a smile. They may say no, but they may say yes. In which case, hand over the cash quickly, thank them, and praise your good fortune.

TAG SALE OR ESTATE SALE

WHAT IT IS: A crapshoot—but a lot of fun, too. Tag sales are the first step in the business. They take anything, which sometimes means nothing interesting.

WHAT YOU'LL FIND: It's about not having expectations! Go with an open mind—and open eyes.

HOW TO WORK IT: Items generally belonged to people who were not collectors, so the pieces often need a little TLC—some have been neglected for years. Score cheap things that you can reinvent.

GO FOR: The adrenaline rush of finding a diamond in the rough.

ONLINE DESTINATIONS

ONLINE AGGREGATORS of smaller auctions from all over the country, like LiveAuctioneers.com. Pro: Tons of inventory at your disposal. Con: If you find something you love hundreds of miles away, you'll need to have it shipped—which can be costly.

1STDIBS.COM, which aggregates the already curated merchandise of hundreds of top antiques shops across the country (and, indeed, the world). You'll have to register (free) to see prices.

MAJOR AUCTION HOUSE SITES. All the biggies, including Sotheby's and Christies, now offer online-only sales.

People often wonder about the financial aspects of the antique-furniture business. Or, to put it more bluntly, they ask me, "How did that $50 desk become $5,000?" Here's a brief explanation.

$50

A picker scores it at an estate sale for $50,
painted and dirty but somewhat interesting.

↓

$150

He sells it at a flea market to a local dealer for $150 at the
end of the day, in bargain mode, as part of a five-item lot.

↓

$500

The dealer cleans it up a bit and puts it on the sales floor in a styled vignette.
A scout for a high-end shop scoops it up for $500.

↓

$1,000

The scout sells it to the high-end shop for $1,000.

↓

$3,000

The high-end shop has three clients who are looking for exactly this kind of piece—
including a decorator who's about to do an install and is desperate for the
perfect piece for an oddly sized nook in a client's den. She buys it for $3,000—
six times what it initially came on the market for, but a deal compared
with having a custom piece commissioned and waiting two months for it.

↓

$5,000

Five years later, the client—a prominent arts patron—
downsizes a collection of possessions at auction.
The piece now has historical cred *and* cachet, and sells
at a prominent auction house for $5,000.

Now, for the son of an antiques dealer, this is an extra-sensitive topic, and I know that the reaction of many will be something like "Easy money!" or "What a rip-off!" Well, consider that all parties in this process were risking their own money, and worked hard to find, move, research, and restore the piece, as well as to give it pedigree and find the right buyer. And for the high-end dealer, consider his overhead, the time and energy involved to build his client roster, and the knowledge to discern a diamond among similar—but not quite—pieces.

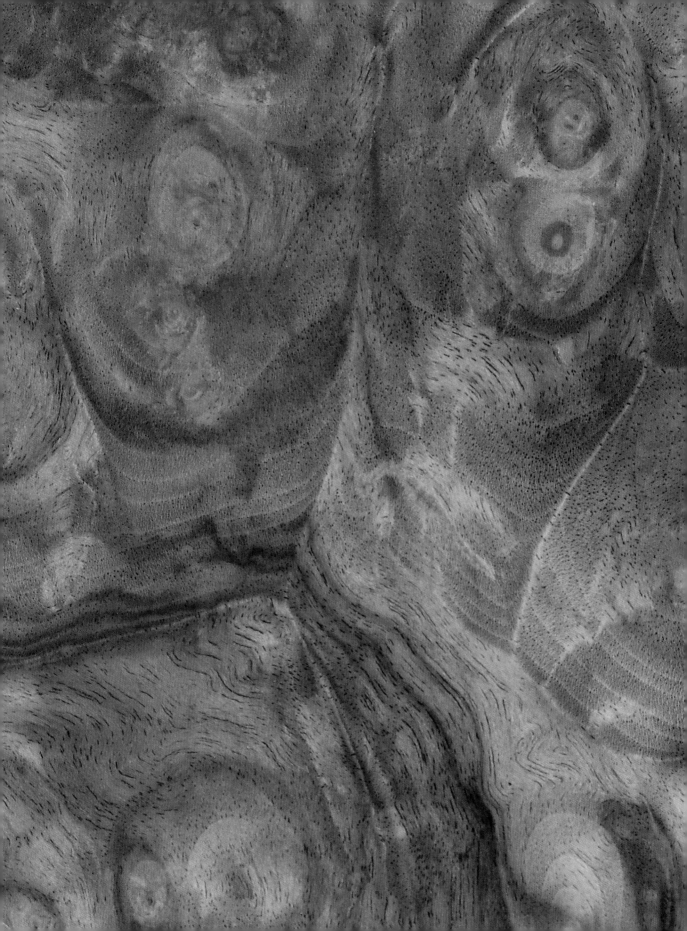

PART 2

FINISHING SCHOOL

Here is an encyclopedic overview of traditional fine-finishing techniques, organized according to medium. It covers the three main ingredients of period processes—oil, wax, and shellac—as well as gilding and paint, the other treatments you are most likely to encounter on antiques. I explain the history behind various techniques, from French polish to dry-wax rub, as well as applications for which they are best suited. Read this section to acquaint yourself with the many methods at your disposal and to better understand the artistry and alchemy involved.

WAX OVERVIEW

When I moved to New York from France, I had just one phone number in my pocket. Luckily, it was that of a former client of my parents', a Greenwich Village septuagenarian whose furniture I systematically started to refinish. Without money for a studio, I had to do all the work in her lovely town house. Wax proved the perfect tool for on-site restoration. The results were achieved without making too much of a mess, and the material is incredibly versatile.

Depending on your vision and the method used, wax can make a period piece look brand-new—or a brand-new reproduction look old. The material can be used in its cold, solid state or its warm, liquid form to bestow an amber glow or even an ebony hue. Use wax on its own to give pieces shine, depth, and patina or in conjunction with other products—oil, pigment, pumice stone—to create decorative finishes such as ceruse and *vernis anglais*. Embrace the chameleon-like quality of this ancient furniture-finishing medium.

IDENTIFYING A WAX FINISH

Wax is most commonly used to finish rustic pieces, from early American and Shaker designs to French provincial and Spanish mission furniture. It's easy to visually identify an antique that's been waxed—it's often rough-hewn, with a country feel. Still, it's good to confirm your guess by tracing a fingernail across the piece; you'll scrape up a bit of brown, greasy residue. (Varnish, in contrast, will flake up.) Another identification method is to put a small amount of turpentine on the tip of your finger and rub a hidden spot; a slurry residue will melt on your finger if it's waxed.

Wax-finished antiques that have been well taken care of over the centuries have a beautiful, deep patina, whereas neglected pieces are often quite dirty or dry-looking, with an absence of shine. The power of the wax has been lost, and the essence of the wood has been effaced by centuries of built-up grime.

WAX TECHNIQUES

Ceruse

To create this wonderfully decorative finish, you open up the grain as much as possible—brushing away the loose fiber—and rub pigment deep into the wood. The action colors the creases but leaves the top surface protruding from the pigment like ridges in a windswept desert. The idea is to create a contrast between the grain of the wood—which you deepen—and the background, which you want as smooth and even as possible. The contrast between high and low augments the distinctiveness of the grain patterning.

THE LOOK: An enhanced grain and two-tone coloration. Although this finish is often executed with gray and white pigment, bolder colors can be used for more exuberance.

SEEN ON: Oak and ash. The favored types of wood for cerusing, they have open and deep figuration and a contrast in texture between the inside and outside of the grain, making it easy to loosen and remove the fiber.

HISTORY: From antiquity until the middle of the 19th century, a white lead called *ceruse* was used to color the space between wood grains in this fashionable technique. It was rediscovered during the Art Deco period, spurring a revival. As is often the case, the origin is utilitarian: Ceruse protected wood against pests and vermin. Lead in ceruse was banned progressively beginning in the 1960s.

GOOD FOR: Ceruse is the perfect special-effect finish to use on furniture with simple, clean lines that needs a dramatic (or more subtly chic) punctuation.

PROS: Easy and fun to do. And unbelievably versatile stylistically, given the unlimited range of color combinations.

CONS: As with all wax finishes, it's not designed for heavy wear and tear.

See page 146 for an example of ceruse.

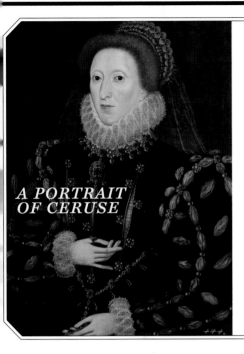

A PORTRAIT
OF CERUSE

The first time I tried a ceruse finish with white wax, I ended up looking like a spectrally pale portrait of Queen Elizabeth I. In fact, the comparison is a fair one. From medieval times to the middle of the 19th century, aristocratic European women used Venetian cerussite to whiten their faces. To apply the lead-based paste, women mixed it with egg whites, which created the unfortunate side effect of cracking when these women smiled—the resulting necessity to maintain a stern visage can be seen in portraits of the Virgin Queen. Furniture ateliers and boat makers, too, used the pigment, in their case rubbing the paste into wood to protect against vermin. Of course, both these women and the artisans were slowly poisoning themselves, as the lead seeped through their skin into their bloodstreams.

Ceruse saw a revival the 1930s with designers such as Jean-Michel Frank. The pairing made sense as the clean and simple lines of the furniture style benefited from the bold, somewhat aggressive finish of ceruse.

Lead pigments are now banned; while the newly formulated white pigment is still known by the name *ceruse*, it is now lead-free and safe.

Wax vs. Oil

Which one is better suited to your piece? A comparison of the two most common mediums.

WAX	VS.	OIL
Imparts a nice warm shine; enhances the details: carvings, balusters, sculpted parts.	WHAT IT DOES	Gives a satin shine; penetrates into the fiber to develop a deep bond with the wood; enhances the grain patterning and coloration.
From light pine and oak to black walnut and ebony; simple and/or rustic pieces; very old pieces built from solid wood.	WHAT IT'S GOOD FOR	Light- to medium-toned hardwood species like walnut, mahogany, tiger maple, or curly maple; Danish, midcentury modern, or Shaker furniture; other pieces with simple lines and an emphasis on the naked beauty of the wood.
Lends a warm patina; is easy to apply; can be mixed with color; is easy to maintain and restore.	PROS	Penetrates deeply to nourish the wood; is easy to apply, maintain, and restore: just clean and then rebuild the finish—no stripping needed; is safe for toys and kitchen utensils (when food-grade products are used).
Dries out and loses its properties; has a lower resistance to liquids; must be reapplied occasionally; may build up gunk if reapplied without care.	CONS	Has a slow drying time; releases some fumes during application; requires repeated applications for a thick coating; can yellow with age.

Ciré Rempli

Ciré rempli (French for "filled wax") captures the rustic look and feel of timeworn solid-wood furniture patinated by repeated waxing, dusting, and shining. The surface looks as if years and years of accumulated grime has filled up the pores and the grain, resulting in a burnished, glimmering aspect—almost fossilized. *Ciré rempli* mimics that effect by filling the grain with a mix of wax and pumice stone, rubbed in with a pad, to create a hard shine and a smooth, flat surface that suggests centuries of use.

THE LOOK: A lustrous patina, almost like that on the handle of a tool that's been worn by repeated use. Think of dark Renaissance furniture that seems to glow from within.

SEEN ON: Old farm tables, medieval and Renaissance furniture, anything massive (chests, tabletops) made of solid wood that's been heavily waxed.

HISTORY: The technique has roots in the 16th and 17th centuries as a glossier and more resistant wax finish used for pieces like tables.

GOOD FOR: Giving character to less interesting woods like pine. But *ciré rempli* is equally well suited to species like walnut and chestnut, whose color and grain react well to polish. Best for large, monolithic pieces with flat surfaces that are not overly detailed.

PROS: Provides waterproofing and ages well; stains, grease, and oil just give the finish more depth and personality—great for heavily used dining tables. Easily maintained with oil or a new coat of wax; you don't have to refill the grain every time.

CONS: Unsuited to pieces with lots of detailing, which makes the technique hard to execute.

See page 142 for an example of ciré rempli.

Dry-Wax Rub

This simple, no-fuss, almost primitive finish is ideal for enhancing raw wood: no fumes, no mixing. While doing it, I always picture old artisans and their scarce supplies, creating beauty out of a little raw beeswax and a burnisher. The technique could not be simpler: Sand the surface extra smooth (with 320-grit sandpaper) and then rub it with a loaf of untreated solid beeswax, going with the grain. Once you've rubbed it all over (there's no need for drying time), burnish with a flat piece of cork or wood—or the favored tool of 17th-century wood artisans (and still made today by The Broom Brothers in North Carolina), a reed burnisher, which is designed to crush wood fibers. In just five minutes, you have a gleaming tabletop and a fairly impervious finish.

THE LOOK: A harsh, stone-like satin shine that enhances the wood's natural character and coloration.

SEEN ON: Clean-lined monolithic furniture, paneling, boiserie, and doors.

HISTORY: One of the most ancient finishes, this method has long been used to polish and burnish wood surfaces.

GOOD FOR: A new or just-stripped piece. Furnishings without abundant detailing, since you need wide, flat surfaces to rub the wax. (Details require burnishing with an agate or stone burnishing tool.) Perfect for kitchen countertops or tables.

PROS: Offers waterproofing with minimal product—and turpentine isn't even required, because you don't heat and melt the wax. Totally foolproof, it takes just five minutes to do. Reveals the beauty of a raw, unique slab of wood.

CONS: Can only be executed on solid, unstained wood.

See page 204 for an example of dry-wax rub.

HAND LACQUER AND SHELLAC OVERVIEW

Before the advent of modern spray-on one-coat varnish, hand-padded shellac-based finishes were used to create a flawless, aqueous gloss. The European methods of furniture lacquering, collectively known as *le laque européen*, evolved from attempts to copy the legendary (and legendarily elusive) beauty and shine of Asian lacquerwork. Shellac-based techniques are the secret behind the transparent finishes seen on museum-quality antiques, the assertive grain distinguishing Art Deco lacquer, and the perfect, mirror-like shine representative of 18th-century French-polished furniture—the ne plus ultra of the genre.

IDENTIFYING HAND LACQUER AND SHELLAC FINISHES

In contrast to varnish, which coats the wood to create a film, historical lacquer techniques like French polish are *integral* to the wood. The giveaway is a shine that appears to emanate from the wood itself, rather than an applied topcoat.

HAND LACQUER AND SHELLAC TECHNIQUES

Shellac

Shellac is used to give wood a protective coating. The solution is a mixture of alcohol and lac, the resinous excretion of a female bug that eats tree bark. Collected from trees throughout Southeast Asia, the lac is cooked, filtered, reduced, and dried to create an amber-hued sheet that's crumbled into flakes and sold by weight. The flakes come in three colors: ruby (also called garnet), amber, and blonde. You can use shellac on its own as a finishing coat, or in conjunction with oil or wax techniques; it marries well with almost everything. Shellac is a wonderful product to work with, so lustrous and versatile. (Read more about the material on page 244.)

THE LOOK: Shellac is more of a process than a look in itself.

SEEN ON: A wide range of 18th- and 19th-century antiques, especially French polish and European pieces.

HISTORY: Shellac was first used in ancient China for varied applications, including as a base for lacquer, as a glue, to pigment cosmetics, and to preserve food. Europeans discovered it when trade routes opened up during Marco Polo's time. It's since been used as a base for finishes and varnishes—and to re-create the look of Chinese lacquer.

GOOD FOR: A sealing coat before other finishes (for instance, a coat of shellac serves as a great buffer between an oil stain and an oil finish). It's also used as the base of many wax or oil finishes and is the main ingredient of French polish.

PROS: Protean product with myriad applications that's nontoxic and dries quickly, yet is quite forgiving to use. Mixed with color, it provides an easy way to repair and upgrade almost any piece or to execute spot touch-ups.

CONS: Does not provide total protection against water, alcohol, or heat.

LACCIFER LACCA

Native to Southeast Asia, this insect feeds on trees and excretes the digested wood fibers in a resinous compound that coats entire branches. This raw material (called sticklac) is collected, cleaned, crushed (seedlac), and finally filtered to form shellac.

French Polish

French polish is a classic historical finish for fine antiques. In terms of beauty, it is without peer. The resulting surface is so pure it seems as though you could reach right inside the grain. The basis of the technique involves shellac, alcohol, pumice, and a few drops of oil, but all refinishers have their own French polish recipe— and are emphatic that *their* way is the *right* way. In my younger days, I ruined numerous furnishings trying to apply this deceptively simple method, but if you're less pigheaded, you can stop at any step in the process and finish the piece with wax.

THE LOOK: A deep, transparent, mirror-like shine. Variations of the technique involve mixing pigments with the shellac or working with a colored background to create intoxicatingly deep hues.

SEEN ON: 18th- and 19th-century European pieces, mahogany furniture from the 19th century, and überglossy Art Deco pieces.

HISTORY: Cabinetmakers have always sought the purest finish to enhance their creation. Efforts to copy the high shine of Asian lacquer techniques achieved the greatest level of refinement in France with this particular process and combination of ingredients.

GOOD FOR: Enhancing the clarity, tone, grain, and patterns of the most refined antiques, pieces with beautifully figured wood or elaborate marquetry. Equally transformed by French polish: Victorian furnishings, which can be found cheaply in antiques stores and flea markets, not to mention vintage pieces with bad finishes.

PROS: Offers unparalleled clarity and beauty: Think water on bare wood. Although technically not the most resistant finish, it doesn't require maintenance. French polish can be repaired, patched up, upgraded, and enhanced without prior stripping or cleaning. Can be used as the base for other finishes.

CONS: Technique needs experience and practice and can be tedious. Offers low resistance to abrasion and liquids as well as heat damage.

See pages 172 and 180 for examples of French polish.

THE FRENCH POLISH MIND-SET

I discovered French polish when I was ten years old. I remember running my finishing pad over an old Oriental lacquer piece and seeing the black color instantly wake up, the gold penmanship and different inlays reappear. It was magic! I knew instantly why it was referred to as "the king of finishes and the finish of kings."

Vernis Anglais

Vernis anglais, or English varnish, is an abbreviated version of French polish, eliminating the tedious pumice-filling of the grain and the difficult alcohol shine that culminates the process. *Vernis anglais* offers a solid, nicely built-up finish ideal for 19th-century furniture, especially those crafted of mahogany.

THE LOOK: A less luminous version of French polish. Think of the decor of an old English country estate or Mayfair town house.

SEEN ON: George III, Victorian, and Edwardian-era furnishings.

HISTORY: I would hate to revive ancient Franco-English quarrels, but *vernis anglais* is a recipe to get a French polish look with less time and expertise—a by-product of the 19th-century industrial mind-set that championed easier, faster production methods.

GOOD FOR: 19th-century furniture, including Victorian designs, as well as antiques crafted of mahogany. Although *vernis anglais* is a wonderful vehicle for imbuing many pieces with an old-world feeling, it's really only appropriate for rather formal pieces made of hardwood and for works dating from the 17th century onward. Not suited to rustic pieces or dark oak.

PROS: Quicker and easier than French polish, as well as more resistant and impervious. Easy to maintain and upgrade. A safe, less toxic way to varnish an old piece of furniture.

CONS: Less transparent than French polish; as a varnish, it's really a coating, not a polish. The finish will cloud with age, potentially obscuring the wood over time.

European Lacquer

In the 16th century, Spanish and Portuguese explorers brought home to Europe the first examples of Asian lacquer, setting off an instant craze—and rafts of imitators attempting to achieve the same aqueous shine and deep coloration without knowledge of (or access to) the ingredients behind them: saps and oils from native trees. The techniques that the European artisans developed, although radically diverse, are collectively referred to as *le laque européen*, or japanning. Recipes included various concoctions of drying oils, shellac, pigments, and more. Some techniques were very similar to refined versions of varnishing, polished to a high shine. Others were closer to a French polish buildup, incorporating pigments in the background and during the finishing phase.

THE LOOK: Deep color, but with great variation and less uniformity than glossy paint. Imbued with a warmth that high-shine modern finishes lack.

SEEN ON: 18th-century European pieces incorporating or reproducing Asian lacquerwork; Victorian black papier-mâché objects and small furniture; Art Deco pieces till the 1940s when chemical lacquers started to take over.

HISTORY: To achieve the effect of Asian lacquer, Europeans imported lacquered panels—low tables, screens—and incorporated them into new furnishings. Cabinetmakers began developing their own techniques, first to complete the surroundings of the imported panels, and ultimately to free themselves from the constraints of borrowing.

GOOD FOR: Furniture with clean, geometric lines that demand the royal treatment; Art Deco–era designs.

PROS: Inimitable gloss and depth; low maintenance—only periodic dusting is required. Can be patched and restored.

CON: Fragile finish. The technique requires practice. Not for ornate or carved pieces.

VERNIS MARTIN

In the 18th century, myriad European artisans and ébénistes developed proprietary methods and formulas to reproduce the high gloss and intense coloration of Oriental lacquers. The most famous were a sibling duo of upscale cabinetmakers, Guillaume and Étienne-Simon Martin, who devised a technique of mixing copal varnishes, shellac, and Venetian turpentine to re-create the characteristic sheen and palette. The vivid colors they used and the delicacy of their painted chinoiserie ornamentation (reinterpreted with European themes and characters) became synonymous with rococo Louis XV style.

OIL OVERVIEW

Traditional cabinetmakers used to call oil finishes "varnishes." Although the term *varnish* is now synonymous with chemical-based coatings such as polyurethane and epoxy, it actually derives from ancient Greek: the word *berenix,* which means "fragrant resin." In Latin, it changed to *vernix,* the origin of *vernis* in French.

The masterful use of oils reached its height with the great Danish designers of the 1950s and '60s. Courtesy of the prevailing vogue for all things Scandinavian modern, and the fact that similar designs were concurrently mass-produced in America, these pieces are a staple of vintage shops. You may even have an aunt's dining set or a perfect coffee table with great lines but a decaying finish that needs restoration. Use the traditional oil finishes that follow to restore such pieces to their original glory.

These oil finishes are also great for a wide variety of other applications, including building a durable yet subdued look and acting as a sealer between coats of other finishes. Oil is also the base of glazes and stains used to envision decorative effects. You can achieve different looks and degrees of shine, depending on whether you hand-rub ten coats or apply two with a brush. Add pigment to oil to create ebonized and driftwood finishes as well as other period looks, or just to enhance the color of a beautiful wood.

IDENTIFYING AN OIL FINISH

The finish has a natural look that you don't get with a modern varnish coating. An oil finish comes across as a *part* of the wood. The glow is more satin and the buildup not very thick.

OIL TECHNIQUES

Ebonizing

This technique stains furniture a deep, rich hue to mimic the inky look of ebony. During the 19th-century Victorian and Second Empire eras, the stand-in for ebony was usually pearwood, a stable variety of timber that could take the stain color very well (counterintuitive, as its natural state is rather blond) and that has a hard, tight grain approximating dense ebony's uniformity. These days, the substitute is often mahogany or—better yet—walnut, whose dark veining is almost identical to ebony's.

THE LOOK: Although people are most familiar with a dark, obsidian-hued variation, ebonizing can also provide a lighter finish, akin to the color of espresso.

SEEN ON: Victorian, Second Empire, and neoclassical pieces, as well as 19th-century copies of 18th-century classics. Lighter ebonized finishes are common on midcentury-modern furnishings.

HISTORY: Ebonizing became ubiquitous in Victorian England and its French counterpart, the Second Empire (the reign of Napoléon III), in the later 19th century. Now almost extinct, ebony was already rare when this technique was developed, and thus prohibitively expensive. It's also a difficult wood to work with, brittle and dense. For all those reasons, it was preferable to achieve its likeness with a faux finish.

GOOD FOR: Pieces in poor condition. Dark stains can hide a multitude of sins! Ebonizing is a very flexible technique, equally suited to a fancy Louis XVI desk or hand-me-downs from your grandparents.

PROS: Relatively easy to execute and looks good on any style of furniture.

CONS: Masks the grain somewhat, so not the best choice for furniture made from a beautiful wood that merits showing off. May require many coats of stain to achieve the desired darkness, and the process can be messy.

See pages 162 and 168 for examples of ebonizing.

Oil Varnishes

The word *varnish* evokes overly glossy coatings generated by harsh modern chemicals—polyurethane, spray lacquer, and catalyzed products—all of which are unfit for antiques. But historically, the term was used to describe a method of finishing wood via various combinations of natural products and solvents: usually tree resin or sap mixed with either oil (called *gum varnish*) or turpentine (called *spirit varnish*, so named because it cures via evaporation). Shellac was often referred to as a varnish, too. Remnants of these finishes, which became prevalent in 19th-century France and England, are easily mistaken for French polish.

As with all traditional techniques and products, restoration and upkeep is easy: Even after they crack, cloud, and lose their protective quality, historic varnishes can be sanded down and cleaned—no need to strip!—and then revived with shellac and wax.

RESINS USED FOR HISTORIC VARNISHES

TYPE OF RESIN	WHAT IT'S MADE OF
Rosin	Pine sap
Copal	Almost-fossilized amber
Sandarac	Derived from an African tree
Gum arabic	Sap from the acacia tree
Balsam	Derived from a type of fir tree

OIL GLOSSARY

There are three different types of oil used to finish furniture.

LINSEED OIL: Before the advent of chemical drying agents, most varnishes were based on linseed oil. Linseed oil sinks into the wood, coating and protecting it—it is hard to build up and should be reserved for less formal, more organic finishes and very simple pieces like teak tables and old, rustic benches. It is also good for maintaining preexisting oil finishes. It takes a long time to dry—up to a week to cure—so build up coats little by little. An old custom suggests that you apply once a day for a week, once a week for a month, and once a month for a year. If you overdo it, the wood surface becomes saturated and gummy. It also has a tendency to yellow with age, so avoid on lighter woods.

TUNG OIL: Personal bias alert: For my fine furniture, I favor a great, pure tung oil. Derived from the Chinese tung tree, this oil variety is more water- and weather-resistant than linseed oil. That makes it great for outdoor applications. In addition, tung oil dries faster. It has a naturally heavy drying agent, so after a few coats, it builds up quite nicely without giving the surface a varnish-y look. Some people layer up to eight or nine coats. (Although over-applying without proper bonding or preparation leaves behind a film and/or iridescent marks; use steel wool to break it down.) Tung oil gives a shine that you won't achieve with linseed oil—and at a much faster pace—so it's suitable for a wide variety of pieces.

DANISH OIL: A combination of poly-merized tung oil, linseed oil, and colored pigments, this oil was the darling of midcentury Danish cabinetmakers—hence the name. Contemporary blends offer superior UV protection and faster drying time. Perfect for exterior use and rustic, dark pieces. Four or more coats are needed for protection.

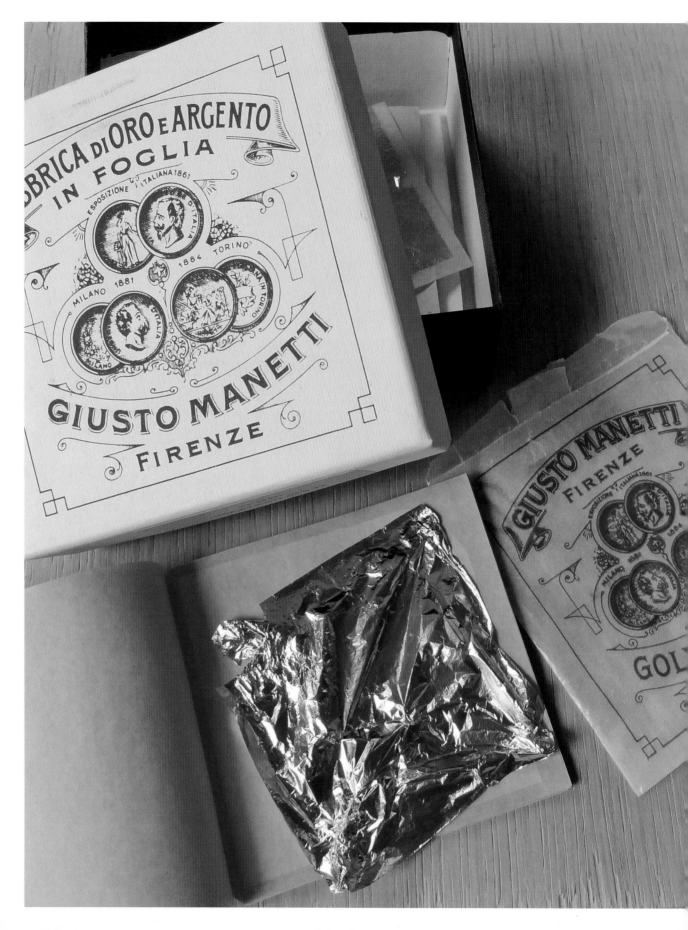

GILDING OVERVIEW

Gilding was developed to mimic the look of solid gold, a precious commodity that was also a currency used by kings to pay for wars and debts. The earliest versions of this ancient technique used thick sheet metal hammered over carved wood, sometimes heated to better marry with the shape of the piece. (Since gold is ductile, it's pretty malleable.) Gold leaf is made by hand-hammering nuggets of gold between two cushions of suede or leather, resulting in a superthin but elastic sheet. Over the centuries, the artistry and materials became increasingly refined: The gold sheet became thinner and the substrate smoother, thanks to a more sophisticated preparation of the wood, involving coats of plaster (gesso) and red clay (bole).

Throughout history, a high-shine finish was most coveted—think King Tut's tomb, the Rosary Chapel in Puebla, Mexico, and Louis XIV's bedchambers; this preference culminated in the 17th and 18th centuries. Today, many favor the aged patina of exposed bole and a burnished hue. There are numerous ways to achieve this effect on newly applied gold leaf, ranging from überfine abrasion to tinting (and jealously guarded secret brews!). Gilding can also be combined with special treatments to create patinas or imbue the gold with coloration. Some of the most popular decorative techniques involving metal leaf, including mecca finish, evolved from clever attempts to imitate gilt with other materials, notably silver leaf and varnish.

IDENTIFYING A GOLD-LEAF FINISH

It's very simple: Gold is inimitable. Any other material will look fake. But on older pieces worn and patinated by age, the true test is to look at the seams, the little lines where the squares overlapped. A leaf of gold is always the same size: three fingers wide. If the seams are spaced farther apart, the piece is finished with composition gold—i.e., brass or copper, which are wider. And if there are no obvious seams, or the gold is too brassy in tone, then the piece has likely been treated to gold varnish or paint.

GILDING TECHNIQUES

Water Gilding

This is the most refined iteration of gold leafing. Water is used to reactivate the trace amount of glue in the preparation coats—the gesso and bole—just before the loose leaf is applied. The water evaporates, so the gold leaf bonds directly with the underlying bole. (Even the thinnest coat of glue would not give the perfect, flawless, flat-metal finish that can be achieved with water gilding!) And because water gilding results in an integral bond versus a superficial application, you can burnish the finish to a high shine and even add varnishes after the gold leaf dries.

THE LOOK: A smooth, flawless gold-metal look.

SEEN ON: First and foremost, religious ornaments—from statues to altars—as well as 18th-century furniture and boiserie, and all frames and mirrors from that time. Italian, Spanish, and French artisans frequently used gold leaf, as did Germans in the Baroque era.

HISTORY: Gold was a signifier of status—a symbol of kings and nobility—and also had overt religious connotations, which is why it was a favorite treatment for architectural elements, statues, and furnishings in ecclesiastical and royal contexts across many cultures.

GOOD FOR: Mirror and picture frames, headboards, wall panels, statues, and chair frames, as well as to embellish carving details on dark-stained furniture.

PROS: A shine that does not tarnish. Repairs and patches to the wood support structure will be rendered invisible, since the gesso and bole will ensure uniformity and flawlessness. Paradoxically, gold also requires no maintenance: light dusting only, and temperate conditions.

CONS: The most difficult gilding technique to achieve, as it requires a flawless application.

See pages 184 and 190 for examples of water gilding.

Oil Gilding

In this technique, the bonding agent between the bole and the gold leaf is a kind of adhesive called *sizing glue*. This glue is brushed on and left to dry until it's a little tacky; then patent gold leaf is applied to the top. Courtesy of the glue's viscosity, the resulting surface is somewhat textured. Many people prefer this slightly rustic look to the glitzier sheen of water gilding.

THE LOOK: Can range from rustic and rough-hewn to a sleek, smooth finish approximating water gilding, depending on the piece and the treatment of the prep coats.

SEEN ON: Italian furnishings, Renaissance pieces, older boiserie (usually oil gilding is executed directly on the wood, rather than on prep coats of gesso and bole), and architectural details like moldings.

HISTORY: The sizing was originally oil-based, with a long drying time. Today, most sizing is acrylic and a light tack is achieved within ten minutes. (The name *oil gilding*, however, stuck.)

GOOD FOR: Beginners! It's a great way to start learning the gilding process. Oil gilding allows the use of patent gold leaf, backed by a paper sheet that's removed after you position the leaf. Also good for creating an antique look. For use with composition leaves or combinations of different metal varieties without the expense of real gold.

PROS: Easier to execute (and more forgiving) than water gilding.

CONS: The resulting surface texture will not have the unparalleled solid-gold look. Cannot be burnished to a metallic aspect (but can be waxed and is perfect for receiving patinas).

See page 196 for an example of oil gilding.

Mecca Finish

Mecca finish started as a cheat, in which silver leaf treated to a yellow varnish substituted for gold. But from there, a number of creative liberties were taken: mixing different metal leafs together in a patchwork, superimposing them, or adding colored pigments to the varnish. Accordingly, mecca finish has become an umbrella term for a category of variations, often used to create a tarnished, variegated patina. Mecca finishes age beautifully: The silver corrodes irregularly under the shellac, cracking it haphazardly.

THE LOOK: Exuberant patinas, metallic hues.

SEEN ON: Baroque furniture, frames, and statues—primarily Italian and Spanish. Although not technically mecca finish, many Oriental lacquers also involved coloring silver and metal leaves to alter their appearance.

HISTORY: Italian artisans developed the technique in the 17th century.

GOOD FOR: Creating a highly antiqued metal-leaf finish; ceilings and other broad surfaces where the variegation between individual leafs will be showcased.

PROS: Highly decorative, and capable of achieving a wide variety of effects depending on the type of leaf (or leafs) you use, and what color varnish.

CONS: Takes time to do properly. The look is also a matter of personal preference— not everyone wants such a "living" finish.

Gold Varnish

An alternative to metal leafing is to use a top-quality gold varnish—*not* radiator paint!—purchased from a gilding resource or high-end art-supply store. I do not recommend this treatment for restoration work, since you could damage any existing gold leaf. But, because it can be treated to various patinas and coatings, it's a great choice for finishing a piece from scratch for decorative purposes.

THE LOOK: There are many varnish tones available, ideal for achieving funky artistic effects: Chantilly, Trianon, champagne, gold, silver, pewter, copper, and pink- and green-tinted gold

SEEN ON: Contemporary pieces.

HISTORY: Today's chemically based gold varnishes are a fairly recent invention. But versions of it have existed for centuries as a way to achieve the look of water gilding without the expense and labor—ground-bronze particles in an oil medium, for example.

GOOD FOR: A new finish only; never use to restore a gold-leaf finish.

PROS: Incredibly easy to use and, if properly applied, a very close stand-in for real gold leaf.

CONS: Cannot be used for restoration of an antique. I can't emphasize this enough: I know it's so tempting to use, but it could damage the piece and undermine its value.

See page 197 for an example of gold varnish.

GOLD-LEAF GLOSSARY

GESSO: A hard plaster-based cream used to prime the wood and build it to a smooth, hard surface. You can make your own gesso from plaster of Paris (or chalk), rabbit glue, and water, but it also comes premixed. Wet gesso has the consistency of crème fraîche; when dry, it's very hard, allowing you to carve intricate details or sand it to a silky-smooth texture. Derived from an animal product—rabbit glue—gesso is also elastic, moving with the wood substrate as it expands and contracts.

BOLE: This colored, water-based clay paste is applied on top of gesso, establishing a neutral base that makes the gold or silver leaf appear more brilliant. It comes in many hues, the most common being classic red, which enhances the gold's depth. Yellow is a better choice if you have a design with lots of carved details; any flaws in the gold leaf application won't be as noticeable. (That's why it's also used to cheat. Clerical ornaments in churches, for instance, are often gilded just on the front; from afar, the eye can't discern between gold leaf and yellow bole.) Black or blue bole also exists, primarily to give the metal leaf a cold undertone.

GOLD LEAF: There are many other varieties of leaf at your disposal: 14, 18, or 24 karat (i.e., double leaf) gold, as well as palladium, white gold, silver, and more. What you choose for your piece will depend on the desired tone, or what variety best matches the item you're restoring. The latter sometimes involves a bit of guess-work, since the material patinates differently on the same piece (consult a specialist for advice here). Sheets are always the same size, and have been throughout history: three fingers wide. *Loose gold leaf*, separated by silk paper, is used for water gild-ing. *Patent gold leaf*, the basis of oil gilding, comes backed by paper and a light adhesive; when applied, the backing separates from the gold.

PAINT OVERVIEW

Paint is composed of colored pigments mixed with either a water- or an oil-based medium. To enhance strength, heighten gloss, or ensure the stability of the pigments, assorted additives have been used in paint over the ages, from simple egg yolks to the sophisticated chemicals that distinguish contemporary products. Although the invention of canned, premixed paint and readily available oil paint was enabled by modern technology, the use of paint on furniture dates back millennia. Certain colors are associated with specific eras and locales— for example, the vivid (and well-preserved) hues of Egyptian artifacts and the patinated historical colors known today as Trianon gray, Empire green, and Gustavian blue. Highlighted here are two products very much anchored in the past, milk paint and hide-glue paint; both predated the introduction of oil-based coatings in the Renaissance.

IDENTIFYING A PAINTED FINISH

This is one of the easiest treatments to identify, as paint obscures the grain of the wood with a semitransparent or solid layer of color.

PAINT TECHNIQUES

Milk Paint

This totally natural, water-based product is a mixture of lime and casein, a type of milk protein. It's sold as a powder that you hydrate. Milk paint is one of the oldest forms of paint (versions of it were used in ancient Egypt and Rome). Centuries later it was ideally suited to a time when professional painters were itinerants traveling from village to village and job to job, carrying only their brushes and pigments. Because milk by-products and a limekiln were found almost everywhere, these painters could mix their product in situ.

THE LOOK: The finish is fairly flat and matte, although you can burnish it to a nice sheen with a bit of wax.

SEEN ON: Early-American furniture, Shaker pieces in particular.

HISTORY: Rooted in ancient times, milk paint in one form or another was used almost ubiquitously across the globe.

GOOD FOR: Shaker-style furniture, Gustavian-period pieces, or achieving weathered finishes (see page 198).

PROS: You can create the exact hue desired by adding pigments to your milk paint—or by mixing colors from scratch. It wears beautifully, fading as opposed to peeling or flaking. You never need to strip the wood and repaint; you can just add more coats. Great for faux aging and makes a good support for patinas.

CONS: Small period of workability: Just like an open carton of milk, it will spoil quickly once hydrated. It's also less resistant to wear and tear than oil-based products. Take extra precautions if you use it for outdoor applications, waiting a number of days in between coats so the paint bonds adequately with the wood.

See page 198 for an example of milk paint.

Hide-Glue Paint

This ancient and venerable water-based paint uses animal gelatin—notably hide glue or rabbit-skin glue—as a binder. Mixed with a tiny bit of clove oil, hide-glue paint was a resistant and versatile product used for artwork as well as cabinetry and architectural woodworking, items that were often painted as a luxury treatment in the Middle Ages and during the Renaissance. It is slightly glossier than milk paint and can be burnished or waxed to a beautiful, deep shine that transcends a painted coating to become a veritable *matériel*.

THE LOOK: Deep and rich in tone; often has a satin shine. Beautiful patinas.

SEEN ON: Old polychrome statues, consoles, and boiserie.

HISTORY: Like milk paint, its invention derived from resourcefulness, a way for artisans to use readily available materials: water and animal rejects.

GOOD FOR: Since hide glue layers well, it's perfect for painted finishes requiring several coats or the addition of painted details and ornaments.

PROS: Beautiful and resistant. Nontoxic and releases no fumes, so safe for toys and eating utensils.

CONS: The mixing process is a bit laborious, since it requires heat. As with all traditional, water-based products, stability depends on adequate proportions.

How Do You Know What Finish Your Piece Currently Has?

*Before you dive into refinishing your piece, you need to determine what finish
it already has—oil, wax, shellac, varnish, etc.—because that will affect what preparation
you need to do and to some extent narrow your options. Consult this table.*

YOU KNOW IT'S . . .	. . . WHEN	HOW TO TEST IT
MODERN LACQUER	The surface seems to have a hard, glossy look—almost vitreous.	Acetone or lacquer thinner will dissolve the finish after a little rubbing.
NEW VARNISHES (polyurethane, etc.)	The coating is tough and hard, almost plastic-like.	Water and acetone will not disturb the finish; paint thinner will dull the shine.
AN OIL-RUBBED FINISH	The finish has a natural look that comes across as a part of the wood.	Linseed oil rubbed with your finger will be absorbed by the wood.
PRE-CHEMICAL OIL VARNISHES	The wood seems to have a coating to it—whether satin or glossy.	Water droplets should bead up and not penetrate. Acetone rubbed for a minute or so will soften the varnish to a muddy gunk.
SHELLAC	A transparent, water-like feel (this will be French polish) or a mellow, old-varnish look (this is a simple coating).	Rubbing a little alcohol on the wood surface dissolves the coating.
WAX	A mellow shine and deep glow seem to emanate from inside the wood.	Scraping your fingernail across the wood lifts up gunk. Turpentine rubbed on will melt the coating.

How Do You Know What Finish It Needs?

*The purpose of finishing is to protect your piece—from use, dirt, light, humidity, dryness, etc.—
and to embellish it by enhancing the grain and the color of the wood. It always serves both a practical and
an aesthetic reason. Here are some pointers for determining what finish makes sense for your piece.*

I WANT MY PIECE TO LOOK...		USE
Cleaner	→	Adequate cleaning, sanding down top layers
Older	→	Glazing, different patinas
More formal	→	French polish or oil varnish
More rustic	→	Wax
Totally different!	→	Stripper, then start fresh
Unfinished	→	Dry-rubbed wax
Natural looking	→	An oil-rubbed finish

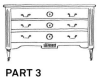

PART 3

PREP SCHOOL

Before you execute any finish work, a few preparatory steps must be taken. Removing hardware as well as any moving or sliding elements, including doors and drawers, will make it easier to maneuver the piece and apply and wipe off products used in the prep and finishing stages. At the very least, a thorough cleaning is then required to remove dust and dirt. Partial or complete removal of an existing finish, via stripping or dewaxing, may also be a necessity; any residue will keep subsequent coats—stain, sealer, etc.—from adhering to and bonding with the wood. Once the wood is bare, you can assess the state of the piece and initiate repair work, patching, and filling. Sand afterward to create a smooth canvas, giving the wood just the right texture to absorb stain and other products evenly and consistently. Stain if desired, and then preserve the work you've just executed by sealing it. This section also covers two optional processes: grain filling, which is done before staining, and glazing, which is done after or in between coats of staining.

I strongly suggest reading this part in its entirety, since it will acquaint you with the basic techniques, methodologies, and philosophies that form the basis of finishing work.

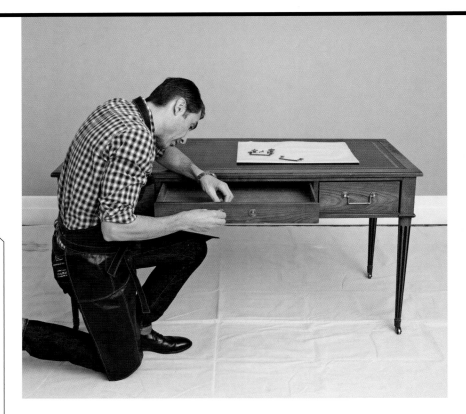

┌─────────────────────────────────┐

─── *TECHNIQUE GLOSSARY* ───

Here's a little more information about a few technical terms you'll encounter in this section.

OPEN TIME: The amount of time you have to work with the product before it sets. Products with a long open time are more forgiving, but there is a trade-off: The longer a solution takes to dry, the likelier it is to absorb dust particles from the air.

CHARGE: Charging means pouring a solution, like alcohol, into or onto a rag or pad.

WITH THE GRAIN: Moving your pad, rag, or sanding block over the wood surface in the same direction that the grain pattern flows, like so:

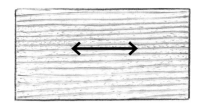

AGAINST THE GRAIN: Moving your pad across or perpendicular to the direction of the grain, like so:
└─────────────────────────────────┘

DISMANTLING

Before any prep work or finishing can begin, it is necessary to remove parts like drawers and as much hardware as possible.

REMOVING MOVABLE PIECES

Be sure to remove drawers, doors, crown moldings, interior shelves, and any other moving parts so they don't get jostled as you maneuver the piece. Doing this also means you can refinish more easily; your result will be even sharper and cleaner!

Label elements as you detach them, noting where they came from. (Don't assume that you'll remember which was the top drawer and which was the bottom.) Use tags or low-tack tape affixed to the underside, inside, or edge. Your smartphone or digital camera can also be an invaluable aid in recording where each element belongs. As you dismantle, you may discover old pencil marks from the furniture maker or subsequent restorers; if these annotations are still relevant, use them. It is common practice to leave these marks as they are and/or to add your own pencil notes on hidden parts of a piece of furniture—all usable for future generations.

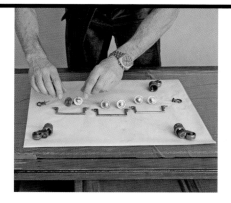

REMOVING HARDWARE

The more naked your piece, the easier it will be to refinish and the more artful the result, so hardware should be removed, too. Nevertheless, some pieces may not come off at all. If you give something a little tug and it sticks, leave it affixed. It is quite common for old hardware to have been tampered with and badly reattached, so don't force it.

That said, I advocate removing as much metalwork as you feel comfortable with. First, you'll likely be cleaning or restoring the hardware anyway (see "Hardware," page 276). Second, an intangible level of crispness and neatness occurs when you remove all the hardware for the finishing process and put it back afterward. The quality of your work will be so much higher, and you reduce the risk of damaging the hardware with various products.

Prioritize the ornamental bits (knobs, ormolu) since they'll be most obtrusive and are generally easiest to remove. Then approach the mechanical, functional stuff (hinges, locks) on a case-by-case basis. Store everything in resealable plastic bags, labeling the contents of each one with indelible marker. Fun fact: It doesn't matter what order you take things off—the last piece you remove will always give you the most trouble!

If you can't remove some or all of the hardware, protect it carefully and execute the finish around it. Cover the metal with white masking tape, the edges trimmed clean with an X-Acto knife. Replace the tape after every step—before it dries—since the tape is inclined to get gunky, and product might seep underneath.

PUTTING HARDWARE BACK ON

The very, very last step of finishing is to place all the hardware back on the piece. Most likely you'll have to replace some broken screws and brass nails; see "Hardware," page 276, for tips and advice. Adjust carefully so that each piece operates soundly and smoothly; drop handles especially will require finessing to ensure that they fall just right. Return casters last so the piece doesn't move—thus reducing the chances of a runaway desk (or squashing your toes!). Remember: A piece of hardware—even ornamental—not secured or placed properly will eventually cause damage to your furniture.

WHAT YOU'LL NEED

- *Gel stripper*
  Stripping is one of very few processes I do in my studio that involves very nasty chemicals. Some natural, eco-friendly strippers incorporate lye, which burns and thus darkens the wood, so are suitable only if you're painting the piece afterward or applying a dark finish. Other natural strippers are citrus-based and—although they don't darken the wood—not so efficient on tough finishes, especially pieces treated to more modern chemical varnishes. For furniture, a gel stripper offers the best control: Unlike liquid stripper, the product stays put and doesn't run off.

- *A plastic scraper*
  Avoid using metal tools, which are too sharp and can scratch the fragile, wet wood. You can buy a proper plastic scraper, but I prefer using old credit cards, which you can shape with scissors to the exact angle needed to clean moldings, details, and profiles. Sand the card before using to give it a nice, smooth edge.

- *A container*
  Use it to catch the gunk you scrape off. I save plastic takeout containers for this purpose.

- *Two pairs of gloves*
  Wear one latex, and a heavier, chemical-resistant pair on top. That way, you can remove the heavy pair when needed for detail work and still have protection (and keep your hands clean).

STRIPPING

Before refinishing a piece, you may have to strip any existing damaged finish—especially varnish, which tends to yellow and cloud over time. Creating an even, consistent base requires fully removing whatever product is already coating the wood, and then cleaning every surface thoroughly. Stripping is dirty and tiresome, but the transformation can be quite dramatic. When it's executed methodically, with the right tools and protection, the job will be fast and clean, and the result rewarding! The removal process also involves a certain poetry, revealing the unique history of the piece by exposing previous repairs, patches, and fillers. Embrace the unexpected beauty of these flaws. As Jean Cocteau said, "Since we have no clue about what happened, let's pretend we initiated it!"

THE PIECE

I'm demonstrating this preparatory step on an unusual 1940s French pearwood console with a scallop-like profile detail that made for challenging stripping. The existing clear finish was also quite thick, necessitating several coats of stripper.

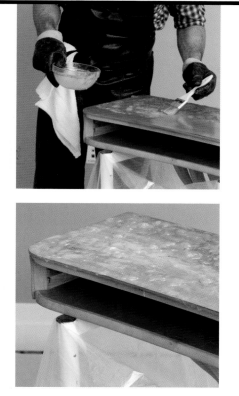

1   **POUR STRIPPER INTO A BOWL.** With a brush, apply a thick coat of stripper to a small surface area at a time—no more than 1 or 2 square feet. Use the brush only to spread the gel and not to more forcefully "paint" the surface; brushing aerates the stripper and makes it less effective.

2   **WAIT FOR THE STRIPPER TO DO ITS JOB.** As long as the gel is wet, it's still working. Sometimes the stripper pulls up the finish and starts bubbling within 5 minutes; other times, you're twiddling your thumbs for half an hour.

3   **SCRAPE OFF THE RESIDUE INTO YOUR CONTAINER.** This is not a mechanical process; you want the chemicals to do all the work, not you. In fact, you'll damage the wood if you scrape too hard. Flat surfaces are pretty easy to clean, but details and crevices can be tricky; this is where the cut-to-size credit card comes in handy.

4   **REPEAT AS NEEDED,** waiting a few minutes between coats, until the piece is absolutely clean. You may need to apply quite a few coats, as I did here. If you get discouraged and aren't seeing adequate progress, wait a day, clear your head, and start again. Nobody said the finish was going to come off all at once . . . except the stripper manufacturer!

5   **OPTIONAL:** For a more thorough cleaning, you can rub liquid stripper into the wood with very fine steel wool.

6   **DRY ALL SURFACES.** Finally, wipe the piece clean with a rag dampened with denatured alcohol.

7   **DISPOSE OF THE RESIDUE SAFELY.** Professional studios have a pickup service for waste, but you should pour the gunk back into the original stripper container and call your municipal offices for a disposal procedure. (Don't pour it down your sink!)

WHAT YOU'LL NEED

- *Turpentine*
  This is my preferred solvent for dewaxing. Whether you plan to execute a light cleaning or heavy wax removal, never use the heavy chemical strippers you find in hardware stores. Since they're designed for kitchen floors or industrial applications, they are much too powerful for antiques and could damage or destroy them. Also avoid any commercial degreaser unless purchased from a fine-woodworking supplier; these are adequately zealous yet safe. But in most cases you're much better off relying on the turpentine in your tool kit.

- *Synthetic-bristle brush*

- *Rags*
  Softly textured terry cloth makes an ideal rag; for more forceful cleaning, use any grade from 00 to 0000 steel wool.

DEWAXING

If your piece is already waxed, you'll probably want to remove some or all of the existing finish before proceeding. Wax has a tendency to dry out and collect dirt if improperly cared for. How much wax you should take off depends on the techniques you plan to execute, as well as your aesthetic preference. If you favor preserving the existing patina and simply applying a new topcoat, initiate a light cleaning. This will remove superficial schmutz and restore crispness to any carvings while leaving the beautifully aged texture undisturbed. (Afterward, avoid water-based stains and finishes on a dewaxed piece.)

Do Not Confuse Patina with Dirt

Years and years of layering wax on a piece without cleaning beforehand creates a gunky coating that mellows the details and obscures the natural color and beauty of the wood. This is dirt, not patina! Reviving the wood's spark requires a full removal of the existing wax and attendant grime, and has to be done properly. It is part of the conservation and restoration process and ensures the longevity of your antique.

STANDARD COURSE OF ACTION

With a brush, apply turpentine section by section. Keep wet for a few minutes. As the existing coating softens or melts, remove with a rag. Repeat as needed, removing as much or as little wax as desired until the richness of the wood reappears.

LIGHT-HANDED VERSION

Apply turpentine gently with a slightly damp cotton rag. This will mostly remove dirt and grime, while preserving the existing patina.

HEAVY-HANDED VERSION

On rustic, solid-wood pieces, you can use 0000 steel wool—super-saturated with turpentine—to enact a more forceful cleaning. Move the pad lightly across the piece, always with the grain, working section by section. Hold a rag in your other hand, and clean up as you go: Rub in the steel wool with your right hand, blot off gunk with your left. Afterward, clean thoroughly with a turpentine-dampened rag.

Variation

An intentionally sloppy dewaxing can help you realize an aged patina. Any water-based product you apply next, such as milk paint, won't adhere to the wax residue, creating peeling, bubbling, or an otherwise worn-by-the-centuries effect that you may desire. See page 198 for an example of this technique.

Troubleshooting

If you can't remove all the wax (or fear damaging the piece) but still want to execute a full refinish, clean as well as you can and use oil-based stains and finish afterward. Because they utilize the same medium as wax, they will penetrate and combine with the extant finish. Then you can safely continue your finish with tung or linseed oil, followed by a topcoat of wax if desired. Alcohol-based mediums are also safe.

WHAT YOU'LL NEED

- *Filler*
  This can be made using a number of recipes—see "Making Your Own Fillers," page 246—to create a product of varying thickness; a dough-like consistency is good for this use.

- *Toothpick*
  Alternatively, you can use a wood stick.

- *100 percent cotton rag*

- *Alcohol or turpentine*

FILLING HOLES AND CRACKS

Rebuild missing elements—broken feet, chipped corners—and patch holes and cracks after you've stripped and cleaned the piece, and prior to any sanding, staining, or finishing. This creates a sound substrate, and a stable canvas for your subsequent craftsmanship. I cover a number of common repairs on pages 260–289, but here's a quickie filler primer.

1   **DAB THE FILLER INTO THE HOLE** or crack with a finger, bit by bit. Fill the bottom of the hole more carefully, using a wood stick or toothpick to force it in if you have to.

2   **PROCEED IN PHASES,** applying over and over; fillers always shrink a bit. Wait until it's dry and reapply. Drying time will vary depending on the filler used, from an hour to overnight.

3   **REMOVE ANY EXCESS WITH A RAG,** dampened with the same medium as the filler, before it totally sets.

4   *ET VOILÀ!* The filled crack will have exactly the same texture as the surrounding wood. You'll smooth the surface flush in the next step, sanding.

Alternatives to Traditional Filler

Wax Sticks

Another handy product for filling cracks and holes is a wax stick, available from good woodworking suppliers. Always keep a few colors on hand, such as light maple, medium oak, and dark walnut. They can be mixed together to create the exact hue needed. The advantages of this product are obvious: It's nontoxic, easy to use, clean, fast, and versatile. You can even apply a finish—especially wax—directly on top. (Because wax will never dry solid, this filler is not suitable for reconstructing a missing part— unless it's something you will never handle or touch.) To use, tear off a piece, knead it between your fingers to warm, fill holes or cracks, and then scrape off the excess carefully with a plastic credit card or even a fingernail.

Hard Shellac Sticks

Hard shellac sticks, which come in different colors, are another classic way to fill a hole. You may encounter this historical filler method when stripping an antique and be puzzled by the strange consistency of the repair. Unlike wax sticks, shellac versions are heated, resulting in a syrup (rather than a paste) that's dropped into the hole and dries almost instantly. Keep this process in mind as a reference, but leave it to professionals: Charred product, heat damage, and a burned-down house are risks you want to avoid!

TYPES OF SANDPAPER

WET AND DRY: The advantage is versatility; use this sandpaper dry or dip it into water or oil for lubrication.

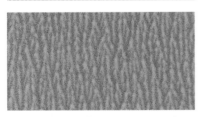

OPEN CUT: Another type commonly used for fine furniture, its surface is coated with a little lubricant for a smoother sanding.

GARNET: Unless you start with very coarse wood that's been barely planed, do not use this ubiquitous hardware-store variety. The texture is too scratchy and not uniform enough for fine cabinetmaking and finishing.

SANDING

When I was grounded as a teenager, I spent many an afternoon sanding furniture in my father's atelier. Sanding is not the most glamorous phase of refinishing, and it's certainly the dustiest. But any artisan will tell you that great preparation is the key to eventual beauty, and sanding is an essential part of that process. You cannot achieve refined results without a refined surface. Sanding is the base of your finish, creating a clean, level canvas in anticipation of a new treatment. Embrace it as a contemplative exercise!

The purpose of sanding is to make the wood as smooth and uniform as possible, bringing it to the level specifically required by the finish you'll be executing and ensuring even absorption of stains or other finishing products. The more you sand, the smoother and more microscopically even the wood surface becomes.

GRITS

Sandpapers come numbered according to their degree of roughness: the lower the grit number, the coarser the abrasive (generally sand and/or glass particles) and the more wood it removes. Higher-grit sandpaper, meanwhile, is better at removing more minute surface asperities. When sanding a piece, you typically start with a low grade and progress upward, following the numbers consecutively. Although you can sand all the way to 20,000 grit—used to polish cars—you'll generally stop at 220, which creates the perfect wood texture for stain to bond with.

Commonly Used Grits

GRIT	USE
50–100	Do not use on fine furniture.
120, 150	Should be reserved only for something really rustic and exceptionally damaged.
180	Start here for fine furniture.
220	Stop here if you plan to stain the wood. A finer grit will tighten the grain and burnish the wood, impairing even penetration of the stain—especially if you plan to go dark.
320, 360, 400	Stop here if you plan to French polish or if you won't be staining the piece.
500, 600	Use for scuff-sanding (see below) in between coats.

SCUFF-SANDING

Scuff-sanding is the term used to describe light sanding executed between coats to remove any fine dust marring your finish. You don't want to abrade the finish in the process or rub through coats; you simply want to remove slight imperfections and dust caught on the wet finish. Using only the weight of your hand, go over the piece just once—30 seconds and you're done. Be sure to use very, very fine sandpaper— never less than 400 grit, and more like 500 or 600 if you've already built up a finish. I suggest starting with 500, and if that doesn't remove the schmutz, go lower.

HOW TO FOLD SANDPAPER

1

CUT A SHEET OF PAPER INTO SIXTHS OR EIGHTHS by folding it a few times and slicing it with a ruler (not your scissors—you could damage the blades).

2

FOLD A SECTION INTO THIRDS, scratchy side out.

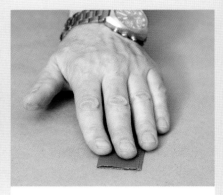

3

USE ONCE AND THEN TOSS. (This is why you keep the pieces small: to save paper.)

HOW TO WRAP A BLOCK

1

I PREFER A SANDING SPONGE, but you can also use a small block sized to wrap a quarter-sheet of sandpaper around.

2

CUT A SMALL PIECE OF CORK TO SIZE. This soft layer will make the block more forgiving.

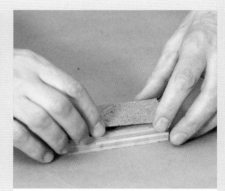

3

AFFIX TO THE BLOCK. Press firmly.

HOW TO WRAP A SANDING SPONGE

1

CUT THE SANDPAPER INTO QUARTERS.

2

WRAP A PIECE OF SANDPAPER AROUND THE SPONGE.

3

THE SPRINGINESS OF THE SPONGE IS SOFTER AND MORE FORGIVING ON WOOD.

4

WRAP THE SANDPAPER AROUND THE BLOCK. The cork goes on the bottom.

5

MAKE SURE THE PAPER IS TIGHT.

6

READY TO USE!

How to Sand

1   **ALWAYS SAND BY HAND.** Power sanding is rough and messy and has no place in furniture refinishing! It can also leave marks, dents, and dirt on the wood surface.

2   **SAND IN A CLEAN ENVIRONMENT.** You do not want specks of dirt or coarse wood dust from previous passes to scratch your surface.

3   **BEGIN WITH THE APPROPRIATE GRIT OF SANDPAPER** (see page 117); then sand a test patch in an unobtrusive spot before tackling the entire piece.

4   **SAND WITH EVEN PRESSURE.** (Pressing harder as you go only removes wood unevenly.) As you progress, you'll notice that the same amount of pressure creates less dust each pass. When the piece feels smoother to your hand, step up to the next grit. Don't overdo it: A little tabletop should take no more than 5 or 10 minutes per grit.

5   **SAND WITH THE PAPER IN THE PALM OF YOUR HAND** for small elements like chair or table legs. But for large, flat surfaces like tabletops, wrap the sandpaper around a wood block or flexible sponge to ensure consistent abrasion (see pages 118–119). As flat as you think your open hand is, there will be a difference between the tips of your fingers and the middle of your palms. A block of wood is the classic method, but if you're a little heavy-handed, the corners of the block could slightly dent your piece. I prefer wrapping my sandpaper around a firm sanding sponge or a block of cork.

6   **USE LONG, CONTINUOUS STROKES,** straight from one end of the piece to the other. Don't scrub.

7   **FOLLOW EACH GRIT CONSECUTIVELY** until you reach your end goal. Never skip grits! Each finer grit refines your future finish results—you don't want to miss that polishing benefit.

8   **IN BETWEEN GRITS, WIPE THE WOOD SURFACE THOROUGHLY** with a tack cloth or an alcohol-dampened rag. (Don't use water, which will raise the grain.) You don't want the coarser wood dust from the previous pass to scratch the more refined surface you're creating.

9   **DO A FINAL CLEANING** before proceeding to your next step, usually staining.

A Little Note About Steel Wool

Steel wool is not for sanding. Its purpose is to clean the wood or to help create a special effect. It doesn't smooth the surface; it actually scratches it, emphasizing the up-and-down texture of the wood grain by removing a bit of wood fiber from the grooves. In contrast, sandpaper is totally flat and stays at the top of the wood surface—the crest of the wave—grinding down the surface evenly (and laterally).

Variations

Weathering

As always, if you want a weathered, antique, or distressed finish, be a contrarian! Do the opposite of what I've just advised, and start with a higher grit, like 220, skipping all lower grits. This will eradicate dust and smaller irregularities only, creating an intentionally uneven surface. As a result, stain will take more in some parts than others, creating a deliberately mottled effect.

Smoothing

To create a supersmooth finish, some refinishers like wetting the grain with a damp rag in between grits so they can really cut it and get a closer sanding; the water raises any asperities they missed. This technique is akin to shaving with a multiblade razor: The first blade lifts the hair so the subsequent blades can cut it lower down. Consider this technique if you are attempting a very fine finish where you want a closed grain or high gloss.

Scraping

Some refinishers use metal scrapers to sand, but they can dent and gouge the wood in the hands of someone inexperienced. I don't recommend using them unless you are a pro. I use scrapers mostly for marquetry and parquetry, which you can't sand, or to address burns or deep staining, which require surgical removal. A perfectly acceptable alternative in both cases is a razor blade.

STAINING

Staining colors the wood's surface in order to highlight its natural tone, enhance it with a decorative cast, or give it a different character completely—for instance, making an inexpensive species look like a precious or richer-hued variety. Staining can also serve a strategic purpose, helping to even the tone between different cuts of the wood used on a piece of furniture, or to help patches and repairs blend in.

In all cases, the key to staining is translucency; the goal is not to obscure the wood like paint, but to add a wash of color that lets the grain show through. You can stain through chemical reactions—bleaching, for one—or through pigmentation, which is more common. Pigments are mixed with one of three mediums: oil, water, or alcohol. I'm partial to water- and alcohol-based stains, which have the greatest bond with the wood, essentially dyeing it to offer the most natural and refined look. Both mediums evaporate after application, leaving behind just the pigment. Additionally, the type of pigments used with water and alcohol dissolve into microscopic molecules, which penetrate deep into the fibers. In contrast, oil-based pigments are made of larger particles that float on the surface of the wood, masking it somewhat; moreover, some of the solvent dries with them, further obscuring the grain.

That said, not all mediums are suitable for all staining jobs. And when choosing stains, you must consider not only the medium, but also how it interacts with different woods. Some species take stains beautifully, others get blotchy; some can get their color altered and pass for another species, some cannot. The more tender a wood is, the more uneven its grain structure—and the greater the risk for blotchiness, a characteristic that can be exploited to give furniture an aged, variegated look.

NATURAL STAINS AND DYES

Beets, coffee, tea, turmeric, blueberries—all can be used to color wood. Although these natural stains are not very light-stable and require several applications to achieve darker hues, they are nonetheless a fun and safe way to involve kids in the finishing process. On a professional level, I use them to nuance alcohol- or water-based stains once dried. In particular, coffee adds a unique dark-honey tone that's just the right shade of walnut!

Wood Stains 101

	WATER-BASED	ALCOHOL-BASED	OIL-BASED	CHEMICALS
DRY TIME	3 to 4 hours	Instant	Overnight	Overnight
APPLICATION	Easy; use a rag and/or a synthetic-bristle brush.	Practice required on large surfaces. Move evenly and keep a wet edge, avoiding overlap.	Easy; use a rag and/or a synthetic-bristle brush.	Easy, but requires protection (goggles, mask, gloves). Use a rag and/or a synthetic-bristle brush.
PROS	Easy and forgiving application; compatible with almost any finish.	Good UV stability. Good with open-pore woods.	The oil medium conditions the wood. Good coverage. Does not raise grain.	Capable of faux aging and other special effects and unique results.
CONS	Raises the grain.	Fumes. Tricky on large surfaces	Long drying time. Less translucent.	Raises the grain. Dangerous!
FILLER	Alcohol- or oil-based	Water- or oil-based	Oil fillers possible; try water-based on samples before.	Oil-based
BEST FINISH	Wax, oil, or shellac	Oil or wax	Oil or alcohol	Almost any

Types of Stains

Each has its pros and cons, as well as applications for which it's best suited.

Alcohol-based (or Aniline)

The great advantages of alcohol-based, or aniline, stain are that it penetrates the wood deeply, creating a beautiful, transparent color, and that it dries extremely fast, almost instantly. This means that immediately afterward you can finish the piece, or apply additional coats to arrive at the desired coloration. You can achieve a perfectly black ebonized stain in a matter of minutes! Best for small surfaces.

PROS: Translucency is unsurpassed. Drying time is instant, so finishing can proceed right away. Doesn't raise the wood grain.

CONS: A little trickier to apply because the medium dries instantly. You have to apply coats very evenly without overlapping, so you have to start a little lighter than the tone you ultimately want to achieve. Use in a ventilated area.

Water-based

The least expensive variety, the easiest to use, and the most forgiving. Water-based stains should be avoided on species with very open pores, as you'd need to flood the wood surface to get adequate coverage—which would then raise the grain that you've just sanded nice and smooth. Water-based stains, even more so than other types, have to be perfectly dry prior to continuing the finish process; otherwise, moisture will be trapped under the finish and ghostly white marks will appear. The upside of the slow drying process is a large open time, meaning greater control of application—thus, it's ideal for bigger pieces. The other advantage is that water-based stains are very flexible. You can dilute them easily and on the spot or keep adding washes until you get the desired look. And if you don't like the color, you can wash it right off.

PROS: Easy to use, easy to mix and intermix, easy to lighten or darken—if you don't like the tone, just mix another batch and correct it.

CONS: The water raises the grain, so you have to sand in between coats. Not recommended on wood that has been previously waxed or finished, unless you thoroughly clean or strip first.

Oil-based

The pigment is typically diluted in turpentine or another oil-based solvent, creating a heavier stain that obscures the wood. It has to dry thoroughly before any subsequent finishing can occur, and the waiting time is long—at least overnight. The petroleum-based solvents emanate fumes that linger, so apply in a well-ventilated area. Because oil-based stains mix well with a number of finishes, they come in handy to revive the tone of a previously finished piece. But do not use them with a heavy hand—think of a veil—so as to reveal rather than obscure the wood.

PROS: Easiest to apply. (Modern versions now come mixed with sealer—but I do not recommend these for antiques or heirlooms.) Longer open time facilitates evenness of application. Repeated coats can obscure the wood's grain and color to artfully mimic another precious species. Does not raise the grain.

CONS: The pigment sits on top of the wood, creating a film. So heavy with product and pigment, these stains must dry overnight. Toxic fumes require ventilation.

untreated oak

water-based

oil-based

alcohol-based

Chemical Stains

Some very common household products—and foodstuffs—are capable of creating wonderful colors or effects without transforming your living room into a chemistry lab (or arousing the suspicion of the FBI!). Wear a mask, goggles, gloves, and appropriate protective clothing when working with these materials.

Ammonia

Brush liberally on wood with a high tannin content—e.g., oak—to darken it to a lovely color. Apply a coat, let dry overnight, and then neutralize with water spiked with 10 percent white vinegar. The process also ages the wood, lending a nice patina. The secret behind Mission furniture's smoky-brown coloration and two-toned grain is ammonia fuming: Pieces were exposed to an ammonia concentrate in a closed room overnight.

Bleach

Will lighten the wood, or in some cases give it a greenish or yellow cast. Pick up a bleaching set from the hardware store, or try household bleach. Apply liberally and repeat as needed—allowing the piece to sit overnight between coats—until you achieve the desired hue (see page 149). You can neutralize the bleach afterward, although it's generally not necessary. Always use a synthetic-bristle brush, since bleach disintegrates natural bristles.

Iron Acetate

This chemical gives a wonderful gray, weathered color to woods rich in tannic acids, such as oak. Soak a steel-wool pad in paint thinner for an hour, let dry, and rinse well with water. (This removes the oil applied by the manufacturer to prevent rusting.) Then soak the pad overnight in white vinegar. Rub the wet pad on the wood, working with the grain; the reaction appears as the piece dries.

(FYI, you can enhance the tannic level of any wood variety using this method: Brew 10 teaspoons of black tea in a quart bowl, infuse, and cool, and then flush your wood with the mixture. Let dry and follow the aforementioned process.)

Sodium dichromate

Readily available at pharmacies, this chemical gives wood a rich, old, dark aspect.

Lye

An effective way to darken cherrywood, which doesn't take standard stains very well. Mix 1 tablespoon of lye in 3 cups of cold water, and then brush on. Wait overnight for it to cure.

Lime

This acid is used to create pickled or whitewashed finishes—and to render wood impervious to bugs, rot, and fungus. It's pigmented but not a solid coat, so it lets the grain show through. It works especially well on pine, which it burns and ages nicely.

Sunlight Exposure

UV rays are another great way to darken woods like cherry. Apply a coat of linseed oil and leave your piece outside in full sunshine for a day or two. The process gives cherry a silky, dark color; walnut, a tan cast; teak, a silvery hue; and pine, an orange coloration. Other woods like mahogany will, on the other hand, bleach over time when left in the sunlight.

Choosing Your Color

Many clients ask, "Christophe, what is the right stain color? Should a piece be blond, ebony, or simply chestnut?" The answer is, there are no hard-and-fast rules about right or wrong; the right color is the one you *like*. Start by sampling. Try stains on wood scraps to see how they react, the color you get, how it applies and dries, and how the finish you plan to apply on top turns out. A few stains and a few woods can create a huge palette of hues with which to work. Here, we applied seven colors to an oak tabletop. See the variety?

SPECIES	CHARACTERISTICS	BEST STAIN	ADVICE
beech	Nicely figured wood	Oil or water	Avoid dark stains
birch	Does not take stain well; gets blotchy	Oil	Consider sealing lightly before staining
cherry	Does not take stain well; gets blotchy	Light stains	Consider sunlight, which darkens the wood naturally, or sealing lightly before staining
chestnut	Polishes well, so do not oversand	Any	Avoid staining too dark (already has a lovely deep brown hue)
ebony	Very hard wood	No stain needed	Sand to a very fine grit to get the best finished aspect
mahogany	Open grain; avoid water-based stain	Oil or alcohol	A light-brown stain will tame its orange-y cast
maple	Does not take stain well; gets blotchy when dark	Light stains	Consider sealing lightly before staining
oak	Very open pores and deep grain; versatile for special effects and aging	Oil or alcohol	Stain thoroughly or the pores will stay light
poplar	Stains unevenly; absorbs a lot	Oil or alcohol	Repeated stain coats can make it look like a different species
pine	Soft. Stains unevenly; absorbs a lot	Oil or alcohol	Repeated stain coats can make it look like a different species
teak	vOily wood	Oil or alcohol	Do not stain (only treat with teak oil or wax)

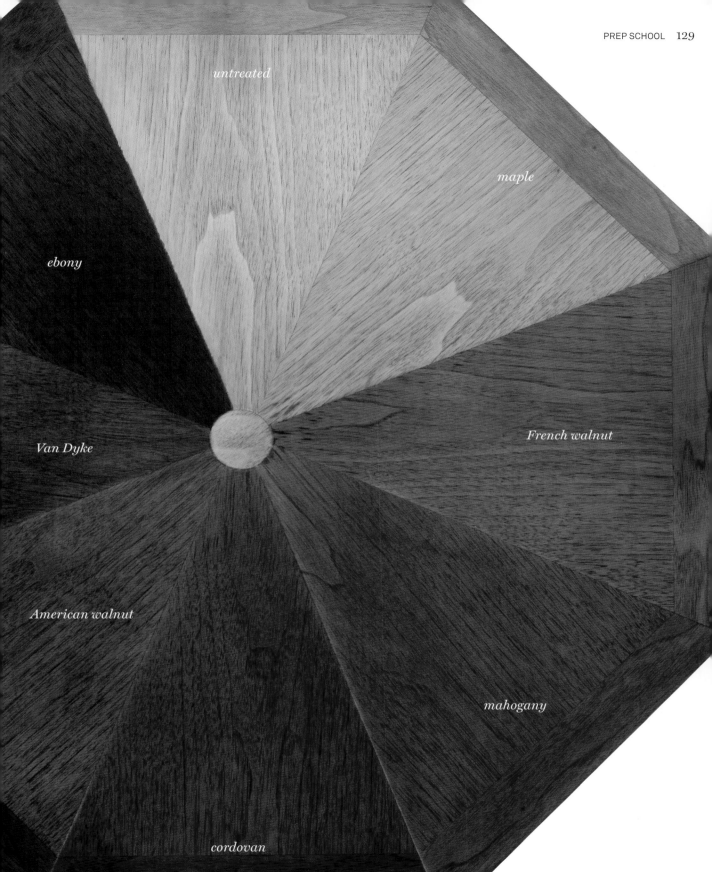

untreated

maple

ebony

French walnut

Van Dyke

American walnut

mahogany

cordovan

WHAT YOU'LL NEED

- *Stain*
- *100 percent cotton rags*
- *Natural-bristle brushes*
- *180–220-grit sandpaper*
- *Sealer*

How to Stain

Staining should be executed only after the proper preparatory steps have been taken to restore the wood to its naked stage. Stripping may be necessary or, at the very least, a good cleaning with alcohol. You must also sand the piece first, but never above 220 grit (I even recommend 180), because oversanding will close the grain too much and inhibit stain absorption.

1   **DO A RUN-THROUGH.** Before staining a piece, I like to do a run-through with a dry brush to rehearse where and in what order I'll be applying the stain. This step is especially important when using products that don't have a long open time—you don't want to get it wrong or to feel rushed.

2   **SEAL THE END GRAIN WITH SHELLAC FOR A MORE EVEN APPLICATION.** Some parts of wood—legs and edges of tabletops, for instance, which are cut in a way that has lots of end fibers—are more absorbent and thus soak up more stain than a flat surface; the wood can turn almost black. Flame mahogany as well as crotch and burl veneers present the same issue. You may want to seal before staining for a more even coloration.

3   **APPLY THE STAIN.** Never pour stain directly on wood. Use a pad for large, flat surfaces and a small brush to get into crevices and corners; always have both on hand. The combination of the two devices gets every nook and cranny saturated to create an even application, which is especially important for woods with very open grain. Always work *with* the grain of the wood, never against.

4   **START WITH THE DRAWERS.** Many finishers advise starting on less prominent parts, but I advocate the opposite: starting with main parts, like drawers and doors, and doing the frame last. Why? Because it's easier to cheat on the frame and the sides! Plus lesser parts should be adjusted to match the front-and-center ones, not the other way around. I like to start with the drawers. That way, you can carry a drawer around the piece as you go, holding it up for comparison to ensure that everything matches.

5   **APPLY STAIN IN A CONSISTENT MANNER.** If you are staining a big piece, be totally linear. You even want the same hand to stain the entire piece of furniture: Please don't have your spouse or roommate do one part when your arm tires.

6   **WAIT FOR THE STAIN TO DRY.** After applying the stain, let the piece dry thoroughly (see the chart on page 123 for drying times of various stains). Put the piece back together—slide in the drawers, hang the doors—after each step of the finishing process to check that everything looks logical and consistent. Just keep drawers and doors open for better drying!

7   **ADJUST AS NEEDED.** You may have to adjust the stain while it's drying or after the first coat has been applied: One leg may not have taken the stain like the others, for instance. So long as you haven't sealed the piece, you can keep adjusting the coloration. Do this by using a rag dampened with its medium. As mentioned previously, water- or alcohol-based stains are much easier to adjust. Courtesy of alcohol's quick drying time, you can add successive coats quickly, whereas with water you can adjust your batch and make it lighter or darker as you go. (If you wash out water-based stain, remember that it will raise the grain a bit more than usual.)

8   **DRY BETWEEN COATS.** Let your stain dry fully between coats or further steps. There should be no reason to sand between stain coats unless the grain is raised. Because the coloring is superficial—less than $1/8$ inch deep—sand only lightly. Readjust the color and tone if needed.

9   **SEAL YOUR WORK.** Once you're happy with the hue, you are ready to finish. The first coat will probably be a sealer, which will protect your stain, lock in the color, and keep it from mixing with whatever product you apply next. Each type of stain demands a finish that does not have the same medium, to keep them from melting together or bleeding into each other.

10   **FINISH AS DESIRED.**

How Do You Know When Your Color Is Correct?

Observe how the stain looks when wet (i.e., just applied); this best approximates what will result once you've properly finished the piece. When the stain dries, it will become dull and ghostly. Don't panic and start adjusting the stain because of that! Adjust only for consistency of tone. Stain is just a color, not a finish; don't judge the color by an effect that you need to achieve via other products—i.e., shine, transparency, protection.

Variation

Stain as a Finish:
You can also use stain as a finish in its own right, in a one-step process. One traditional technique involves adding pigments to pure, high-quality tung oil (1 to 2 ounces per quart), creating a beautiful finish. This product is different than an oil-based stain: It's technically a finishing stain. Apply just as you would a standard oil-rubbed finish.

A Note About Drawers

Unless you are staining your piece to mimic another wood species, I advocate leaving the insides of the drawers unstained. It's very French—they never treat the inside of the piece the same as the outside—and also more practical. If you want a decorative effect inside, try a pretty paper drawer liner.

Turn to the following sections for examples of staining:

EBONIZED desk, page 162: The most dramatic transformation, using an alcohol-based stain to make a light walnut desk look like ebony.

EBONIZED dresser, page 168: This was also a heavy stain, but for a different purpose—to mask damage and flaws.

CERUSED nesting tables, page 146: Involved bleach, a chemical staining.

Staining Order

Although certain rules usually apply, every piece is different. So always start by mapping out your game plan via a dry run with your pad/brush. Start with the large, flat, prominent surfaces, which will determine the look of the piece, and then move to lesser areas. Apply an even amount of stain and, without rushing, make long, straight, and slightly overlapping passes from one end to the other, trying to keep a wet edge. For consistency, rewet your pad as it dries. On panels and details, stain any carvings, moldings, and corners first, evening them out, followed by the flat inside part of the panel. Stain the frame next, beginning with horizontal parts and progressing to verticals. Don't forget the insides of the lateral frames of the drawers, lest unstained wood be exposed when you operate them. As you stain, move around the piece repeatedly to correct, even the tone, and lighten and darken as needed. Everything is still possible at this stage, so take advantage!

Which Stain to Use?

DESIRED EFFECT	USE THIS STAIN
A darker color	Repeated alcohol (or water-based) stain coats; dark water-based stain
A lighter color	Diluted coats of water- or alcohol-based stain
Hiding the wood grain	Oil-based stain

Stain Troubleshooting

PROBLEM	CAUSE	REMEDY
White veil, blush	Condensation or humidity: water-based stain is not dry enough, or the wood stock is too green.	Work in a drier environment and respect the product's drying time. Unfortunately, there is no solution for improperly dried wood, a source of much consternation for cabinetmakers.
Uneven tone	Different cuts of the same wood were used to build the piece.	Apply more coats of the same stain on the lighter parts.
	Different types of woods were used on the piece.	Use an oil-based stain, which will have a better concealing effect.
Stain inconsistency	Old product, evaporation of medium, coagulation of pigment	Check products regularly and discard them if they are old. Store products away from light and heat, and stir them well before each use.
Problems with application	Uneven application, wipe-off, drying time, or penetration of the stain	Try rehearsing your application technique more. Use natural-fiber rags, and avoid humid, cold, or overly hot environments.

SEALING

Sealing is more a process than a product per se: the act of containing and sterilizing the work that you've done, preserving it in its current state. A seal is like a lid. As such, it has to be impervious to what you've done before, which means using an incompatible product so they don't mix. Alcohol- and water-based stains and treatments are quite movable, fragile, and more easily removed, so a sealer based on another medium is a must. Oil-based stains are an exception, because their solvents are pretty stable and more impervious once dry; an oil sealer is acceptable for them. But for its versatility and ease of use, I almost universally recommend sealing with shellac. The only time it's inappropriate is following an alcohol-based stain, of course, in which case use a light coat of tung oil, which sinks deep into the wood to fix and harden everything.

Pro Tip

You can find sanding sealers on the shelves of Home Depot, but as always, steer clear of these over-the-counter products for fine-woodworking applications. The only time I use them is to seal an unstable or complicated staining job; a light spritz with a spray bottle will do in such cases, when you don't even want a brush to disturb your work. A better solution is matting spray, designed for watercolor or chalk and found at fine-art-supply stores, which acts more like a fixative.

WHAT YOU'LL NEED

- *Wood-filler paste*
- *Burlap or canvas rags*
- *100 percent cotton rags*
- *220- or 320-grit sandpaper*

FILLING THE GRAIN

Filling the grain is an invaluable technique for open-pored woods like oak and mahogany. The process closes the pores—literally filling them up—to protect against moisture and dirt. It is also a necessary step for achieving a glossy and formal finish, for which you need a totally flat, polished surface.

You can purchase grain fillers from the hardware store or make your own oil- or water-based version (see pages 247 and 249 for the recipes). The slurry-like paste is forced into the grain via vigorous rubbing, eradicating surface asperities. Some people fill the grain before staining, others prefer doing it afterward. I advocate staining *before* using oil filler, which acts as a sealer and may complicate subsequent staining. With water-based fillers, staining can be done *after*. Personally, I like the best of both worlds: I stain and get my desired color prior to grain filling, and then adjust the stain a bit after.

Filling the grain is an essential part of techniques like *ciré rempli* and French polish, which utilize a mix of fine pumice, wood particles, and oil to do the trick; see pages 142–145 for an example and a full tutorial. And see page 157 for a variation of the technique, self-filling, which fills the grain with wood dust generated from sanding the piece.

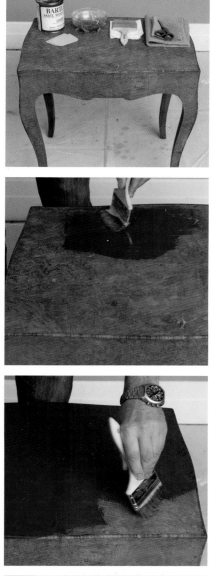

1   **APPLY THE PASTE.** Use a generous amount, rubbing it inside the pores in every direction with a spatula or an open hand.

2   **WAIT.** Let the filler set a bit; it will get opaque.

3   **SCRAPE** against the wood grain with a flexible plastic scraper (never metal). Wait 15 minutes.

4   **RUB OFF THE EXCESS.** Using a rough fabric like burlap or canvas, work energetically against the grain so the filler stays inside the pores only.

5   **LET THE SURFACE DRY THOROUGHLY.** Ideally, wait overnight. Oil-based fillers take longer to dry; I always wait a few days to be safe, but I sand the next day (see next step) before it gets too hard.

6   **SAND CAREFULLY AND METICULOUSLY.** Use 400-grit sandpaper and a light hand, followed by a soft rag to get a totally smooth and even surface. If some filler has dried on the surface or been improperly removed, scrape it off with a razor blade, being careful not to go through the stain or indent the wood.

7   **REPEAT AS NEEDED.** It's okay to do a second pass of filler to achieve a totally filled grain—especially if you're new to the process.

8   **ADJUST THE COLOR AS NEEDED.** Be sure to use the appropriate stain.

9   **YOU ARE READY FOR THE FINISH!**

WHAT YOU'LL NEED

- *Glaze*
- *Natural-bristle artist's paintbrushes*
- *100 percent cotton rags*

GLAZING

Glazing is a translucent, pigmented coat—brushed atop or in between coats of finishes—used to create decorative effects and give the wood surface a sense of depth and dimension. Applied to wood that's been sealed or otherwise finished, it stays on top of the previous coating rather than mixing with it and penetrating the wood. It's an especially beautiful treatment for light-stained oak, a slick of dark glaze animating the grain to create a cerusing effect. (In fact, ceruse is technically an extreme version of glazing.) Glazing is also a great way to give wood age and patina, re-creating the look of accumulated dust or stain in moldings, doors, and so on.

Use glazing to:

- Add a dark, smoky film to a light wood background

- Give a dark finish pale highlights

- Heighten grain patterning

- Capture the effect of a centuries-old patina by applying the glaze to just the profile of the molding, and leaving flat panels as is

The pigments are carried by a medium, generally oil or water. My strong preference is oil-based glazes, which have a longer open time—up to six hours for some. You get very nice control, and the product is quite forgiving. Work it at your convenience, manipulating the glaze or even removing it with a solvent-dampened rag if you dislike the result. The disadvantage of a long open time is that dust can mar the glaze unless you're in a very controlled environment.

Found in art stores and fine-woodworking catalogs, oil glazes come as a transparent medium to which you add oil-soluble pigments of your choosing (usually Universal tinting or japan color). Make your own glaze if you prefer to precisely customize colors or the duration of the open time (see page 255 for the recipe).

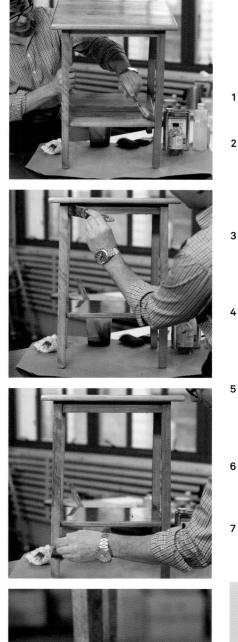

1   **IDEALLY, DON GLOVES AND GOGGLES** and protect your floor with a tarp. Glazing can be messy.

2   **APPLY THE GLAZE.** With a natural-bristle brush, apply the glaze to the stained, sealed wood surface. Rub it all over, working it deep into corners, profiles, and details, and against the grain if you want the glaze to penetrate the wood pores. Evenness of application is unnecessary at this stage since your artistry and precision come in subsequent steps.

3   **WORK THE GLAZE.** When you are done coating the entire surface, the product should still be wet. Maneuver with a rag, leaving color or buildup only as desired: a little bit in the corners for an aged effect, or in the grain crevices to create contrast and depth.

4   **ALTERNATIVELY, DRAG A FLAT BRUSH OVER THE GLAZE** to create a uniform haze that artfully mimics an aged finish. The more you drag your brush, the smaller the resulting striations—rendering the brushstrokes invisible and creating a cloud of color.

5   **ADJUST AS NEEDED.** If your application is not uniform—too much here, not enough there—you can correct by reapplying. If you are not satisfied with your result, wash it off with a clean rag dampened with turpentine or naphtha. (Again, this is why you want a long open time for the product!)

6   **WAIT AT LEAST OVERNIGHT.** The large amount of solvent extends the drying time. You want to be sure the glaze is totally dry, especially if you are using oil glaze and the next coating will use the same medium.

7   **REPEAT AS DESIRED.** You can add several coats of glaze—just seal your previous glaze prior to applying a new one—before your subsequent finish.

Variations

Colored Wax

As an alternative to oil-based glazing products, use a topcoat of colored wax at the very end of your finish. It's a great way to create faux aging, applied in a manner that mimics stains and wear. Dry overnight and buff for a shine, or leave matte as is. The disadvantage is that you can only use wax as a topcoat and not in between coats of stain.

Gel Stain

Another option is to use gel stain as a glaze. What makes them only okay stains—they don't sink well into the wood, coating it more than anything else—makes them great for glazing. The consistent medium is very spreadable, allowing you to get just the effect and transparency that you want. Let dry thoroughly and seal.

PART 4

TECHNIQUES

Here's what you've been waiting for: a demonstration of my favorite refinishing and restoration techniques! As you'll discover, finishing is a layering process. But if you want something to look beautiful, it cannot *look* layered. The key is to use compatible products that mix without melting one another, so they relate seamlessly. Like everything refined in life, the result should look effortless and continuous; you don't want to see the process.

Because these tutorials address specific pieces that came through my studio, with their unique quirks and features, you may not be able to follow the steps verbatim when executing the technique on your own. You are allowed—nay, encouraged—to take creative liberties. If I've learned anything in my decades of working with antiques, it's that no two pieces will be the same; each one presents its own unique challenges. Accordingly, the key to refinishing is improvisation. There are no strict rules, only guidelines—and your own sense of logic and intuition. Most of these techniques are explained in greater detail in Part 2, so I advocate reading the corresponding overview before embarking on your project. In fact, the goal of Parts 1 through 3 was to provide context to help you make informed (and empowered) decisions on the spur of the moment. That's the true foundation of artistry.

CIRÉ REMPLI

Dresser

Typically, you use wax by itself or as the topcoat of another finish, and buff it to a high shine. In contrast, *ciré rempli* utilizes wax as a medium to create a patina and a smooth, polished-by-age texture. The technique incorporates fine pumice powder to fill the wood grain and polish the surface, imparting a deeper, harsher shine than you can achieve via wax alone.

THE PIECE

This nice old dresser boasted clean lines and great detailing. But it had a weird and unappealing finish, sort of half-painted—and pine isn't the most noble of woods. Also, I thought the wood knobs were dumb-looking. Accordingly, it was the perfect piece to upgrade, giving it a complete makeover and a more distinguished mien.

THE LOOK

I wanted to capture the rich, dark patina of 17th-century furniture. My goal was a reddish-brown, oxblood hue—what the French call *sang de bœuf*. This unpretentious yet lovely finish works really well for rustic pieces because you fill up the grain but still preserve a sense of texture.

THE PROCESS

After the piece is stained, a coat of wax is applied, followed by a dusting of pumice; the resulting slurry is rubbed deep into the wood pores and then buffed to a luminous shine.

category
Wax

degree of difficulty
Easy to medium

prep work
I removed drawers, realigned and repaired stuck slides (see "Drawer Slide Repair," page 266), fixed a cat scratch, and lightly stripped the piece. Then I sanded until grit 220.

THE HISTORY OF OXBLOOD

Prior to the advent of modern pest repellents, animal blood—readily available in the countryside—was frequently used to treat wood. (There are differing opinions about whether actual ox blood was used to stain furniture.) The rich, dark hue of sang de bœuf *also inspired the North American trend for crimson-painted barns (achieved via red ochre and linseed oil), a practice that originated in Pennsylvania in the 19th century.*

WHAT YOU'LL NEED

- *Alcohol- or water-based stain*
- *100 percent cotton rags*
- *Colored wax (I used dark mahogany for its deep, cordovan hue; colored waxes are usually quite liquid, but a thick paste-like variety will be key to your success!)*
- *Coarse natural-bristle brush*
- *Pumice 4F*
- *Powdered pigment (optional)*
- *Linen-wrapped French polish pad (see "Making and Using French Polish Pads," page 250)*
- *Denatured wood alcohol*
- *Wool or felt rags*

1

DARKEN THE PINE WITH AN ALCOHOL-BASED STAIN. Note that you can skip this step if you're working with walnut or a similar deep-toned wood. (In that case, sand a little farther down than usual—to about 320—so the grain is very close, almost polished.) Achieving this cordovan tone required two coats, since pine is pretty light and absorbs a lot of stain. Wait a few hours before proceeding to the next step.

2

APPLY A THICK COAT OF COLORED WAX. Then let it sink in overnight.

3

APPLY A SECOND COAT OF WAX. Wait an hour for it to dry. With a coarse natural-bristle brush (a shoe-shine brush is great), go over the finish as if you want to shine it.

6

FILL THE GRAIN. Force the wax/pumice mix into the wood grain with the alcohol-charged pad, rubbing in a circular motion; when you start feeling like you have to force the pad, every 10 minutes or so, recharge it with alcohol. This step "closes" the grain and creates a polish-like effect. Right away, you'll notice an integral shine—more of a sheen, really—that emanates from inside the wood grain.

7

GIVE IT A FINAL BUFF. I like waiting overnight so the wax dries thoroughly, especially when executing this finish. Buff lightly with a soft wool or felt rag, and voilà: a magnificent shine, worth centuries of use and patina!

4

APPLY PUMICE STONE. When you have a subtle shine, sprinkle the surface with a cloud of powdered pumice stone, spiked with a bit of powdered pigment (the kind used for staining, to be diluted in oil) if you want enhanced coloration. Massage in lightly with your hand—but don't press, which could rub off some of the wax.

5

CHARGE YOUR PAD. Pour a light amount of wood alcohol onto the outside of a linen-wrapped French polish pad. Tap it gently on the back of your hand to evenly distribute the alcohol. Your pad should be damp, not dripping wet.

8

REPLACE THE WOOD KNOBS. The piece probably had handles originally, since there were two holes, one of which was patched. The simple brass drops give the rustic piece another layer of sophistication, introducing metal to complement the look (see "Hardware Makeover," page 279, for more on hardware replacement).

Troubleshooting

If you have problems achieving a shine (cause: too much alcohol) or have rubbed through the wax coating (cause: a dry pad or not enough wax), it's no big deal. Just reapply wax on the specific trouble spot or the entire section. Wait 1 hour, brush it, and start from Step 4 again.

CERUSE

Midcentury-Modern Nesting Tables

Ceruse can be used to achieve very decorative, high-contrast effects. But this project is emblematic of a more classic ceruse, in which light oak provides a mellow, honey-toned background for gray or white pigmentation within the grain—creating a soft, maze-like pattern that never ceases to enthrall me.

THE PIECES

Made from the highest-quality white oak, these classic Parsons-style nesting tables are unbelievably well crafted—they fit together like a glove. I'm especially enamored of the precise reveal detailing the top edge. Commissioning a custom set like this would cost a lot, but I scored these for $50 each at Housing Works, my local thrift shop. The original finish was most likely oil or wax; the derelict gray paint is more recent. It's sacrilegious to cover up such beautifully figured oak—especially with a bad paint job! I wanted to save these great little tables from their ill-advised "makeover."

THE LOOK

Coarsely applied paint had penetrated the wood grain, creating a sort of ceruse. It was only logical to augment that effect by using the same-color pigment. Cerusing also suits this genre, reminiscent of a 1930s Jean-Michel Frank design. I abided by his preferred ceruse combination—blond wood with light gray pigment—to achieve a slightly weathered, driftwood feeling.

THE PROCESS

Ceruse is typically an applied process, whereby you add pigment into the grain after having sealed the wood surface. But here I started by taking away, using sandpaper to remove the paint from just the top surface, and leaving it in the grain. Bleaching the oak afterward heightened the contrast between the newly exposed wood surface and the gray-pigmented creases, which I augmented with wax.

category
Wax

degree of difficulty
Easy

prep work
I lightly stripped the paint, then cleaned and sanded the piece.

JEAN-MICHEL FRANK

The French Art Deco designer (a cousin of Anne Frank's) was renowned for elegant furnishings that combined pureness of line with luxurious materials. He almost single-handedly revived techniques and treatments like straw marquetry, ceruse, shagreen, and parchment. The success of his legacy—which includes the Parsons table—owes much to the classicism and sophistication of his taste.

WHAT YOU'LL NEED

- Chemical-resistant gloves
- Glass bowl
- Hydrogen peroxide: a two-solution set (this can be found easily in hardware stores)
- Synthetic-bristle brush
- Wire brush
- Dust mask
- A range of fine (0000) to coarse (4) steel wool
- Plastic scrub brush
- Denatured wood alcohol
- 100 percent cotton rags
- Tack cloth (optional)
- Gas torch (optional)
- Blonde shellac
- Pigmented wax: store-bought or homemade (see page 240)
- Paint thinner (optional)

2

"OPEN" THE GRAIN. Wire-brush the wood vigorously, brushing with the grain—this will loosen and remove the tender end fibers, widening the crevices in the process. (Use a dust mask: Dried particles of bleach are not safe to breathe.) Don't neglect corners and edges; a smaller wire brush or a little piece of coarse (4 or 3) steel wool can help open the grain in these areas.

4

REMOVE ADDITIONAL FIBERS. Optional: If your skill level allows and your piece is made of a darker (not pale) wood, you can remove leftover fibers by lightly passing a gas torch over the entire piece. This will help you achieve a greater contrast between the darker wood and the lighter wax. Clean away the burned fibers with coarse (4) steel wool, followed by an alcohol-dampened rag. Safety note: Do not scorch your wood or set it on fire! And never use a gas torch in close proximity to alcohol.

5

DON'T TOUCH. Whether or not you used the torch, your wood should now be completely clean and devoid of grease; henceforth, avoid touching the piece with your bare hands.

1

BLEACH THE WOOD. Wearing chemical-resistant gloves and following the directions on the two-part solution, prepare the hydrogen peroxide in a glass bowl. Apply the hydrogen peroxide liberally with a synthetic-bristle brush (bleach will eat through natural bristles). Repeat as needed to keep the wood wet for about 15 minutes. Let dry. Wait overnight to see how bleached the wood gets; depending on how light you want to go, you may want to repeat this step.

I could have stopped here and sealed the piece for a weathered, bleached look that's quite chic!

3

CHECK YOUR PROGRESS. You know you're done when the act of wire-brushing stops creating a significant amount of dust. The more fiber removed, the more dramatic the result! The surface of the wood should feel very textured, with a contrast between the tops of the grain and the creases; you can even feel the indentations with a fingernail. Wipe the surface with a plastic scrub brush to dislodge any residual dust. Then wipe with a clean cloth, followed by an alcohol-dampened rag or a tack cloth.

I happen to like the burnished look of a piece at this stage, and you may decide to stop right here.

6

APPLY THE SHELLAC. You'll need two good coats to seal the wood surface; this will ensure that the pigmented wax—the ceruse, which you will apply next—stays only in the creases. Here I used blonde shellac, which has a neutral coloration, but your choice of sealer will depend on whether you've stained the wood or not, and what type of stain you used; the point is to use products with different solvents, so they never touch or remove each other. (Shellac's medium is alcohol, while wax uses oil or paint thinner.) Apply the shellac with a pad made from a folded scrap of cotton T-shirt to ensure that the product touches only the surface of the wood and not the grain crevices; think of it like snowcapped mountain peaks versus the valleys.

7

APPLY THE WAX. Shellac dries very quickly, so you can apply the wax almost immediately afterward. I chose a gray hue to match the existing paint residue (see page 243 on coloring wax). Using a rag or your fingertips, rub the wax in powerful circles—a more aggressive version of how you'd moisturize your face. Don't worry about evenness of application; the point is to saturate the grain by coating the entire piece in wax, forcing it into the corners and crevices. Continue until you've thoroughly filled every pore—you'll no longer see any open grain showing through.

8

WAIT A FEW HOURS. Let the wax dry and settle into the wood grooves for at least 8 hours and preferably overnight.

10

OPTIONAL: APPLY PAINT THINNER. If the ceruse proves especially tenacious, try a cloth dampened with paint thinner; however, this method is almost too efficient, and you must be careful not to remove too much ceruse.

11

STOP WHEN YOU ACHIEVE THE DESIRED CONTRAST. For added protection, apply another light coat of blonde shellac, which seals your work and imparts shine.

9

WIPE OFF THE WAX. Rub against the grain with medium-fine (0) steel wool in small, circular strokes to remove the wax from the top surface of the wood without abrading any more wood fiber. (If you do, just add a little more wax and let stand for a while.) Apply even pressure and let the steel wool do its job. Rather than obsess about eliminating all the wax in a small area, make multiple passes, removing a little wax from the entire piece to ensure a more even result. This step rewards patience and a light hand! The bleached ridges will slowly start emerging from the sea of ceruse. As it does and you need to remove less and less wax, switch to finer grades of steel wool: 00 to 0000, depending on the desired result.

Variations

Use a darker ceruse against the light background, or stain the wood a dark color and use light ceruse. There are also many color combinations to consider: gold against a black background, green against white, etc. You can create novelty by playing with colors—both of the ceruse itself and the wood tone, via staining:

- If you opt for staining the piece, use an alcohol-based product, followed 10 minutes later by an acrylic sealer. Apply two light coats of sealer with a rag, as you'd do with shellac; no need to sand in between.

- If you use a water-based stain, seal with blonde shellac or an oil/alkyd sealer. Again, the point is to use products with different solvents.

- Follow an oil-based stain with a water-based sealer or blonde shellac.

Ebony stain, gold ceruse

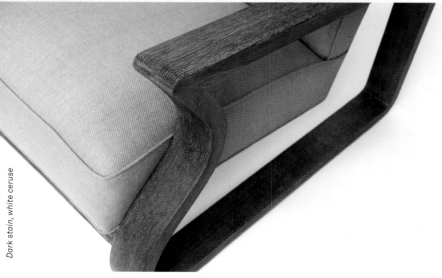

Dark stain, white ceruse

TUNG-OIL QUENCH

Chinoiserie Plant Stand

I use this cool technique to revive boiserie, old refectory tables, oak paneling, even floors—anything that needs refreshing but that you don't want to bother stripping. Just be sure the wood has no existing modern varnish that would prevent it from absorbing the oil (although any old, worn-down coating will let this process do its job). The oil serves not only to finish and protect the piece, but also to clean it. The more beat-up the piece is, the better it will look after!

THE PIECE

This chinoiserie plant stand is a prime example of Chinese export furniture, typically crafted of rosewood or a similarly hard species. You often see such pieces in this state: very dry, very gray, and with intricate dirt-caked carving that makes you think, *How am I going to refinish this? It will be hell!* But I promise it's quite easy. There's slight damage to this piece, but it's structurally sound.

THE LOOK

I didn't want to reinvent this plant stand so much as clean and nurture the timeworn wood to give it a new lease on life. The goal was to make it look quenched, not crisp and new; a patina and a little dirt lend authenticity to the finish.

THE PROCESS

This technique works perfectly with tung oil, which was made specifically for this genre of furniture. (If you prefer to add tone or coloration, choose Danish oil.) Hardwood takes oil so beautifully: The inherent color, depth, and richness shine through almost immediately.

category
Oil

degree of difficulty
Easy

prep work
None!

CHINESE EXPORT FURNITURE

"Made in China" is not such a badge of honor today, but prior to the 20th century, Oriental furniture was prized throughout the Occident. In the 17th century, China began developing and exporting furniture, dishware, lacquerware, and other goods made specifically for the western market. In the 19th century, pieces imported to America mostly came through San Francisco, which became a hub for the diffusion of those items.

WHAT YOU'LL NEED

- Glass bowl
- Tung oil
- Pure gum turpentine
- One-quart container
- Hot water
- Superfine steel wool (0000) and/or an old toothbrush
- 100 percent cotton rags
- Pigmented wax (optional)

1

PREPARE THE TUNG OIL SOLUTION. In a glass bowl, make a mixture of 2 parts tung oil to 1 part turpentine. The turpentine dissolves and cleans dirt, while the oil acts as a rubbing agent to prevent scratching and both nourish and finish the wood.

2

FILL A QUART CONTAINER HALFWAY WITH HOT WATER.

4

SCRUB THE PIECE THOROUGHLY. Dip the steel wool or toothbrush into the solution and begin scrubbing, trying to get into every nook and cranny—use the toothbrush if needed. As you clean, the oil treats and finishes the wood. See how it already looks fabulous?

5

PROCEED SECTION BY SECTION. Rub your piece dry with a clean rag as you go.

7

APPLY TUNG OIL. With a brush, apply a coat, let it sink in for 5 minutes, and then wipe away the excess. (Here I used my homemade tonic.) Let dry and repeat once if you wish to enhance the shine. Wait overnight for the oil to penetrate. You're done!

3

ADD THE OIL/TURPENTINE SOLUTION. Pour the mixture into the container. Since oil and water don't mix, your product stays on top. The hot water below warms the solution, making it work more effectively. (The point being, of course, that you should never *ever* heat oils and solvents directly!)

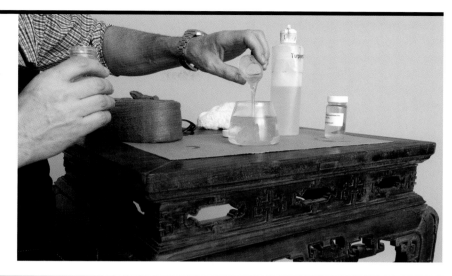

6

REPEAT THE ENTIRE PROCESS UNTIL YOUR DRYING RAG COMES AWAY CLEAN. Depending on its condition, your piece may require one or two more passes. (Don't worry, the process goes quickly; a huge piece like this takes only an hour or so start to finish.) Let it dry overnight.

8

OPTIONAL: TREAT YOUR PIECE TO A COAT OF WALNUT-COLORED WAX. It will accentuate the depth of color, the level of protection, and the degree of shine. For lighter woods, use amber-colored wax instead.

Maintenance

Wax or moisturize with oil annually.

TUNG-OIL BUILDUP

Midcentury-Modern Dining Set

This rubbed-in formula is a wonderful all-natural alternative to brushed-on polyurethane or marine varnish. Oil penetrates and bonds with the wood rather than coating it, as varnishes or spray lacquers do, while wet sanding between coats fills the grain and allows more buildup. It's the perfect medium to upgrade an already finished midcentury-modern piece or to finish one anew.

THE PIECE

A good friend of mine bought this European walnut dining set on eBay. It's a classic (and space-saving) 1950s Danish design by Hans Olsen: The three-legged leatherette-upholstered chairs tuck snugly under the tabletop. The wood was a bit dry-looking—a condition in which you'll often find midcentury-modern furniture. It needed rejuvenation and protection, especially the eating surface. But although the tabletop had some wear, it wasn't damaged; the existing oil finish had protected it well.

THE LOOK

Oil rub was the favored finish of the midcentury Danish design movement, which celebrated the natural beauty of wood—a reaction to the sophisticated finishes of the Art Deco period. I felt that the technique, with its slightly satin sheen, was the ideal way to highlight the warm European walnut and emphasize the clean-lined design of the pieces.

THE PROCESS

I'll demonstrate two versions of the technique: a full refinish for the tabletop, which also involves filling the grain to protect and waterproof the wood, and a simple application of tung oil for the chairs, which was acceptable since the surfaces were smaller and less worn. The latter is also the process that you use for maintenance and to upgrade any oil finish.

category
Oil

degree of difficulty
Chairs: easy
Table: easy to medium

prep work
Chairs: If the seats are removable (these were not), take them off for the neatest possible result. You can also protect your seats with carefully taped plastic. That wasn't necessary here: Oiling the wood is not a messy process and, because the upholstery is leatherette, I could just wipe off any errant drops as I went.

Table: In anticipation of a full refinish, I started from scratch, sanding the wood to get a nice, even base.

WHAT YOU'LL NEED

- 100 percent cotton rags
- Denatured wood alcohol
- Sanding block or sponge
- 180- through 320-grit sandpaper
- Tack cloths
- Clear tung oil, or colored Danish oil
- Natural-bristle brush

- Steel wool (000 or 0000)
- Razor blade, plastic scraper, and/or old credit cards
- Wet-and-dry sandpaper, 320- or 400-grit silicon carbide
- Burlap or jute rags
- Wax
- Wool or felt rags

TABLE

1

CLEAN ALL SURFACES. Use an alcohol-dampened rag to remove any loose dirt.

3

CLEAN. Use an alcohol-dampened rag or a tack cloth to wipe away any dust.

4

APPLY TUNG OIL. With a cotton rag or a natural-bristle brush, apply a liberal coat of tung oil to all surfaces. Wait 15 minutes. If the oil soaks in quickly and the wood looks dull in spots, apply another coat. Keep wet by reapplying for about 30 minutes. When the oil stops sinking in, wipe off the excess with a clean, lint-free cloth to create an even base. Let it dry overnight.

7

MAKE SURE THE SURFACE IS EVEN. Between coats is also the time to remove any bumps in the wood and/ or lingering gunk and caked-on dirt. Scrape off the spots carefully with a razor blade or scraper (this is always preferable to using sandpaper, since it lets you slice off just the gunk and leave the wood surface undisturbed). Wipe afterward with a clean cloth.

8

APPLY ANOTHER COAT IF NEEDED. If you have built up a nice finish, proceed to the next step. If the surface of the wood still looks a bit patchy, apply one more coat of oil with a rag, wait 15 minutes, and then wipe up the excess.

2

SAND WITH SUCCESSIVE GRITS. Using a sheet of 180-grit sandpaper wrapped around a flat sponge, sand thoroughly and evenly. (Avoid sanding flat surfaces directly with your hand, as the pressure—and therefore the result—will be uneven, and the finish will vary in tone.) Continue with consecutively finer grits: 180, 220, 240, 280, and then 320 grit; you can afford to burnish the wood with an extra-smooth sanding since you're not staining the table. Stop when you have a smooth, even result.

5

APPLY ANOTHER COAT. Use a clean cotton rag to apply another coat of oil. Wait 15 to 30 minutes, and then wipe clean. Let the table dry overnight.

6

ROUGH UP THE SURFACE. In between coats, you can rub the surface with 0000 steel wool or scuff-sand with very fine sandpaper, which roughs up the surface a bit so it will absorb more oil, creating a deeper finish.

9

WET-SAND TO CREATE A SLURRY. Apply a new coat of oil, wait until it gets a little tacky, and then start sanding the surface. Sand in the direction of the grain, using a very fine grit wet-and-dry sandpaper (ideally 320- or 400-grit silicon carbide) wrapped around a flexible sponge or sanding block. I even recommend saturating the surface of your sandpaper with oil. The point is for the wet oil to mix with the previously applied coats and the fine wood particles that the sanding generates, creating a slurry paste that you distribute evenly. There is no point in applying excess pressure; be light and consistent, and work the entire surface for 15 minutes. If the surface gets too dry, rewet with more oil.

10

SCRAPE OFF THE PASTE. Once you've done a good job moving the slurry around and it gets tacky, take a credit card (or a plastic scraper) and scrape against the grain to remove the slurry, leaving only the paste that's filling the grain.

11

REMOVE MORE PASTE WITH ROUGH BURLAP. When you have removed as much as you can with the scraper, switch to a rough burlap or jute rag, still working against the grain, to finish removing the slurry. The goal is to leave the oil paste in the pores but cut it off at the surface. Let the piece dry fully, at least a day or two.

14

REPEAT. Because the buildup becomes unstable and difficult to work with, finishers typically execute two or three slurry-paste sessions to build up the oil coating. Repeat the process—steps 8 to 13—once or twice, waiting a day in between each application. The more you fill the pores, the shinier the finish and the greater the protection. Some fine woodworkers will tell you that a good rubbed-oil finish requires at least eight coats; the result is divine, but three or four coats will leave you very satisfied and create a safe enough finish—and the execution is more forgiving.

15

A QUICK NOTE ABOUT DRYING TIME: The more coats of oil you apply, the more days you have to wait in between. Also: Avoid applying oil on humid summer days!

2

APPLY TUNG OIL. Using a cotton rag, apply oil on all parts, as you did for the first coat on the table. Let the piece sit overnight.

3

CLEAN. Use superfine (0000) steel wool, then clean with a tack cloth.

4

APPLY A NEW COAT OF OIL. Wipe on, wipe off.

12

SCUFF-SAND THE PIECE. Remove any residual dried paste by scuff-sanding just those spots using dry, 320-grit sandpaper, working with the grain. Do this very carefully. You don't want to "burn" through the finish you have created—remember, it's dry but not cured! And then scuff-sand evenly, all over.

13

CLEAN. After each sanding, clean well with a tack cloth or an alcohol-dampened rag prior to applying a new coat.

16

FINISH THE PIECE. When you have achieved the desired look and level of protection, wait for the finish to fully cure—about 5 days. You can leave it as is or apply paste wax with a clean linen rag (or superfine 0000 steel wool, fully soaked with wax so it doesn't scratch the wood). Rub with very little pressure, in very straight lines, always working with the wood grain. Wait a few hours and buff to a shine with a wool or felt rag.

CHAIR

1

CLEAN. Remove dust, dirt, and crumbs from all surfaces with a dry tack cloth. Follow with an alcohol cleaning.

5

STEEL WOOL AND WAX. After a few coats of oil—the amount determined by the level of shine and coating you like (I stopped after three)—lightly rub with superfine (0000) steel wool and then wax the piece.

6

ADD AN OPTIONAL GLOSS: If your coating and surface are perfect and you're feeling a bit cocky, after the last rub-down with steel wool, apply a coat of oil very evenly with a rag in straight lines, and leave as is (i.e., wet) to dry! The gloss will be higher and the coating a bit more varnishy. Before using, wait 2 days for the piece to fully dry and cure.

Variation

You can execute this technique with linseed, tung, or Danish oil. Linseed oil will take much more time to dry between coats and has a tendency to get yellow with light. Tung and Danish are much better choices.

Maintenance

Once a year (or as needed), clean the surfaces nicely with alcohol and apply a new coat of oil—wipe on, wipe off.

EBONIZING

Leather-Topped 19th-Century
Neoclassical-Style **Bureau Plat**

This technique is used to stain furniture a deep, rich hue, one that mimics the inky look of ebony. Historically, the stand-in was usually pearwood, a stable and tight-grained timber that stains exceptionally well (and was much more affordable than exotic ebony).

THE PIECE

I bought this leather-topped ash desk for a song—$200!—at Capo Auction in New York. The favorite desk of French officials, this genre is often called *bureau ministre* or *bureau plat* (which translates to "flat desk"). It is elegant, perfectly shaped, and very well constructed. The piece was sound structurally, with only superficial damage: a white ring on the leather top and additional water damage on the wood. The only flaw was a worn dull-brown varnish.

THE LOOK

Because the desk featured ebonized accents, it wasn't a stretch to extend the treatment to the entire piece. I knew ebonizing would smarten it up, drawing out its neoclassical looks and lending a more formal character.

THE PROCESS

When ebonizing, it's best to use an alcohol-based stain, which penetrates the wood fibers, changing the color of the wood in depth—as a dye—rather than pigmenting just the surface like icing on a cake. Dye is also more transparent, letting the grain show through so the result looks like black wood, not black-painted wood.

category
Oil

degree of difficulty
Easy. This is a fairly forgiving technique.

prep work
I removed the hardware, from the handles to the casters. Then I took out the drawers and stripped the entire desk.

WHAT'S THE ORIGINAL FINISH?

To determine if the finish on a piece is original, look underneath the hardware, where the original finish has probably not been perfectly removed in previous makeovers. Or check out the underside of the piece, where finishes are applied and removed less carefully over time.

WHAT YOU'LL NEED

- *Plastic tarp*
- *Low-tack painting tape*
- *Latex or nitrile gloves*
- *Alcohol-based stain*
- *100 percent cotton rags*
- *Bristle brushes*
- *Linseed or tung oil*
- *Shellac*
- *Tack cloths*
- *Containers*
- *Very fine (0000 or 000) steel wool*

1

PROTECT THE LEATHER WRITING SURFACE. Put a piece of plastic tarp—a smidge smaller than the size of the top—on the surface and affix it with low-tack painting tape. Always test your tape on an unobtrusive corner first to ensure that it doesn't flake or peel the leather. (Protect your leather this way before stripping, too, using a fresh sheet of plastic for this step.)

2

APPLY THE STAIN. Wearing protective gloves, use a pad or brush to apply the stain in even lines. Don't glop it on too much—it's better to apply many light layers than one big smear. Continue to add coats until you achieve the desired degree of darkness. Since alcohol-based stain dries almost instantly, you can do several passes in a short period of time. You want to achieve a totally flat black stain—but you still want a visible grain patterning.

4

LET THE PIECE DRY. Put the drawers back in—so you can check that all the surfaces look consistent—and then let the piece dry for about 1 hour. You may have to adjust, adding a bit of stain here and there, since various parts will absorb differently, depending on what cut of wood they're built from. Legs, for instance, have more end grain, and thus soak up more stain.

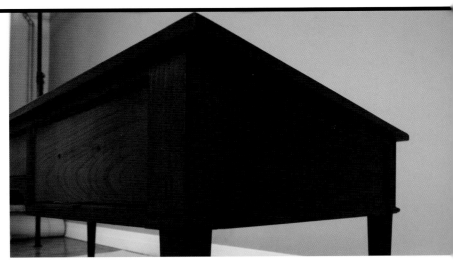

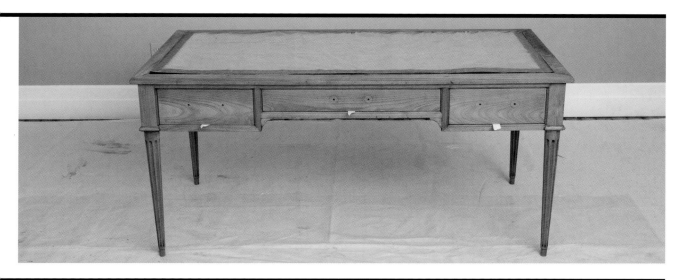

3

BE SURE TO STAIN EVERY SURFACE.
When staining, especially when
darkening a light wood, make sure
you go over the drawer edges and the
underside of the piece, lest you end
up with a visibly unfinished section.
Use a rag for flat surfaces and a
brush for corners and crevices.

5

SEAL THE STAIN. Lock in the base color with a sealing coat of
linseed or tung oil. (The two mediums—alcohol and oil—don't
mix, so none of the stain will rub off when you apply the shellac
later.) To prime, dip your pad in oil, apply everywhere, allow to
penetrate for 10 to 15 minutes, and then blot off the excess. As with
most oil techniques, the first coat may sink in almost entirely, with
little excess to wipe off. Be sure every surface gets treated to the
same amount of product, and that it dries evenly. You may want to
even the surface by rubbing it with very fine grade (0000 or 000)
steel wool; use a light hand and clean carefully afterward with a
clean cotton rag or a tack cloth to remove any steel wool fibers.

6

APPLY THE SHELLAC. Now it's time to add shine and depth to approximate the wet look the piece had while being stained. Do this with a shellac-and-alcohol solution. Add a small amount (10 percent) of the black alcohol-based stain to liquid shellac; here, I used ruby garnet shellac. Fold a cotton cloth into a pad, dip it into the shellac, and apply the moderately wet (not supersaturated) pad evenly to the wood in long, straight passes. Rewet your pad as it dries. Once applied, the product dries instantly, so you can build coats repeatedly. Little by little, you will get the desired depth and finish.

7

LET THE PIECE DRY OVERNIGHT. You can repeat the shellac application a few times if you want a high gloss. Scuff-sand in between coats with superfine (0000) steel wool.

8

PAY ATTENTION TO THE DETAILS. Afterward, if you wish, detail the fluting of the legs with gold leaf or gilt wax—which is what they would have done in the 18th century; see page 196.

9

PUT THE HARDWARE BACK ON. See page 109 for hints on doing this.

10

CLEAN THE LEATHER. I also addressed the leather top, removing the water mark, giving it a new stain, and enhancing the shine.

Ebonizing Tips

- When staining, always keep a pad *and* a brush at the ready so you can reach into the corners and moldings.
- Always keep a clean rag, dampened with the proper medium, on hand to quickly wipe up the inevitable drips and boo-boos.
- To create extra-glossy highlights, apply copal varnish to the edges and moldings with a natural-bristle brush, or apply a light coat of varnish with a rag.
- You can also use a thin, fine artist's brush to apply shellac in the details and recesses.

1   **DUST THOROUGHLY WITH A CLEAN RAG.**

2   **CLEAN.** Using a cotton rag dampened with soapy water, wipe the spot as well as you can.

3   **ASSESS.** If soap and water doesn't do the trick, wait until the leather is dry and repeat. Then buff well with a wool or felt rag.

4   **ASSESS AGAIN.** Stubborn spots may require spot cleaning with a mild chemical. I like rubbing alcohol, which is diluted and free of grease. Apply with a clean cotton rag—this should really do the trick.

5   **TIME FOR THE PROS?** If none of the above has fully fixed the stain, consult a professional.

6   **FEED AND NOURISH.** Once the stain has been removed, treat the surface to a coat of feeding cream or leather treatment.

7   **SHINE WITH WAX.** Be sure to use the appropriate color. Wait a few hours for the wax to sink in.

8   **BUFF TO A SHINE.** If the surface looks dull, apply more wax, waiting an hour after application before buffing.

9   **AN OPTIONAL BUFFING:** Once your piece is in good, clean condition—and only if the leather is pristine, not patinated—you can lightly sprinkle with 4F pumice after waxing. Rub with a wool or felt rag to create a hard, glossy shine. Some people prefer polishing with Renaissance wax (also called museum wax).

LIGHT EBONIZING

Midcentury-Modern Bed Set

Although ebonizing is frequently used to create a dark hue approximating black, a lighter-handed version of the technique is just as lovely and much easier to accomplish—perfect for a piece requiring significant rehab. After painstaking prep work, you want a relatively painless finishing process.

THE PIECES

This midcentury-modern bed set, comprising a dresser and a nightstand, was a disaster: ugly brown hue, numerous broken parts, veneer missing, cracks and other damage . . . the list goes on. My client, who'd purchased the pieces on Craigslist for $45, didn't realize how beat-up the set was until she saw it in person. Desperate, she considered tossing it, but I assured her that this was the perfect scenario for ebonizing. A simple version of the technique looks exceptional—with minimal effort.

THE LOOK

Such a problematic piece leaves you little choice but to go dark! If you can't show it, hide it—and make it look like a million dollars in the process. In contrast to the desk featured on page 162, which I stained almost black, here I wanted an espresso hue.

THE PROCESS

This low-key and informal version of ebonizing is very easy to execute and is well-suited to simple, clean-lined pieces like these.

category
Oil

degree of difficulty
Easy

prep work
I stripped and sanded the pieces. Then I fixed the mahogany veneer—patching in some locations, regluing in others—and built up missing parts with wood filler to create a flush, totally flat surface (see page 276). When you darken a piece, you can be less professional with your repair standards—no need to be a purist. Fill and patch, and have fun!

PICKING A PIGMENT

Hint: You generally use black pigment when ebonizing. But to get this oh-so-slightly lighter hue, mix equal parts black and Van Dyke (a very dark brown that gets its name from Old Master painter Anthony Van Dyck).

WHAT YOU'LL NEED

- *Latex or nitrile gloves*
- *Alcohol-based stain*
- *100 percent cotton rags*
- *Inexpensive natural-bristle brushes*
- *Linseed or tung oil*
- *Black wax*
- *Containers*
- *Superfine steel wool (0000)*

1

START WITH DARK STAIN. Wearing protective gloves and using a pad or a brush, apply a single coat of dark, alcohol-based stain to every exterior surface. (Oil-based stain would be appropriate here, too; just avoid water-based stain.) Use just enough product to make the surface look neat and uniform—you don't want to obscure too much of the wood.

3

SCUFF-SAND. Using superfine (0000) steel wool, scuff-sand the piece to even your finish.

4

WAX AND SHINE. Finish with a light coat of dark-colored wax (see page 243 on making colored wax). Not too much: just enough to lend uniformity and create a satin shine without obscuring the grain. Wait an hour, and buff to a shine. Or, as I like to do with wax, wait overnight, reapply a light coat, wait an hour, and then buff to a nice, richer satin shine.

2

SEAL WITH A COAT OF OIL. Depending on how much protection you want, you can reapply the oil (see page 165) a few times, waiting overnight to dry between coats. The oil darkens the wood a touch and imbues it with an aqueous sheen.

5

REATTACH THE HARDWARE. You can polish the hardware or transform it with a patina.

THE UNEXPECTED BEAUTY OF A "DISASTER" PIECE

A piece in such an advanced stage of decrepitude presents the perfect opportunity for honing your repair, patching, and filling skills. Because any work you do will be an improvement, the execution doesn't have to be flawless. Moreover, you are liberated from adhering to proper restoration methods, so can use whatever glue or color will fix the damage. All the more reason to take creative liberties and choose a finish that suits your aesthetic completely (versus taking cues from the bones of the piece). Use your imagination and flex your artistry and creativity to transform the piece into something fantastic. Remember: You are salvaging what would otherwise be discarded, so anything goes.

One request: Avoid the knee-jerk temptation to paint the far-gone piece. Paint should be your last resort. A good paint job requires just as much prep work—sanding, patching, filling, etc.—as does a nice finish. So painting is not the easy way out. And unless your prep work is meticulous, the result will just look like a bad paint job. In contrast, not only will staining the wood draw out its beauty, but the process is often more forgiving and will better disguise damage. Stain and wax will always look lovely, and natural-wood finishes connote quality.

FRENCH POLISH

Marquetry Table

A traditional 18th-century marquetry piece is the perfect one on which to demonstrate French polish. Its signature glass-like shine gives ornate marquetry an inner glow and crisp definition. The technique is similar to polishing a car or jewelry: What creates the glossiness is a repeated abrasive action that renders the wood surface microscopically smooth, leaving no surface asperities to trap light.

THE PIECE

This neoclassical Italian table is embellished on every surface with ornate veneer marquetry, depicting tools of classical studies. (It reminds me of a scenic boiserie-paneled period room at the Metropolitan Museum of Art in New York—the Studiolo from the Ducal Palace in Gubbio—but in miniature.) The existing French polish was almost gone, dulling the wood.

THE LOOK

One glance at this gem and I knew that only French polish would do it justice. With French polish, technically there is no finish; the shine comes from a smoothing process versus an added-on coating, so you preserve and enhance the purity and depth of the wood. It creates the feeling that the piece is wet, and draws out the intricate decoration.

THE PROCESS

The piece was in subpar condition, both superficially and structurally, and little remained of the existing finish. Plus, sun damage had bleached the top layer of the wood. So it made sense to strip it and start from scratch.

category
Shellac/lacquer

degree of difficulty
The process requires absolute patience, and you need to get the feel for it—listening to the product, developing a sense of when you have too much or too little on your pad. However, while French polishing is tedious, it's not painstaking. It's also relatively forgiving; if you mess up irreparably along the way, just sand down and start over—unlike when using modern commercial varnishes, which need to be stripped if improperly applied.

prep work
First, I stripped the existing finish. The good thing about a piece that's been previously French polished is that you can strip the finish simply by rubbing it with a coarse rag dampened with denatured wood alcohol, until the surface is totally clean. Creating a smooth and level base necessitated replacing veneer where it was missing, scraping other parts smooth, and staining spots with surgical precision. (Note: Do not sand intricate marquetry, because the direction of the grain changes with every piece of veneer and you could end up scratching the wood.)

WHAT YOU'LL NEED

- Latex or nitrile gloves, several disposable pairs
- Shellac
- 100 percent cotton rags
- Numerous French polish pads (see page 250 on making them)
- Pumice 4F
- Rubber band
- Denatured wood alcohol
- Baby oil (or other mineral oil)
- Small artist's brush (optional)
- Small plastic container with a tight lid

I have met French, Italian, Russian, Spanish, English, and Chinese artisans who have shared their unique techniques with me. These varying methodologies speak to the fact that with French polish, you develop your own style. It's all in the hand and in the process. And in the mind: When you're in the zone, you feel like you could do it for hours. The act is meditative—I'm convinced this is the next yoga!

2

APPLY PUMICE. Some finishers prefer to administer the pumice with their hand, but a pounce bag offers better accuracy and utilizes less product. (To create a pounce bag, put a moderate amount of pumice in the center of a small square of cotton T-shirt, wrap the ends together, and secure with a rubber band.) Lightly tap the pounce bag onto the surface of the wood to produce a fine pumice dust, which you distribute evenly by rubbing it lightly into the pores with your palm.

4

START RUBBING THE WOOD WITH THE PAD. As you rub, the pumice and the alcohol start to mix with the previously applied shellac, creating a microscopic slurry that will build up in the pores, and at the same time abrade the wood surface. Work evenly over the entire piece, making sure not to neglect the edge and details (see step 11). Refill your pad with alcohol when it gets too dry, but not with too much at a time! The feel of the pad gliding will tell you if you need to refill or recharge; feel is more accurate than look. Once in a while, use straight lines to even out the circle marks that appear.

1

SEAL THE PIECE WITH SHELLAC. Wearing gloves, pour a medium amount of shellac onto a folded cotton rag—this is called "charging"—and squeeze it to fully distribute. Apply the shellac to the wood surface in continuous, straight lines, from edge to edge, with light pressure. (I used ruby shellac, whose smoky coloration is well suited to antiques—it gives wood more depth and contrast.) Continue executing those long strokes, slightly overlapping one another, until you've coated the entire surface two or three times. Shellac dries fast—almost to the touch—but wait an hour for it to sink in. No need to be overcautious about creating an even appearance; the goal here is to seal every square inch, not to have the shellac look good.

3

POUR ALCOHOL INTO A NEW PAD. Charge a fresh, rough-linen- or canvas-wrapped French polish pad with alcohol. (The rougher fabric is sturdier and more resistant—vital for the next step.) Tap the flat surface of the pad on your hand to evenly distribute the alcohol and test that it's not overly damp.

5

A NOTE ABOUT TECHNIQUE: Never stop moving the pad (this applies to both filling the grain and building up the polish). As soon as you stop for even a second, the pad will catch and you can mar the surface. Take a break and lift off the pad every 20 minutes so your arm doesn't tire. (Or, better yet, learn to French polish with both hands!)

6

WATCH FOR THE SHINE. Over the course of an hour or so, a glass-like surface will start to appear. The shine comes from the action of grinding, which is almost like honing. If you don't have the beginning of a shine after an hour, apply a little more pumice, put a drop or two of alcohol into your pad, and work it in. You may stop at any time—go do your taxes or tuck in your child for the night, and then come back and start again.

7

LET THE PRODUCT SETTLE. Stop when your grain is nicely filled and a smooth, light shine animates the wood surface. Some people wait a day or two at this point, as the product may sink in more, and tackle another session of grain filling.

8

START BUILDING UP THE SURFACE. Charge a new cotton-wrapped French polish pad with shellac solution; tap on the side of your hand to distribute the shellac evenly and test that it's not too wet (a classic beginner's mistake). Rub the piece in tight circles. Since the pad is freshly charged with shellac, rub lightly so you don't apply too much on the wood, which would melt the shellac-based grain-filler. As the pad dries, move to wider figure-eight motions (see diagram on page 179) and apply more pressure. Remember that you are polishing, not varnishing; accordingly, it's not the amount of product you apply that builds the finish, but the continuous motion that blends together the alcohol, shellac, pumice, and wood. When you tilt your pad (without stopping; remember, keep moving!) at a 30-degree angle, you should see a trace of alcohol drying behind. This is called a healthy ghostly trail. The execution is slow, but you can multitask: Once you get the feel for the technique, you don't even need to look at your piece while you're polishing. Let the ease of the glide guide you.

9

DON'T LET THE PAD DRY OUT. As you polish, you'll have to recharge your pad with shellac. When? As it dries, it does not glide as easily, and you have to use more pressure; recharge when you feel like you're forcing it. Always test the dampness on your hand first, and then polish very, very lightly for the first few passes after recharging; the abundance of product could also make the pad stick.

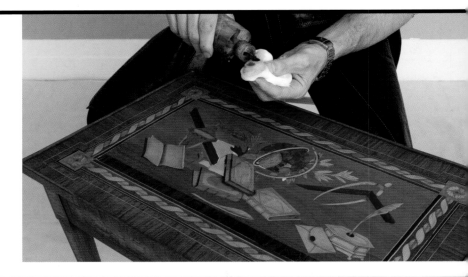

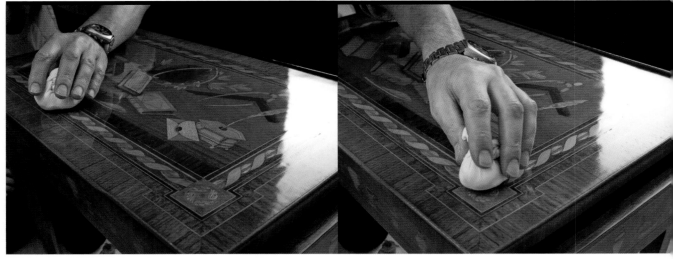

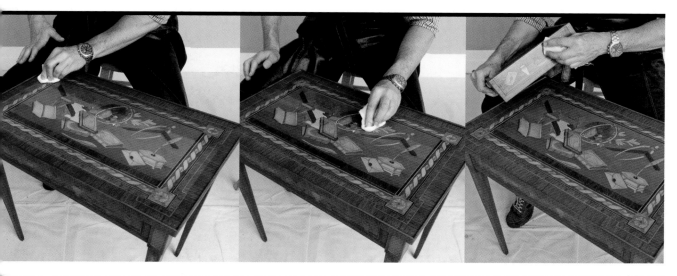

10

ADD A DAB OF LUBRICANT. When your pad stops gliding nicely, even after it's been recharged, add one tiny, tiny drop of baby oil to the outside of your pad. You may be tempted to add more oil once you see the shine it gives, but don't get seduced. The oil is not for appearances, just to help gliding, and you'll have to remove it completely in the last step. (From this point on, you may need to charge your pad less often.)

11

GET INTO THE NOOKS AND CRANNIES. Pads are great for flat surfaces, but anything curved—recesses, corners, crevices, carvings—requires a different technique: cheating! Set aside a little bottle of shellac solution, and leave it unscrewed for a day or two so that some alcohol evaporates. Using a little fine-art brush, apply this slightly concentrated shellac solution to all the detailing. Then polish with a pad. Another method is to open your pad, tear off shreds of the damp cheesecloth filling, and polish loosely with them.

12

LET THE PRODUCT SINK IN. After an hour or so, stop polishing and wait a few days for the product to be fully absorbed. It may be depressing to see that all the nice buildup you created has sunk in, but that's the name of the game. Go over the piece again; it will take two to four sessions to execute the perfect French polish (although some finishers swear by the number seven!). Subsequent sessions may not take as long, since you have more and more shellac on the piece to polish with and it won't sink in anymore.

13

REMOVE THE LINGERING OIL. When the product doesn't sink in anymore, and you have achieved the level of buildup you like, let the piece cure for a few days. Charge a new pad with a touch of pure, denatured alcohol—your pad should be barely damp—and trace it very delicately over the top of the piece. Work in a succession of light, straight lines for a few minutes to remove all the lubricating oil until you have a flawless, wet-looking surface.

You will invariably fail at this process, but it is the only way to learn. Your pad will be too wet and melt the finish; your pad will be too dry and scratch it; your pressure will be too light and you will not remove any oil; your pressure will be too strong and you will imprint your moves onto the finish . . . or all of the above. Take heart: Practice makes perfect.

14

REATTACH THE HARDWARE. Afterward, I delicately reattached the bronze and the ormolu detailing onto the piece.

For Professionals Only

To add shine, some refinishers add a hint of sulfuric acid (yes, car-battery acid!) when removing the oil. Dilute 1 or 2 drops, no more, in a glass of water and pour a drop or two on a fresh pad. This is to be done after step 12, and only by professionals. (Neophytes, pretend you never read this.)

Troubleshooting

- Oversaturated pad: If you have some stickiness, recharge your pad with alcohol instead of shellac, and continue as normal after letting your pad dry a bit.

- To remove surface asperities, rub down the surface with superfine (0000) steel wool or sand it with 1000-grit sandpaper, and then continue polishing on and around that spot until it's even with the surrounding surface.

Variations

- You can stop at any time and wax over your work, which will give the piece a satin shine and an antique feeling. In that case, you can skip the oil-removing step, which is the trickiest to execute.
- Another alternative is English varnish, *vernis anglais.* Brush the wood with animal glue diluted in warm water, which creates a warm syrup that fills and seals the pores. When dry, sand with 400-grit sandpaper, and then execute a French polish—skipping the pumice and filling part. Finish with a coat of wax to give the wood a more satin shine and enhanced resistance.
- If the idea of applying a coat of glue to your furniture doesn't appeal, do a French polish that's half-ragged-on, half-polished: Fill up the grain with a regular filler, brush on a few coats of shellac (with fine sanding in between), and then initiate one or two sessions of French polishing with a pad. The result is decent and will fool many.

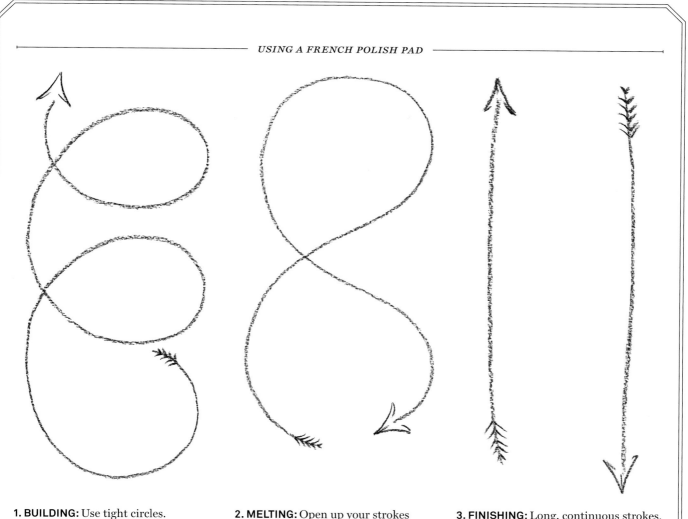

1. BUILDING: Use tight circles.

2. MELTING: Open up your strokes to form figure eights.

3. FINISHING: Long, continuous strokes.

- Always charge (or feed) your pad from the inside. Untie the top (or open from one of the tucked-in corners), pour a little shellac mix into the filler, and then retie. Before applying the pad to your piece, test the moisture level by tapping the pad on the back of your hand. This helps disperse the shellac evenly while allowing you to gauge the amount of product inside. The pad should feel damp, not wet. (If it gets too saturated, just wait a few minutes for some alcohol to evaporate.)

- As you rub the pad on the wood surface, the product should discharge evenly. Keep the pad totally flat.

- When your French polish is done, place the pad in a glass jar, add a drop of alcohol, and close the lid tightly. The pad, which is reusable, will keep for weeks—or even months—if properly stored. (However, do replace the outer fabric if it's gotten gunky or has started to wear.) The beauty of an already broken-in pad is that it fits your palm perfectly and has just the right flatness.

- If you *do* reuse a pad, be sure it's impregnated with the right color shellac; keep a different one for each hue.

FRENCH POLISH RESTORATION

Cuban Mahogany Table

Now that you've learned how to execute a traditional French polish from scratch (in Technique 7), I'll show you how to restore an existing finish. The processes are quite similar, although depending on the state of your piece, you may be able to skip some of the initial steps.

THE PIECE

Crafted of rare Cuban mahogany, this majestic drop-leaf table resides in New York's City Hall, where it was damaged by flooding during 2012's Hurricane Sandy. The top of the table and each drop leaf are crafted from a single unique slab of solid mahogany. This size slab is rare today for any species, but extinct for Cuban mahogany—the most beautiful variety—which has been totally eradicated by overlogging.

THE LOOK

The goal was to revive the table—which I'd previously restored for the city—with a high shine, and erase those pesky water stains.

THE PROCESS

Reviving a French polish entails fine sanding and cleaning, rather than stripping, the piece; as such, you don't reopen the grain. So after cleaning, only a light filling session (with the shellac-sealing and pumicing step) may be necessary before rebuilding the polish with a pad.

category
Shellac/lacquer

degree of difficulty
Medium. Although repair is always daunting, it's easier to rebuild a French polish than to initiate one.

STAIN WITH A LIGHT HAND

During a French polish, you can obscure a repair, blend mismatched parts, or just enhance the color of the wood by adding a drop or two—no more!—of alcohol-based stain to your pad during the process. (You may be tempted to add a bit more color, but don't: Before you know it, the wood becomes smeared with trails of stain!) The act of polishing will move around and evenly distribute the color. But be forewarned: This technique requires a lot of practice and moderation.

WHAT YOU'LL NEED *(see also Technique 7, page 172)*

- *Denatured wood alcohol*
- *100 percent cotton rags*
- *400- to 600-grit sandpaper*
- *Baby oil (or other mineral oil)*
- *French polish pads (see "Making and Using French Polish Pads," page 250)*
- *Shellac*
- *Pumice 4F*
- *Wax*

1

CLEAN. Use an alcohol-dampened rag to clean the wood.

2

SAND. Sand the entire piece—both the damaged and untouched areas—until you have a level, blended surface. Use wet-and-dry or free-cut sandpaper, which has a little lubricant so it doesn't scratch the wood. Damaged areas will require more abrading; use the same grit sandpaper in those spots, but for a longer period of time. The great thing about French polish—as well as alcohol-based finishes in general—is that it doesn't layer as separate coats: The coats melt together, making it easier to sand down to an even base. Use the finest grit possible to do the job, the goal being to clean and smooth, not strip back to bare wood. Use your touch as the judge.

5

SHELLAC AND PUMICE. Start with your shellac sealer followed by the pumice step. Even if the grain is nicely filled, the goal is to microscopically abrade the wood and create a flawless foundation for your shellac buildup.

6

REBUILD THE FRENCH POLISH. See page 176 for instructions.

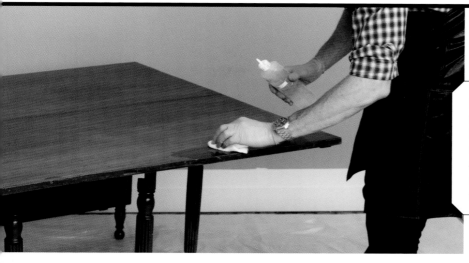

This light alcohol wipe is the only prep work involved—no need to strip the piece. That's the beauty of French polish: Even when the finish fails, as in the case of significant moisture damage, all that's required is to take it down a bit and then rebuild it.

3

CLEAN AGAIN WITH ALCOHOL. You want to create a dry and dust-free surface.

4

INITIATE ANY NECESSARY REPAIR WORK. The wood is now basically clean and smooth, although the grain is filled. At this stage, you may want to make various adjustments to the wood. If you have a water ring, for instance, you can bleach the surface. I don't recommend staining, however, since it's challenging to match the repair to the rest of the piece.

7

SEAL WITH SHELLAC. On an antique, ruby shellac will probably best match the rest of the furniture. To further the overall match, you may want to introduce some alcohol-color in the pad. When restoring a French polish, you might also wish to finish with a coat of wax: The softer, satin look that results is more faithful to an antique than is a full-on gloss.

WATER GILDING RESTORATION

Round Mirror Frame

It is quite common to encounter a gold-leafed mirror or picture frame in need of TLC. With age, the wood substrate and the thick coat of gesso above it move and separate, causing the gilt finish to flake off. Restoration is no different than executing the technique from scratch. The process might seem unnerving, but if you break it down, it's not daunting. Just stick to decaf the day of!

THE PIECE

Dating from early to mid-19th century, this gilt mirror was in decent shape, with a lovely patina. It just had a few patches of flaking that needed fixing, including the 4-inch-long section on which I'm demonstrating the restoration process.

THE LOOK

Rendering the repair as invisible as possible meant patinating the newly applied gold-leaf sections.

THE PROCESS

I rebuilt the frame layer by layer where it was damaged, restoring the profile of the ornamentation. After applying the gold leaf, I faux-aged it with jute (to expose the undercoat in some spots), coloring stains and wax (to temper the shine), and an application of rottenstone (for a matte, dusty look). Note: You need to apply gold leaf in a place with absolutely no ventilation. You can't even breathe on the sheets of gold leaf, or they'll crumple or fly away!

category
Gold leaf

degree of difficulty
Water gilding is the most difficult type of gold leafing to execute: You are judged by the purity of your finish and its level of flatness and shine. An aged patina, however, is a great entry point to the technique. It's forgiving in that you "muck up" your work a bit afterward to make it look older. And don't be intimidated by the material itself. While gold leaf may look brittle and delicate, it's actually sturdy and elastic; the more pure it is, the softer it is.

ROTTENSTONE

Called terre pourrie—*"rotten soil" in French—this superfine powder is a fossilized marine sediment made of limestone mud and algae. It's been used for centuries to polish brass and jewelry as well as fine furniture, namely in French polish, and to fill the grain for an oil buildup. Rottenstone is also called* Tripoli powder *(whose name, incidentally, has nothing to do with the Libyan city; it derives from the Old French term for fine polish).*

WHAT YOU'LL NEED (see page 232 for full description of many)

- Small scraper
- X-Acto knife
- Gesso
- Small synthetic-bristle artist's brush
- Carving tools
- 320- to 1000-grit sandpaper
- Red bole

- Small natural-bristle artist's brush
- Linen
- Baby powder
- Loose gold leaf
- Gilding knife
- Gilding cushion

- Various soft-bristle brushes, such as squirrel hair, called gilding combs
- Agate burnishing tools
- Jute
- Alcohol- or water-based stain
- Rottenstone
- Colored wax

3

RE-CREATE THE MOLDING PROFILE. Use carving tools and chisels to shape the gesso, mimicking the existing details. Professional refinishers have a tool to fit every little crevice, but you can buy just those you need. Bring your piece—or a photograph of it— to a gold-leaf supplier, who can advise which tools (and which variety of metal leaf) will work best; as with all fine-craft suppliers, they are passionate about their trade and will be delighted to share resources and advice!

5

PREPARE AND APPLY THE BOLE. Add about 10 percent of water to the bole and stir well; it should have the consistency of thick cream. Brush on the bole in a single light coat using a smooth, natural-bristle artist's brush that you have wet and patted dry; this keeps the fast-drying bole from caking on the bristles. (When working on larger surfaces, clean the brush regularly during application to keep a constant quality of application and product.) Bole, which will create a hard, supersmooth surface for the gold leaf, dries in a few minutes, so you can reapply immediately where needed. Wait a few hours for it to cure.

1

REMOVE ANY FLAKING. Using your hand or a small scraper, remove as much flaking as possible. Use the tip of an X-Acto knife to probe the gesso. Be conservative, but any loose part has to go. This step can be messy!

2

APPLY THE GESSO. With a small synthetic-bristle brush, liberally apply gesso to the wound. Really fill every nook and cranny to smooth over any roughness. Let the first coat settle for about 30 minutes, and then—before it's fully dry—apply a second coat. Gold leaf experts might apply ten thin coats of gesso, but the number of layers required depends on the damage and how refined you want the result to be. Let the piece sit overnight.

4

SMOOTH THE SURFACE THOROUGHLY. Sand the gesso with a consecutively finer and finer grit; start with 320 grit if you have to remove a lot of gesso and continue to about 800 (or even 1000) grit. Follow by rubbing the gesso with a rough piece of linen to create a totally smooth, paper-like surface; any defect will show through the gold leaf.

6

BURNISH THE BOLE. Using coarse linen, brush the bole until it's totally smooth. You can also rub it with a wet finger or sandpaper (as fine as 1000 grit) to eradicate any flaws.

7

KEEP YOUR HANDS DRY. Before applying the gold leaf, sprinkle baby powder on your hands so that they're totally dry: Do not subject loose gold leaf to moisture or grease (or wind)!

8

PREPARE THE GOLD LEAF. Using a gilding knife, lift a few sheets of leaf from the booklet and drop onto a cushion made of suede or chamois. I used just two sheets of leaf for this entire frame, which had three or four bad parts. (Save any leftovers to garnish chocolate or desserts; yes, gold leaf is edible, as it does not get digested.)

9

CUT THE GOLD LEAF. Flatten a square gently with the wide part of your knife, then cut the square to the dimensions you need; smaller pieces work best for intricate details.

11

APPLY THE LEAF TO THE FRAME. Using a squirrel-hair brush, pick up a square of leaf from the cushion. (First, pass the brush over your forehead or a touch of Vaseline dabbed on the back of your hand, which provides a little tackiness.) Release the leaf onto the frame. It should unfold and flatten perfectly onto the wet bole. As you apply the squares, overlap them about $3/16$ inch so there's no gap in between.

12

WAIT FOR THE LEAF TO ADHERE. The alcohol evaporates immediately and the water gets absorbed by the porous clay below, bonding the leaf to the surface. Wait 10 minutes, and then tap the gold leaf lightly with a very fine natural-bristle artist's brush. This will help adhesion and remove any leaf that didn't stick adequately. Apply more gold leaf where the red bole shows through too prominently, although you do want to leave some bole exposed to create an aged patina. Let the piece dry overnight.

14

EXPOSE THE RED BOLE. Re-create the appearance of a centuries-old finish by using a light abrasive to uncover the red bole—as much or as little as desired. I rubbed the surface with rough jute.

15

MAKE THE PATINA UNIFORM. Use an alcohol- or water-based stain to darken the new patches (which will, of course, fade and age naturally over time—you're just accelerating that process). You can also apply a bit of brown-tinted paste wax with your finger to dull the gold leaf's shine. Bit by bit, add a little stain, a little wax, until you've matched the existing patina.

10

WET THE FRAME. Prepare a mixture of water and alcohol (3 parts water to 1 part alcohol; a pro will dissolve one or two pellets of animal-skin glue for a little more tack) and brush it onto the frame. Work in small sections because the water dries pretty quickly (in which case, it's fine to reapply—but do not oversaturate the polished bole surface).

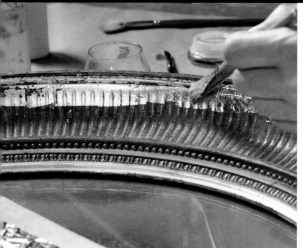

13

POLISH. Polish the gold leaf with agate burnishing tools to forge a flawless bond between the gold leaf and the clay. This step creates a metallic sheen; skip it if you prefer a matte-gold aspect. You'll be amazed how strong burnishing renders the gold-leaf surface!

16

FINISH. Finally, apply powdered rottenstone to mimic an accumulation of dust. Blow or tap it on with a brush, and then wipe off any excess.

TECHNIQUE 10

WATER GILDING

WITH PATINA AND MOLDING REPLACEMENT

Gilt Mirror with Polychromy

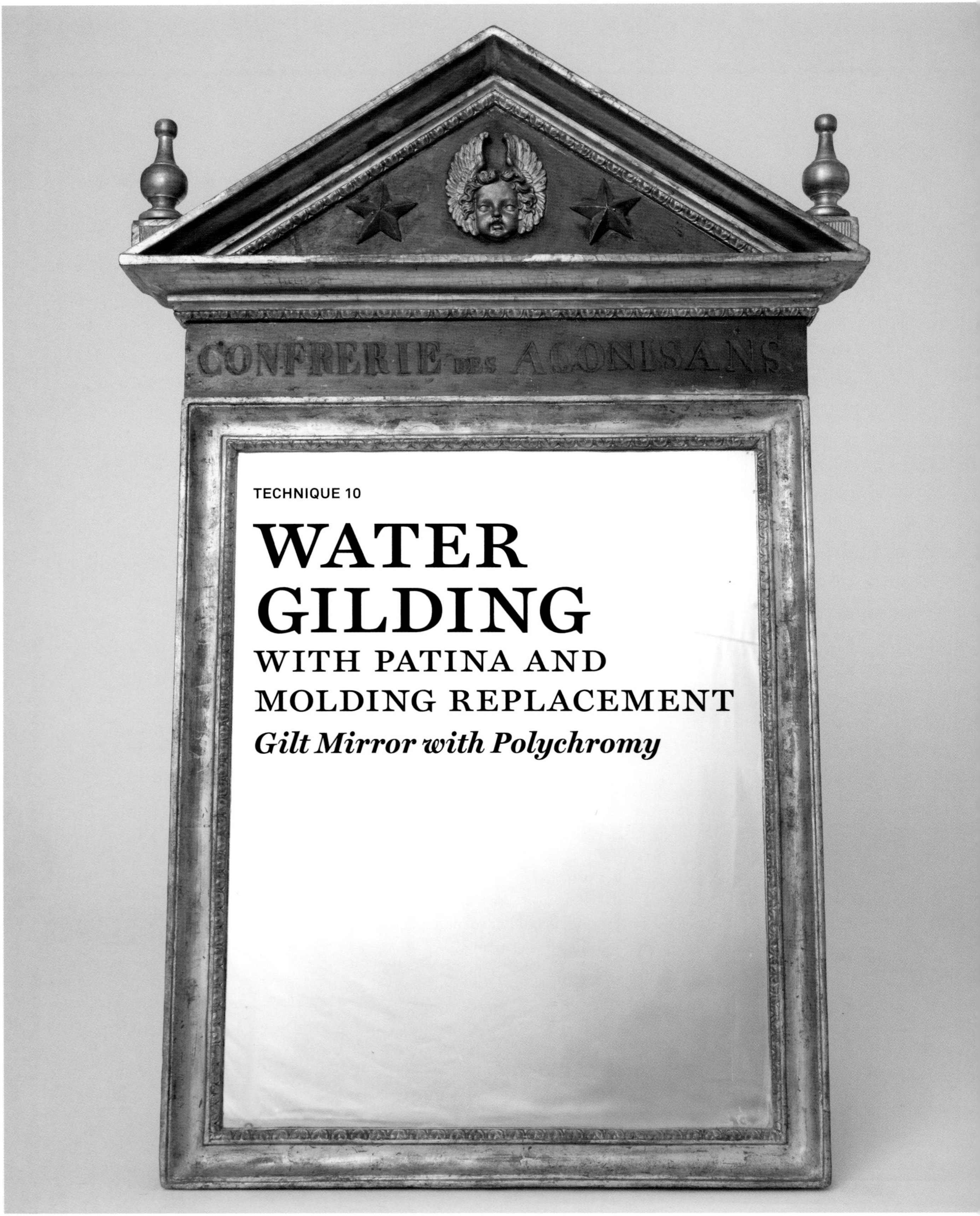

Like Technique 9, this project involves water gilding followed by faux aging and distressing to match the surrounding period gilding. Restoration, however, was more complicated, since the existing molding was largely unsalvageable and required wholesale replacement, and two finials were missing.

THE PIECE

Sarah Scott Thomas, the proprietor of Balzac Antiques in the Garden District of New Orleans, scours markets throughout France in search of unique period furnishings. Among her recent finds was this gilt mirror, embellished with exuberant polychromy (a fancy industry term for multicolored decorative painting). The frame boasted an intriguing design but was a total mess: missing gold, peeling paint, chipping gesso, broken moldings, missing finials . . . a former owner had even applied bronze radiator paint, a major no-no.

THE LOOK

Many of Sarah's clients like distressed pieces, so she didn't want an overzealous rehabilitation. Not limited by having to execute a strict period restoration, I took some liberties, including replacing the derelict molding with one featuring a slightly different profile. (In a historical restoration, I could have matched the molding exactly by having an extant section reproduced via casting.)

THE PROCESS

After removing all the loose parts and rebuilding the woodwork—patching some sections, replacing others—I performed traditional water gilding: applying gesso, bole, and then gold leaf, which I later patinated. (Oil gilding could have been appropriate here, because I aged and distressed the piece rather heavily. In this case, use more easily applied patent gold leaf.)

category
Gilding restoration

degree of difficulty
Medium

prep work
Be safer than I was: Take the piece apart and remove the mirror before restoration!

BEFORE IT WAS
A MIRROR . . .

. . . This piece was a plaque. Confrerie des Agonisans *means "fraternity of the martyrs," which was a society of religious knights. The original panel that the mirror replaced was most likely engraved with the names of the society participants, and would have been carried during Catholic processions.*

WHAT YOU'LL NEED

- Small scraper
- X-Acto knife
- Water-based putty (optional)
- Hide glue (optional)
- 320- to 1000-grit sandpaper
- Gesso
- Soft synthetic-bristle artist's brush
- Coarse linen
- Carving tools (optional)
- Red bole
- Fine natural-bristle artist's brush
- Composition molding
- Kotton Klenser
- 100 percent cotton rags
- Cotton swabs (optional)
- Loose gold leaf
- Gilding knife
- Gilding cushion
- Various soft-bristle brushes, such as squirrel hair
- Agate burnishing tools
- Superfine (0000) steel wool
- Jute
- Rottenstone
- Alcohol-based stain
- Colored wax

3

ATTACH ANY FRAGMENTS.
Reattach any loose sections of the molding profile that are salvageable by using wood or hide glue.

4

SAND. Using 320-grit sandpaper, sand smooth any newly applied wood or wood-composition elements.

5

APPLY GESSO. Any parts that were filled, rebuilt, or added—including moldings and finials—will need an application of gesso. Then sand smooth, progressing from 400- to 800-grit sandpaper. (See Technique 9, step 2.)

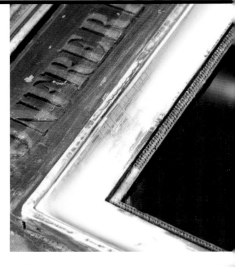

7

REPLACE THE MISSING MOLDINGS with new composition molding. Warm it over a steaming hot plate until the underside gets malleable and a bit melt-y; this reactivates the glue in the composition. (Alternatively, you can heat the molding over a water-filled pan covered with cheesecloth, held in place with a rubber band.) Then simply press it onto the frame. Because the material is slightly malleable, it marries well with the contours of the frame and at the corners where sections adjoin; it also cuts easily with an X-Acto knife. Afterward, you only need to apply bole, not gesso.

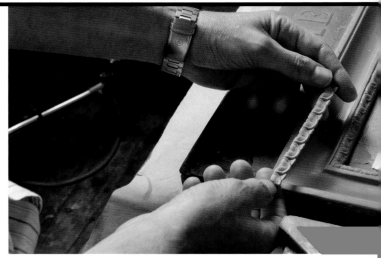

1

PREPARE THE PIECE. Remove all loose parts: flakes, chipped gesso, peeling-off moldings, etc. (see Technique 9, step 1, for more on this process).

2

PREP THE HOLES. Fill in any holes or divots using water-based wood putty.

6

APPLY THE BOLE. Brush on where needed with a soft synthetic-bristle artist's brush, and then burnish the bole using coarse linen until it's totally smooth. Rub with a wet finger or 1000-grit sandpaper to eradicate any lingering flaws. (See Technique 9, steps 5 and 6.)

8

CLEAN THE POLYCHROMY. Kotton Klenser is the only thing I trust to clean polychromy; it's similar to what professional painting restorers use. (The alternative is warm water with a natural soap like Castile or Marseille, mixed with a drop of ammonia.) Apply with a rag or a cotton swab, and rub off any excess with a clean cotton rag. You'll notice that I removed the top pediment and protected the mirrored surface to execute this step.

9

REPLACE THE FINIALS. Here, I replaced the missing finials with new ones. Since both were MIA, I had no way to know what the originals looked like. So I chose a profile that corresponded to the style and scale of the frame. You'll need to apply both gesso and bole before gilding.

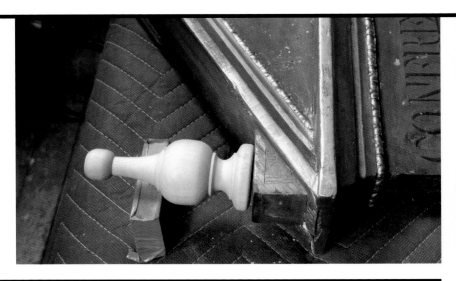

10

APPLY THE GOLD LEAF. Use the water-gild method (see Technique 9, steps 7 to 11). Follow with a nice burnishing.

11

FAUX AGE. Create a patina by abusing the cured gold leaf with superfine (0000) steel wool or jute to match the rest of the piece and following with a dusting of rottenstone.

12

ADD COLOR AND DISTRESS. Use alcohol-based stain to color the leaf as needed, and then apply colored wax to re-create the appearance of dirt and age (see Technique 9, step 15).

WHAT IS COMPOSITION MOLDING?

Historically, frame moldings were hand-carved out of solid wood—traditionally basswood—which was a time-consuming process. During the Industrial Revolution, English artisans developed an efficient, mass-producible alternative to handcrafted ornamentation: composition molding. Although the recipe varied from maker to maker, it was made by mixing plaster of Paris or regular chalk with a binder (typically, animal glue, pine sap, or linseed oil) plus either cotton or hemp fiber or wood dust. The mix was pressed into a mold to form beading and other repetitive motifs, which were sold by the yard. Once these composition moldings were painted or finished, they looked just like wood.

Although rudimentary composition elements had existed since the Italian Renaissance, it wasn't until the 18th century, when the technique was refined, that they were used extensively. Irish artisans began ornamenting wood fireplace mantels with them. At the same time, the British neoclassical designer Robert Adams patronized composition makers in developing his popular furniture style, which was adorned with Roman and Greek ornamentation. The technique was immediately successful in America, always embracing of innovation. In France, however, composition ornaments had a slightly negative connotation, being of subpar quality than wood carving, and were therefore relegated to less expensive furniture—although widely used for frames. Any frame dating from the early 19th century onward is probably made from composition. The way to tell: When composition gets damaged, an entire section will pull off, versus wood, which cracks right through the motif.

Variations

COMPOSITION LEAF

To get a feel for the technique, try your hand at composition leaf, which comes in brass (to mimic gold) and aluminum (to imitate silver). Composition squares are a little bigger, thicker, and firmer—and thus more workable.

PATINA WITH UNDERPAINTING

A designer client brought this chaise to me for a makeover. The initial frame finish had a two-tone effect—cream-colored paint highlighted with gold leaf—that was deemed too matchy-matchy with the upholstery. I suggested gilding the entire frame and giving the gold leaf a nice rubbed patina with superfine (0000) steel wool. The treatment uncovers some of the cream-painted undercoat, just as you would expose the red bole in a typical faux-aging process.

OIL GILDING

Oil gilding typically gives a somewhat rustic look, but this baroque-style headboard is a perfect illustration of how sleek the finish can be—even though the gold leaf can't be burnished. Easier-to-apply patent gold leaf is capable of creating a very flat surface if applied on a well-prepared substrate. I had to execute the technique from scratch on the newly crafted piece, designed by decorator Jamie Drake, a longtime client and friend of mine. The trick was in the prep work: lots of sanding to create a supersmooth prep coat, followed by a very thin application of sizing with a rag—a technique that's only possible on long, flat surfaces like these. Afterward, I treated the gold leaf with superfine (0000) steel wool, and then added wax to further enhance the patina.

GILT WAX

I used this product—a cream version of gold varnish—to showcase the carving details on a chaise. It is a very fast and clean process to highlight detailing or spiff up a boring, too-uniform finish; just follow your inspiration! Here, I applied it to the highlights with a brush and finger, and let it dry overnight.

INVERSE PATINA

This frame already had a gold-leaf finish, but it begged for a hint of patina. The gold leaf was a bit too unstable and fragile for a surface abrasion to uncover the bole, so I mimicked the process by dabbing a bit of a red cream on top of the gold. (Made specifically for this effect, the specialty product can be purchased at a gold-leaf supplier.) This decorative technique fools the eye: The red looks like it's below, rather than above, the gold leaf.

GOLD VARNISH

To give this pair of nightstands a whole new look, I executed an easy imitation gold-leaf finish, achieved via gold varnish. (Never use the cheap gold paint you find in the hardware store—the metallic particles are coarser and tarnish more easily, and your piece will end up looking like a radiator!) The product is made of microscopic particles of brass, bronze, or aluminum. Since the metallic pigments are suspended in varnish, they won't tarnish. They do, however, sink straight to the bottom of the paint can, so you have to stir vigorously prior to dipping in your brush. The technique was executed in three coats, with sanding in between.

1

A MATTE WHITE OIL-BASED PRIMER approximates the gesso. Be sure to choose one that sands well.

2

A COAT OF RED OIL PAINT, in a flat or eggshell finish, stands in for the bole. Pick an earthen red, with a little ochre to it—almost a brick-like tone.

3

A TOPCOAT OF GOLD VARNISH—THE MORE EXPENSIVE THE BETTER—ACTS AS THE GOLD LEAF. Apply with a soft brush. After letting the paint cure, you can expose more of the red undercoat if desired by sanding with steel wool. An even rubbing with 0000 will create an opaque gold veil with just a little red showing through; use coarser grades (00 or 0) for a more scratchy and damaged effect. You can also distress, stain, or color-wax the piece to age it, or apply a varnish coat if you prefer a glossy sheen.

WEATHERED FINISH

18th-Century Dutch Linen Press

A weathered look can be achieved via a number of techniques, from acid bleaching to cerusing. The results can veer from quite shabby-chic to more old-world depending on your piece and chosen medium. Here, I used milk paint to capture the timeworn patina of Gustavian furniture. To re-create a faded effect, you have to mimic the timeline of the original process—as if it had been painted, stripped, and repainted—in an accelerated fashion.

THE PIECE

The provenance of this 18th-century hutch is Northern European, probably Dutch or Swedish. It was likely used as a linen press or to store china or other valuables under lock and key and would have been designed for a middle-class residence, perhaps the home of a merchant. This was painted originally, probably several times over the centuries. A rather plain and unassuming wood, pine was not the most desirable essence at the time, so people typically painted it or stained it to fake a more exotic species—a cheaper alternative to using mahogany or walnut. At some point the hutch was stripped and waxed to look like *pitchpin*, a resinous and highly figured pine native to Europe.

THE LOOK

I wanted to create a finish reminiscent of the original, with a Gustavian feel, so I started with the traditional gray-and-white palette of that period but worked in warmer overtones. The inspiration for the new finish was the austerity of a winter landscape, dappled with quiet tones of blue, gray, and light brown. More than the color, I tried to capture the texture of the season—the dryness and desolation. It's not a rich, deep finish but almost flat and one-dimensional.

THE PROCESS

I used traditional milk paint, which can faux-age quite well if you mix a lower-than-usual ratio of water to powder (which is typically one-to-one) and apply these extra-thick coats quickly. The top layer cracks as it draws moisture from below, resulting in a peeling effect that lends historical authenticity.

category
Paint

degree of difficulty
This is a fairly forgiving technique, since you don't need to apply the coats evenly; the variegation and flaws are part of the beauty.

prep work
I removed the hardware and drawers and dewaxed the piece. Being a bit cavalier with the latter helps enhance the feeling of age: A little wax residue will prevent an even adhesion of paint and spur the peeling process.

GUSTAVIAN FURNITURE

Named for King Gustav III, who ruled Sweden in the last quarter of the 18th century, this style adopted the neoclassical lines of French, Italian, and English furniture—Louis XVI designs in particular. Very representative of the northern courts, Gustavian furniture was more pared-back than its Continental counterpart, the profiles simpler and the finishes mainly gilt or painted white, pale blue, or gray.

WHAT YOU'LL NEED

- *Milk paint*
- *Water soluble pigments*
- *2- to 4-inch natural-bristle paintbrushes*
- *100 percent cotton rags*
- *Plastic scrub brush*
- *Wax*
- *100 percent cotton rags*

1

PRACTICE AND PLAN. Whenever I paint a piece, I do a run-through with a dry brush. This step is critical when using milk paint: Water-based color doesn't have a long open time—15 to 30 minutes—and you don't want to make mistakes, nor do you want to feel rushed once you've mixed the paint. A dress rehearsal puts you in the right mind-set. When painting or staining, cover corners before flat surfaces and move from the center to the periphery; for door frames and panels, paint horizontal parts first followed by verticals.

3

APPLY THE FIRST COAT. Using long and fast strokes, apply a very light coat. Don't fuss too much, since you want the grain to show through and to leave some parts underpainted. Start with the inside corners—you have to stuff the brush in a little bit—and take your time, as this is the hardest part. Then paint the flat panels, working from the inside out, followed by the sides. For the drawers, paint the front and side but not the interiors; if you *must* paint the insides, keep them white, clean, and uniform—no fancy finishes. Let the piece dry for a few hours.

5

APPLY THE SECOND COAT. Feather on the second coat, following the grain. Note that you'll use less paint than with the base. You can be less exacting with the corners as well, to re-create the appearance that paint has rubbed off over time.

I learned this technique from designer John Saladino, a master of classical elegance who commissioned me for my first major project. We were standing in the middle of a newly paneled room, and he asked me to envision an invented history, which I would then re-create. I imagined that the room—just like this piece—had probably been painted initially, repainted several times (to cover use and abuse like stains, smoke, grease, and scratches), and then stripped to expose the wood finish, time having taken a toll on the panels. The result is the witness of what happened though history, and what you want to be loyal to in order to create an aged, distressed look.

2

PREPARE THE PAINT.
The first coat, or *base*, should always be white—the color of primer—but subsequent coats are pigmented.

4

PREPARE THE SECOND COLOR. Here, I spiked gray with blue, green, and burnt umber. Always make samples first and assess the result in situ. And always write down your recipe and proportions, keeping it handy as a reference. (I archive recipes in case a client needs a repair or a touch-up, or to match other pieces to it. Consider doing the same: Archives are always useful and can be stored in a nice decorative box, on the same shelf as your design reference books.) Don't be stingy: better to mix too much product and waste some than to deplete your supply midway through your piece. Once you've mixed your paint, you'll never be able to replicate the color exactly—even if you're faithful to your recipe!

6

LET THE PIECE SIT OVERNIGHT.
If you were painting a piece in earnest and wanted good coverage, you'd wait a few days between coats so everything cures. But for this technique, you want unevenness, so just wait overnight (or a couple of hours, if you feel adventurous) before applying the third coat. In the morning, you'll notice subtle cracking in the top layer.

7

APPLY THE THIRD COAT. The first and second coats are the main colors; the role of subsequent coats is to enhance the patina and capture the appearance of dirt or wear. That's why I chose a brown pigment for this step. Counterintuitively, the result should look less like a new coat has been added and more like the coat below has rubbed off. You really discriminate with this layer since you want the lower ones to show through. Dab slowly, assessing as you go, and use very little paint; the brush should be almost dry.

9

FAUX-AGE. When the piece is dry, you can use a plastic scrub brush to fake more wear-and-tear patterns. Brush the joints, the cracks, the top of drawers, around the handles—everywhere the hands have touched during centuries of use. The paint rubs off knots very easily, which you want to be prominent. If you want greater removal of paint, switch to a wire brush (versus using the same brush and trying to apply more force).

11

APPLY WAX. A final coat of pigmented wax neatens the piece while sealing it to stop the flaking. Wax also "wets" the finish, giving the flat milk paint shine and depth—and a greasy, worn feeling for verisimilitude. You can buff the wax for a light shine or leave it untouched for a drier, matte look. Wait a few days for everything to cure before using.

8

WIPE AS YOU PAINT. Wipe off a bit of the paint here and there with a rag, which gives you better control than does a brush. The wiping process also removes a bit of the cracked, peeling paint, exposing the primer and even some wood below—to which you can add more paint. Letting paint pool a little in the corners gives the desired effect of lazy stripping or a bit of dirt. Take your time with this step; it's where the artistry comes in.

10

LET DRY FOR A FEW DAYS. After applying the desired amount of coats—three or four max—let the piece dry for a few days to halt the peeling process. You'll notice that the colors start to meld together; see how the gray looks like it's aged into brown?

See how closely the results approximate the inspiration: an austere winter landscape.

Notes

- The first coat applied soaks into the wood and dries almost immediately; subsequent coats absorb a bit more slowly, but you still have only 15 to 30 minutes of workability.

- Stored in a container, good milk paint has a shelf life of 1 or 2 weeks max; inferior products should be used within a few days.

- Milk paint is nontoxic and doesn't have fumes, so you can execute this technique pretty much anywhere in your house. And although you're flaking off a bit of paint, the process isn't messy; the flakes are heavy, so they fall straight to your drop cloth.

Variation

If you want to execute a regular milk-paint finish, prep the piece by carefully dewaxing it (versus my cavalier approach above) to create a uniform substrate; otherwise, the paint won't adhere properly. Mix the paint according to the manufacturer's specifications. Then apply a single, thick coat—versus many lighter ones as you do in the weathering technique. Let it dry and then seal your handiwork with oil or wax.

DRY-WAX RUB

Paneled Door

This low-key, fail-proof process is particularly recommended for rustic furniture, like refectory or farm tables or provincial armoires. It can be applied on raw wood or on a previously waxed finish that has lost its shine, and it renders a wood surface more impervious to stains and liquid—great for tabletops and other dining surfaces.

THE PIECE

This door is made of an alpine fir, called *mélèze* in France. It's a great quality of pine, with a nice honey-blond coloration, and quite sturdy. As such, it was often used for paneling and Provençal armoires.

THE LOOK

With pine, you have limited finishing options. The wood takes stain very poorly, becoming blotchy and fake looking. And liquid wax, shellac, or turpentine would darken its dark-honey hue. A dry-wax rub is the best technique to enhance the wood's natural glow and preserve its dry look. Although pine is not a noble wood, it can take a hard shine for a wow factor.

THE PROCESS

Requiring only pure beeswax and elbow grease, this process is not messy, emits no fumes, and can be executed without moving or dismantling the piece first. It uses only pure beeswax (without any solvents), making it totally food safe, too. The act of burnishing smashes the grain and the wood fibers, creating a bold shine that's protective. Although I used a special tool here, a small agate or stone burnisher would be fine for a more petite piece.

category
Wax

degree of difficulty
Easy

prep work
I sanded the surface extra smooth with 320-grit sandpaper.

BURNISHING TOOL

In the 18th century, Parisian cabinetmaker Monsieur Roubo, a descendant of master ébénistes, *wrote a comprehensive guide to furniture styles and techniques that remains an authority. He was also one of the first to divulge a savoir faire that was jealously guarded by artisans of his day. In the search for the elusive perfect wood finish, he invented (or at least describes) a burnishing tool that employs solid wax as a medium and lubricant for a hard satin-polished shine. It is my opinion that Roubo's tool may be a rougher variation of the horsetail (i.e., the plant) polissoir used in traditional French polish.*

WHAT YOU'LL NEED

- *Tack cloths*
- *Cotton cloths*
- *Pure gum turpentine or denatured wood alcohol*
- *A loaf of pure, natural beeswax*
- *Burnishing tool*
- *Buffing felt or wool cloth*

1

CLEAN THE SURFACE CAREFULLY.
If the wood is unfinished, use a tack cloth. If the surface has been waxed previously, wipe it with a clean cloth, dampened with gum turpentine or alcohol, to remove caked-on dirt or old, loose finish. (Each product has its advantage: Alcohol dries instantly, so you can continue to the next step; gum turpentine remoisturizes and nourishes the wood but needs to dry overnight.)

3

ASSESS YOUR COVERAGE. Once you have covered the entire surface, the wood should have a fine, almost invisible coat of wax, sprinkled with a few loose specks of dry wax here and there.

4

START BURNISHING IMMEDIATELY.
Pure wax, unlike paste wax, requires no waiting or drying time, since no solvent is used. Rub the burnishing tool on the dry, waxed surface. (If the tool is brand-new, break it in first by rubbing in dry wax.) Instantly the burnished wood fibers will emit a hard, deep glow.

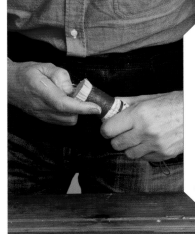

This small, hard brush-like tool can be purchased from The Broom Brothers, or make your own by trimming a natural-bristle broom or using a flat block of cork.

5

BURNISH WITH A RAG. Once the piece has an even shine, continue polishing with a felt or wool rag. Work any carved details or profiles with your fingers to dislodge any lingering specks.

2

RUB IN THE WAX.
Take the solid wax firmly in hand and rub generously on the wood surface. Don't miss a spot. To coat details and molding profiles, break the block and rub with broken edges of the wax loaf, working with the grain.

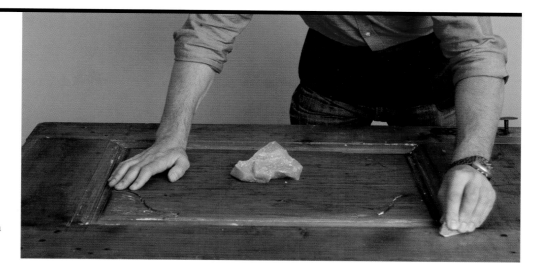

Maintenance

Other than the occasional buffing with a light wool cloth, the finish should require no maintenance for years to come. Tabletops subject to more abuse should be cleaned with alcohol or gum turpentine, and the entire process repeated.

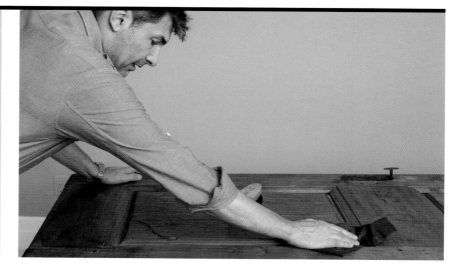

WOOD REPAIR

18th-Century Gueridon

This neat tilt-top table showcases a number of common structural issues you're likely to encounter when refurbishing old pieces: a sheared-off leg, a disjointed leg, and a split top that had already been repaired once with butterfly joints, now broken. Don't be intimidated; these are all relatively quick fixes.

THE PIECE

Crafted in the late 18th century, this mahogany gueridon may appear at first glance to be quite derelict, but it just needed straightforward mending and a little buffing to enhance the wood. I could see that the piece had been previously restored: Butterfly joints are a traditional restoration technique for split panels or flat tops, as is the use of wood glue; those elements date the restoration to 19th-century woodworking (or a contemporary artisan using those techniques). Woodworkers today use stronger glues that do not require butterfly joints, although they're often used as decorative elements on newly crafted rustic tabletops.

THE LOOK

The client was something of a purist and wanted to keep the piece as original as possible. His desire to preserve the historical integrity meant I could use only traditional glue and fillers. He also didn't want me to refinish, sand, or even clean the top. So after repairing the breaks, I treated the tabletop to just a light coat of colored wax, which I also used to diminish—but not eradicate—the crack. This is a nice example of an exposed restoration that gives character to an antique, evidence of its long and enduring life.

THE PROCESS

I assessed the breaks to make sure the pieces fit perfectly together, which luckily they did. (A missing part or unstable wood would have meant grafting a new piece onto the leg, a job that always requires the services of a professional woodworker or restorer.) Then I removed all the old glue to create a clean surface for an application of new adhesive. This step is vital to ensure a proper, long-lasting glue job—as is taking your time, organizing tools in advance, and executing every step in the right order.

category
Repair

degree of difficulty
Medium

prep work
None, other than removing the worn green-felt pads from the bottoms of the feet.

WHAT'S A GUERIDON?

It's a small stand or table, ornate yet light in weight, and thus easily moved around. In French, gueridon *refers to a comical vaudeville character—hence the connotations of lightness and whimsy.*

WHAT YOU'LL NEED

- *Rubber mallet*
- *Scrapers and an X-Acto knife*
- *Paint thinner or warm water*
- *100 percent cotton rags*
- *Denatured wood alcohol*
- *Water-based wood filler*
- *Toothpicks, dowels, and shims (optional)*
- *Hide glue*
- *Glue brush*
- *Clamps*
- *Chisel*
- *Stain*
- *Wax*
- *Plastic credit card*

1

DISASSEMBLE THE PIECE. I started with the disjointed leg, which I easily knocked out of its slot with a rubber mallet. Then I unscrewed the tilt top from the base so the two pieces could be repaired separately.

2

REMOVE THE BUTTERFLY JOINTS. Number each one as you go to remind you which went where. Use the old, broken butterflies to create new ones, tracing their exact shape onto a new piece of wood.

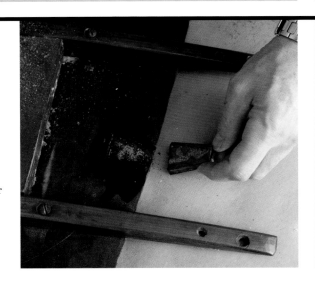

3

REMOVE ANY GLUE. Using a scraper (rather than sandpaper, which could alter the surface of both parts and affect how tightly they fit together), remove any glue residue in the wounds. Traditional hide glue dries and flakes into a crystal-like powder that's easy to clean up; use paint thinner or warm water to dissolve intractable clumps. Clean up afterward with an alcohol-dampened rag. A perfectly clean wound is a must for a successful glue job!

5

PREPARE AND PLAN. Do a dress rehearsal for the gluing process. Put the entire piece together, paying special attention to how you'll affix the clamps. (You don't want to be mulling this over after you've already applied the glue and it's starting to dry!) I decided to tackle the base first, and then the tabletop.

6

OPTIONAL: REINFORCE LEG REPAIRS. Use a wood dowel as a pin through the fixed crack to ensure strength in the legs and any other places subject to a lot of pressure or heavy use. (Never use a metal rod, screw, or nail, which will eventually tear apart the wood.) Pinning in this way is a common and historically proper way to fix this type of damage. Drill perpendicularly through the wound and insert the dowel so that it "bites" into both parts.

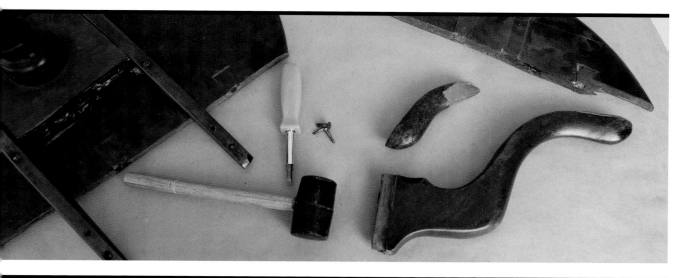

4

FILL THE HOLES. Patch any existing screw holes, since they're most likely worn and abused. I created my own filler, a mixture of sawdust, water, and glue (see page 249). Apply it little by little, using a finger or a toothpick to push the product all the way down into the holes. You can even leave the toothpick inside—breaking it off flush with the surface—so your screw has something to grip onto. Clean with alcohol or warm water.

7

APPLY THE GLUE. Using a coarse-bristle brush reserved for this purpose, apply hide glue to both faces of each break; it goes on wet-looking, so you'll be able to see that it's adequately covering the surface. The glue tacks quickly to hold the piece in place yet takes time to fully bond—which means you can reposition if needed. Clean up around the wounds with warm water and a rag.

8

ATTACH THE NEW BUTTERFLIES. First, glue both edges of the cracked tabletop and push them together. Then adhere the butterflies in place, brushing glue on the bottom and sides of the new sutures. Tap them with a mallet to wedge them in all the way.

9

USE SHIMS WHERE NEEDED. Joinery needs to fit perfectly. Here I used a little shim to re-create the perfect fit between the leg and its slot. The shim stays in; cut it flush. Glue is not even required for this fix!

11

CLEAN. Once everything is clamped in place, clean any excess glue with a damp rag and warm water.

12

LET THE PIECE DRY FOR A FEW DAYS. When you're ready to resume work, remove all the clamps.

13

LEVEL THE BUTTERFLIES. Once the glue has dried, chisel out the excess wood so the butterflies lie flush with the underside of the table. Use the chisel upside down so you don't gouge the piece, and tap the mallet lightly, working with the grain.

15

MINIMIZE THE CRACK. To make the tabletop crack less obvious, I filled the line with hard wax in a matching shade. They come in several colors to match your furniture, are reversible, and can be used where damage is light and the holes too shallow for filler to hold. Warm a bit of wax between your fingers, like you would putty, and rub into the crack with your fingernail or a plastic credit card. Scrape out any excess.

10

CLAMP. Using multiple clamps to ensure that the piece is in the right position from every angle, clamp each break. Be creative: Curved elements like legs can be tricky, so try using big rubber bands instead. Some cabinetmakers even use pins, electric tape, springs that have been cut open . . . anything flexible. To keep flat surfaces like the tabletop from buckling, affix the clamps over wood planks for horizontal and vertical reinforcement. Even if your clamps have plastic pads, place cardboard under them so as not to damage the wood.

14

ADD A TOUCH OF FILLER. After the glue dries, you can dab filler around the break (this depends on the look you like and how deep the break is; I did this for this table's broken leg). Conceal the fix via brushed-on stain and a coat of colored wax to help the filler blend with the wood. (See page 274.)

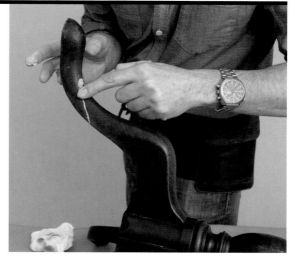

16

REASSEMBLE THE PIECE. Screw the top back onto the base, replacing any screw that's torn, damaged, or mismatched from the others. Be sure to use a flat-head screw for period authenticity.

17

WAX AND BUFF. Apply a light coat of wax to the tabletop, buff lightly to a shine with a soft, clean rag—and you are good to go!

VENEER REPAIR

Late-18th-Century/Early-19th-Century
Side Table with Geometric Veneer Patterning

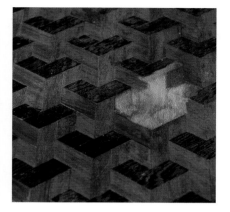

The most common types of veneer distress that I treat in my studio are surfaces that have bubbled or peeled up but are otherwise intact. Also common are chips and dings, most often on corners, drawer edges, tops of tables, and other parts subject to wear and tear and general abuse. But complex patterns like this are a bit trickier, necessitating a patching process.

THE PIECE

This petite 18th-century neoclassical side table is characteristic of the type of repair work that cycles through my studio. Small, lightweight furnishings were common at the time, when servants carried things to their masters: food, drink, stationery, a sewing kit. Pieces could be moved around within the room more easily—which of course subjected them to more abuse. The top is quite decorative, with a geometric marquetry collage of three different woods. People didn't have TV as visual entertainment in the 18th century; they had art . . . and furniture! Hence the elaborate motif: You can literally lose yourself in the intricacies of this pattern.

THE LOOK

I wanted to restore the table to its original appearance, which necessitated a careful patching job and then further disguising the patch via staining to match the exact hue of the existing marquetry veneer.

THE PROCESS

Fixing it is a complex puzzle, but not that tricky. It just requires patience.

category
Repair

degree of difficulty
Medium to very complex depending on the intricacy of the veneer pattern.

prep work
None

> ### VENEER ANTAGONISTS
>
> *The damage here most likely resulted from a significant event, such as water staining, or perhaps a burn (normal wear wouldn't have created such a wound). Most often you'll see water damage from a glass or vase. Too much water and voilà! The marriage is over and the veneer peels up.*

WHAT YOU'LL NEED

- *Veneer sheet(s)*
- *X-Acto knife*
- *Ruler*
- *Razor blades*
- *100 percent cotton rags*
- *Denatured wood alcohol*
- *A few sheets of paper*
- *Water-based paper glue*
- *Veneer saw (optional)*
- *Hide glue*
- *Coarse-hair glue brush*
- *Bone burnisher*
- *Veneer tape and/or a heavy weight*
- *Paint thinner*
- *Very fine-grit (320 or 420) sandpaper*

1

MATCH THE VENEER. Find a veneer piece in the same wood and thickness if possible. I always keep handy a few veneer-sample booklets, sold through woodworking websites or catalogs. In addition to being a great way to identify different species, they are perfect for patching: Pick the piece you need for any repair at a low cost and without the inconvenience of ordering a full sheet (which is generally several square feet).

3

BOX THE WOUND. Reshape the missing veneer wound with an X-Acto knife and a ruler, creating straight edges.

4

REMOVE THE OLD VENEER FRAGMENTS. Clean the wood by scraping it with a razor blade, being careful to leave straight, untouched edges of veneer around the wound.

7

DRAW THE OUTLINE OF THE PARQUETRY. On one photocopy, draw the inside pattern pieces of the parquetry by juxtaposing it along an extant section of the pattern. Carefully number the pieces on the sheet and make a photocopy for reference. Then cut the "puzzle" pieces carefully. Place them in the wound, cutting to adjust as needed. You may have to redo the template to get it just right; hence the photocopies.

2

WORK WITH THE WOOD SURFACE UNREFINISHED. Structural work is usually the first thing to address on a piece of furniture. Addressing the finish *after* the repair is done will allow you to blend the parts more cohesively.

5

CLEAN. If the veneer has been loose or missing for some time, dirt has probably accumulated. Using a clean rag dampened with warm water, wipe away any residual glue or dirt. Then clean with alcohol to remove any lingering grease.

6

MAKE A TEMPLATE. Place a sheet of white paper or tracing paper on top of the wound and mark the exact contour of the missing piece by rubbing a pencil over it. (Do not try to cut the new veneer piece freehand; you will not be precise enough! Make a few photocopies of this rubbing in case you mess up the first go-round.

8

CUT THE VENEER. Once you have a perfect fit, adhere the template to the new veneer sheet(s) with water-based paper glue. Let dry, and then cut the exact shape with an X-Acto knife or a blade. Professionals use a veneer saw, which slices perfectly through the wood fibers and is sturdy enough to not deviate from a straight line, as a light razor blade does. (Avoid this problem by running your blade several times lightly on the veneer until you create a proper guiding groove.)

9

APPLY THE GLUE. Using a glue brush, apply hide glue on the wound. Set your patch on top.

11

WEIGH DOWN THE PATCH. Using a bone burnisher—or any smooth, hard surface—apply constant, even pressure; be careful not to crush the wood fibers. Then place a heavy weight on top or affix a piece of veneer tape, which contracts and stretches with the wood as it dries. Let the piece dry overnight.

13

BLEND THE PATCH. Clean and scrape the entire piece—or sand lightly with a very fine grit sandpaper. Although sanding veneer is not recommended, since the grain runs in a different direction on every piece of wood, here it was possible since I could carefully sand each one individually piece. Stain as needed, using a fine artist's brush, to match the existing veneer.

10

CLEAN EXCESS GLUE. Apply pressure from the center of the piece to the edges to squeeze out any excess glue; clean with a damp rag.

12

FINISH. Rewet the tape and paper template and remove carefully with a damp rag, razor blade, and/ or sandpaper; this will also ensure proper edge blending. Be sure to peel up the tape at a 45-degree angle. Clean with a touch of paint thinner.

14

AFTER REPLACING THE MISSING VENEER, clean, strip, and/or prep the furniture for refinishing. To ensure that the repair will blend perfectly with its surroundings, any further matching will be done via dyes, stains, colors, etc.

General Tips

- Professional woodworkers avoid sanding veneer—especially marquetry designs featuring more than one wood type, or with grains running in different directions. (Sanding should always be uniform and executed in one direction only.) Instead of sanding, prepare veneer for refinishing by scraping it smooth with a razor blade or a wood scraper for veneer, only use thinner versions.) Run the blade at a 45-degree angle, with the edge perfectly flat against the wood, maintaining good pressure control in order not to scratch.

- When patching an antique with new veneer, you sometimes have to build up the substrate, since old veneers were hand-cut and generally thicker. (Today, the wood log is peeled like a pencil in a pencil sharpener with a mechanical blade, creating a superthin sheet.) Use two or more layers of veneer, ensuring the grains run perpendicular to each other.

PART 5

TOOL SCHOOL

Following is a glossary of ingredients, products, tools, and materials that are handy to have in your studio—whether said studio is a 500-square-foot atelier or just a rolling cart stashed in a closet. (Either way, I'll show you how to set it up.) Some items have many uses, while others are more specific to a particular technique. Almost all can be purchased from fine purveyors like Woodworker's Supply, Garrett Wade, and Highland Woodworking, but many can be found at your neighborhood hardware store, too. I've also included easy recipes for some of the natural products I use most frequently in my own studio, including paste wax and wood filler.

SETTING UP YOUR ATELIER

If you are new to furniture finishing, you might assume that an airy, loftlike space and abundant products will be required to execute your handiwork. Not so! Indeed, in the beginning of my career, I didn't even *have* a studio to speak of, just a bag of supplies that accompanied me as I traveled from client to client. In most cases I restored precious antiques on-site with just a drop cloth below, sometimes in a kitchen—but often right where the piece lived (i.e., in a living or dining room).

So fear not: renting a commercial studio is not a prerequisite, nor is having a dedicated room. On the following pages, I walk you through three common residential scenarios and itemize the essentials you need, whether you can devote a corner of your garage to your practice or have only one drawer to spare. In each case, the core elements are the same. You'll want brushes, rags, steel wool, sandpaper, scissors, and a few common tools, plus the building blocks of all period finishes: oil, wax, and shellac. I now operate from a 6,000-square-foot studio, but my setup is remarkably similar to what it was when I started out, just vastly scaled up.

Scaling up is simply a matter of expanding the variety and quantity of each genre. Wholesale reinvention of your studio is not required—everything from your drawer still has its place when you graduate to larger digs. Be open to expansion: You may start with a small rolling cart and, as you get addicted, find yourself converting a guest room into a full-blown workshop. Now instead of having one color you have three; instead of two brushes you have ten. As your tool kit broadens, so does your roster of techniques—and thus the finishes that you can achieve.

No need to be a neat freak; better to have things set up so that what you use most frequently is easiest to reach. Do consider proper ventilation. An open window and a fan or proximity to a door is generally enough for most products and techniques demonstrated in this book. Follow your state's rules for storage and disposal of chemicals. And avoid storing chemicals indoors unless in a metal storage cabinet designed for this.

if you have a drawer

Keep things simple with high-quality tools and products in small quantities.

1 **ASSORTED CLOTHS:** cheesecloth, tack cloth, cotton, and a fine-dusting cloth (reserved exclusively for this use)

2 **RUBBER MIXING BOWL:** easy to clean

3 **SPECIAL SOAP** to clean tools and fine brushes

4 **PLASTIC TARP AND ZIPLOC BAGS**

5 **NITRILE GLOVES**

6 **GREAT-QUALITY SCISSORS**

7 **CLEAR WAX:** you can color it as needed

8 **STEEL WOOL:** only the finest grades

9 **BUFFING BRUSH**

10 **GLUE BRUSH**

11 **TOUCH-UP CRAYONS AND FELT PENS**

12 **WOOD GLUE**

13 **LIGHT-COLORED FILLER**

14 **COLOR WHEEL**

15 **WHITE AND GREEN PACKING TAPE**

16 **STORAGE CONTAINER**

17 **A FEW OTHER NICE-QUALITY TOOLS**

18 **SMALL CLAMPS:** always buy in pairs

19 **SMALL JAPANESE SAW**

20 **4-IN-1 SCREWDRIVER**

21 **SMALL HAMMER**

22 **GUIDING SCREW TOOL**

23 **TAPE MEASURE** graduated in both imperial and metric systems

24 **STEEL RULER:** choose a nice, heavy graduated one

25 **A FEW HIGH-QUALITY BRUSHES**

26 **ONLY A FEW COLORS:** sienna, ochre, umber, black, white

27 **SOLVENTS AND LIQUIDS** stored in small bottles

if you have a shelf

Supplies from the drawer will have a place on the shelf as you expand; you only need to add, not replace or upgrade, tools. Consider an adjustable metal shelf unit, which will last longer.

1   **A SECOND SET OF CLAMPS,** longer and stronger

2   **SET OF METAL SPATULAS, STICKS, AND VARIOUS PICKS** to clean, apply, carve, etc.

3   **A SECOND JAPANESE SAW:** longer and more flexible (for making longer cuts and flush cuts)

4   **A NICE SET OF CHISELS** (they'll last you a lifetime)

5   **A GOOD RUBBER OR WOOD MALLET**

6   **MULTIPLE BRUSH SHAPES AND TYPES**—use the right one for each task and label them

7   **MORE CANS FOR STORING SOLIDS AND LIQUIDS**—the more you mix, the more leftovers you'll have

8   **A NICE BLOCK PLANE,** which doesn't take up much room and suits many tasks

9   **A STOCKPILE OF SPECIFIC FINISHING PRODUCTS** (here: shellac, mixed and ready to use)

10 **SANDING SPONGES:** good for wrapping sandpaper around and for cleaning, too

11 **OIL STAIN** (here, mixed with tung oil, ready to use)

12 **AN EXPANDED COLOR SELECTION:** oil, acrylic, dry pigments, etc.

13 **AN EXPANDED SELECTION OF WOOD FILLER, WAXES, ETC.** in different colors and hues

14 **A FEW CLEANING PRODUCTS** devoted to studio use, always at the ready

15 **A NICE NATURAL-BRISTLE BRUSH WITH A LONG HANDLE** (and soft bristles)

if you have a wall

Graduating to a wall unit allows you to store and stockpile more products. Consider coupling it with a worktable.

1   **A LARGER ARRAY OF CANS AND STORAGE ITEMS** (disposable cans, jars, containers, etc.)

2   **SANDPAPER BY THE SLEEVE**—you'll always have the right grit handy

3   **WHITE PAPER PLATES** for mixing colors

4   **FEATHER DUSTER**

5   **ROLL OF MEDIUM-WEIGHT CRAFT PAPER** for protection and wrapping

6   **STACKABLE OPEN BINS** for neatly storing and moving around products

7   **MORE SAWS AND MORE TOOLS** for the tasks you perform most often

8   **SMALL EXTINGUISHER:** Safety first!

9   **FIRST-AID KIT**

10   **PAPER RAGS** to wipe off and clean tools

11   **BLEACHING SET**

12   **CLOSED AND COMPARTMENTED STORAGE,** labeled in front, for smaller items and pieces

13   **ALL THE TOOLS YOU DID NOT HAVE ROOM FOR BEFORE:** funnels, brush holders, etc.

14   **DOCUMENTATION:** catalogs, folders, notebooks, magazines, etc.

15   **STACK OF SMALL WOOD PIECES,** in various species, for making samples

16   **BIG BOX OF COTTON RAGS**

17   **STEPLADDER**

18   **CLAMPS:** even bigger (buy two)

19   **YOUR THREE MAIN FINISHING MEDIUMS**—oil, alcohol, and water—on their own shelf

20   **AN EXPANDED SELECTION OF STEEL WOOL**

21   **MOVING BLANKETS AND PACKING MATERIAL**

22   **OFFICE RACK:** for drying samples or stacking finished ones

ASSORTED PRODUCTS

AMMONIA: Ideal for cleaning wood and brass, ammonia can also be used to darken highly tannic woods like oak. Ammonia does emit toxic fumes, so always use it in a properly ventilated area.

BABY OIL: A type of mineral oil used as a lubricant for French polishing: A tiny drop on the outside of your pad keeps it gliding smoothly across the wood surface.

Chalk powder

CHALK POWDER: Also called *blanc d'Espagne* and *blanc de Meudon*. Use chalk as a binder or an abrasive or to make filler paste or hide-glue paint, or mix it with wax to create ceruse.

COPAL VARNISH: A staple of historical oil varnish recipes—particularly those used on fine violins (think Stradivarius). Copal is fossilized sap that is ground and then dissolved in either gum turpentine or drying oil. Add a teaspoon to a pint of tung oil for a shinier effect or use as part of a homemade finish.

DANISH OIL: A blend of tung oil, varnish, and colored pigment that was the favorite finish of midcentury-modern designers. It's sold over the counter, but you can also make your own. (The recipe: 90 percent tung oil, 10 percent oil varnish, plus oil pigment at your discretion.) See more information on page 93.

DENATURED ALCOHOL: The term *denatured* means that additives have rendered this alcohol unfit for consumption. The solvent is a great cleaner: It's not aggressive, it doesn't leave residue, and yet it removes grease. For most woodworking purposes, the denatured alcohol sold in hardware stores is of adequate quality, but some suppliers sell extra-dry refined alcohol, which can be used to eliminate any remnant of oil and impurities from the wood surface—thus giving your French polish a totally crisp finish.

FILLER AND PUTTY: These products share the same ingredients (pigment, drier, and pumice, plus either oil or water) but have different consistencies. Filling wood pores requires a thick, syrup-like consistency, whereas a more dough-like product is needed to fill big holes or missing parts. Buy over-the-counter products, or make your own; see pages 247 and 249 for recipes.

GUM AND SPIRIT VARNISHES: This category includes traditional varnishes made from plant-derived saps and gums, damar, sandarac, rosin, and copal among them. The materials are distilled, infused, ground, dissolved, reduced, and extended according to various proprietary recipes.

HYDROCHLORIC ACID: A chemical stain that can be used to fade wood, making it look older. Also called muriatic acid, it's very corrosive.

HYDROGEN PEROXIDE: A bleaching solution used to lighten wood, hydrogen peroxide offers better control than household bleach. It's usually sold as a two-part solution that gets activated by mixing. See page 149 for a how-to.

LINSEED OIL: Often called *boiled linseed oil* (raw linseed oil is seldom found in stores other than art-supply resources), this self-polymerizing product is made of heated and treated flaxseed oil. It has been used for millennia as a finish and as a medium for paint and varnish.

MORDANT

This blanket term describes any liquid that binds or fixes dye or color to the wood via a chemical reaction: Alcohol, vinegar, lime, and oxalic acid are prime examples. The word derives from the French mordre, "to bite"—and so it does! Before the advent of modern chemical stains, most mordants were derived from tree roots and insect by-products.

MURIATIC ACID: See hydrochloric acid, above.

NAPHTHA: Use this slow-drying solvent to extend the open time of oil-based fillers.

OXALIC ACID: A traditional bleaching product used to lighten wood. It is sold as a powder to be mixed with water.

PAINT THINNER: Avoid using this petroleum distillate directly on furniture or as a mixing solvent—it's not refined enough! Save it for cleaning your tools.

POLYMERIZATION

You will discover this term on the labels of drying oils and varnishes. Self-polymerization means that the product has its own drying or binding agent: The chemical structure of the product changes when exposed to air, causing the molecules to grow and bind to coat the wood.

PUMICE: Made from pulverized volcanic stone, pumice powder comes in different degrees of coarseness. Use the finest grade, 4F, for French polish and as a grain filler/polishing compound. Pumice can be mixed with oil or wax, creating an abrasive slurry that "finishes" your finish—without scratching the surface. Or use it to tame a too-glossy finish.

PURE GUM TURPENTINE: Distilled from the sap of live, resinous trees like pine, this traditional solvent is omnipresent in fine finishes and woodworking. Pure gum turpentine nourishes wood and is used to mollify wax, helping it penetrate the fibers. It can be mixed with oil-based products. Buy and use only the highest quality: If it does not smell like pine, it's not pure. (This high-quality product is also found under the name oil of turpentine.) Do not substitute regular turpentine, which is petroleum-based and chemically processed, or oil of turpentine, which is more concentrated.

Rottenstone

ROTTENSTONE: Made from ground, decaying limestone, this powder—also called *Tripoli powder*—is used as a very fine abrasive and to polish. (It's even finer than pumice.) Use it dry or mix with oil or wax. Rottenstone is great for faux-aging a newly gilt piece—it's like fake dust!

Hard shellac sticks

SHELLAC: A resinous product, originally from Asia, derived from the excretion of the bark-eating lac bug. Mix the flakes with alcohol to create a versatile solution ideal for everything from sealing wood to building up a French polish. Shellac also comes in a hard stick form that's ideal for small repairs. Read more about its use and applications on pages 85–89.

TUNG OIL: A self-polymerizing oil derived from the nut of the Asian tung tree. (Legend has it that Marco Polo brought it back to Europe.) Originally used to waterproof wood—even ships!—it dries faster than linseed oil and does not yellow with age. Tung oil penetrates deep into the wood fibers and also builds up nicely to form a coating. See more on page 93.

Veneer sheets

VENEER SHEETS: You can buy individual sheets as needed for repairs and patches or, better yet, purchase a sample booklet or kit that includes swatches of many wood species.

Clear paste wax

WAX: A popular and versatile product used as a polish or paste to finish wood and create decorative effects. See pages 79–83 for a full overview on the medium and its applications, and page 240 on making your own furniture wax.

WHITE VINEGAR: An easily accessible, fume-free cleaner that's great for disinfecting drawers and armoires and neutralizing wood-bleaching acids like hydrogen peroxide and hydrochloric acid, as well as many other chemicals and corroding processes. When making water-based stains, add 10 percent white vinegar to the water before stirring in the pigments; the added bite helps fix the color in the wood.

ASSORTED TOOLS

Clamps

CLAMPS: Get an array of sizes—you will be surprised at how helpful they can be around the house. Buy ones with plastic pads so you don't damage the wood surface and, for added protection, tape a piece of cardboard on top before clamping. Be firm but gentle when clamping parts together for gluing. Do not squeeze like a maniac—or you will squeeze out all the glue! Be confident in the power of your adhesive. (And if the glue doesn't hold on its own, no problem: Hide glue is reversible. Clean the wound, insert a wood peg or a structural rod, and try again.)

Hand plane

PLANES: There are dozens of sizes and varieties, one for every use. While I do not expect you to start fussing with myriad planes, I do recommend buying a nice block plane. Choose a small- to medium-sized version, light enough to be used with one hand. A good hand plane will last a lifetime. Purchase from a reputable source, and expect to spend between $100 and $300. Call a supplier or specialist, explain your needs, and ask which one is best for you; they will provide the safest, most versatile and useful tool. A plane is very handy for fixing sticky doors and drawers, smoothing rough surfaces, getting rid of splinters, trimming joints and edges . . . you might become addicted! You can also do the opposite, deliberately denting and scarring the wood to create aged effects. When planning, be aware of hidden nails.

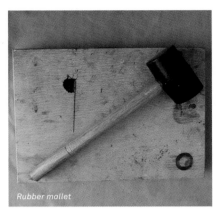

Rubber mallet

RUBBER MALLET: An absolute necessity. A hammer is only for hammering nails! Use a rubber (or wood) mallet for everything else: dismantling, unlocking tight joints, moving elements, etc. For enhanced protection, place fabric on top of the wood before tapping. Always be gentle; if what you're tapping doesn't come loose, it was not meant to. Try another approach.

Wood stirrers

STIRRERS: For most purposes, wood or plastic stirrers are preferred. Metal should be avoided, as it reacts with various products. Among my favorite implements: traditional paint stirrers, coffee stirrers, tongue depressors, plastic spoons and forks (the latter are particularly good for breaking up lumps when mixing), and chopsticks.

TAPE: Just because it's sticky doesn't mean you can use it everywhere. Tape damage is very common. Nonetheless, it's an indispensable tool for refinishing; use tape to protect hardware, for instance. The safest variety is green tape or other similar low-tack products sold in art-supply stores; consider splurging for museum-quality wrapping and handling products. After applying it, run your nail along the edge to ensure proper adhesion and keep product from seeping in below. To remove tape, pull very slowly at a 45-degree angle (both vertically and horizontally). Some tape tips and no-nos:

- Packing tape is for packing only; it should *never* touch the piece itself.

- White tape is for rough use only: on unfinished parts, on the underside of furniture, for labeling. Never affix this type of tape to finished wood or leather (although it's okay on stone and metal).

- Blue tape is generally safe for most applications, but test it on an unobtrusive spot first. Good for unfinished surfaces. Always remove this tape at the end of the task (or the day) and reapply it before the next step (if necessary). Never leave painter's tape affixed to the wood overnight, even if it's labeled safe to leave in place for 4 or even 7 days.

- Gummed paper tape and gum tape should be used only for gluing and holding things in place, such as repair work where clamps wouldn't be feasible. It has a strong hold yet can be removed gently with a warm, wet cloth.

- Veneer tape is a specialty gummed tape, used to hold veneer patches in place while they dry. Remove delicately after patting it with a warm, wet cloth.

Wood chisels

WOOD CHISELS: If an artisan had to flee a fire with only one set of tools, it would be his chisels. Partly because a good set is (justifiably) expensive, partly because they are very time-consuming to maintain in top-notch form. Innumerable shapes and forms exist for carving, sculpting, planing, shaping, and thinning wood without damaging it. Marks of a good one: It feels nice in the hand and has a sharp blade.

Veneer saw

VENEER SAW: Mastering this saw requires practice; it cuts veneer slowly and evenly without spinning out of control on straight lines the way that a razor blade or an X-Acto knife can do if you go too fast.

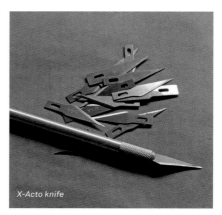
X-Acto knife

X-ACTO KNIFE: So versatile, and a true precision tool. Use it to cut veneer, to remove errant particles from a finish, or to scrape off old glue residue from joinery. Change blades frequently, but save the old ones for rougher use.

CLOTHS AND RAGS

Linen

BURLAP, JUTE, AND LINEN RAGS: These rough, coarse-weave fabrics are great for removing caked dirt and excess filler. (Burlap and jute are often used for packing potatoes and other food goods—save them for your woodworking projects!) Scraps of artist's canvas serve the same purpose. They are also good for aging—without scratching—gold leaf.

Tack cloth

CHEESECLOTH: Use open and closed (i.e., loose and tight weave) cheesecloth as filler for French polish pads and to accomplish many other jobs around the studio.

COTTON RAGS: I use cotton rags for most applications—about a shopping bag full for every piece. Cut them from used 100 percent cotton T-shirts or white socks—these should never go into the garbage. Wash them several times so they are devoid of lint. Fold them flat, versus crumpling them into a ball, so you disperse product evenly.

French polish pads

FRENCH POLISH PADS: To execute French polish, you need a special pad, made of linen or cotton wrapped around an absorbent filler, usually cheesecloth. Learn how to make them (and use them) on page 250.

Fine dusting cloth

TACK CLOTH: A lint-free cheesecloth pad, coated with a slightly tacky material derived from a resinous compound. Use it to remove dust and sanding debris, for a final cleaning, or to perfect your wood surface between finish coats. Fine dusting cloths are nice for cleaning, too.

Wool rag

WOOL AND FELT RAGS: Both materials are great for buffing wax. Nice tweed fabrics in particular are the best for a sharp shine! Or wool from old sweaters only—no virgin wool. Be sure to wash felt before using it. Discard rags when they get too caked with dry wax.

CONTAINERS

Once you start properly caring for your furniture and embracing woodworking, you will accumulate a lot of wood parts, open product jars, custom mixes, old screws and nails, small tools, and the like. Stains and finishes should be stored away from light, in opaque containers, but clear containers can be used to organize practically everything else. Label each container neatly with the contents, the date, and the job it pertains to—never assume you will remember (trust me)! You would be surprised at the amount of documentation and archiving I do in my studio: Clients often call after many years to ask if I still can match a finish or lost hardware; I'm always proud to say yes!

You'll also use containers for mixing stains, fillers, and many other products. There's no need to purchase specialty products; repurposed household containers are ideal for the studio. Although it is helpful to have on hand a few containers with gradients for measuring product amounts. Here are some great items to have on hand.

Glass jars

GLASS CONTAINERS OF ALL SIZES: I prefer working with glass containers for most uses. It's a matter of feel: they are harder, heavier, and sturdier and hold their shape better than plastic. (But they are also more easily breakable.) Give old jam jars and drinking glasses a new lease on life in your studio.

Graduated plastic containers

PLASTIC CONTAINERS: I save all pint- and quart-sized deli and takeout containers. They resist chemicals, especially lacquer thinner, and can be discarded after use.

PLASTIC SQUEEZE CONTAINERS: I love them. I have them in every size from a few ounces to 34 ounces. Small bottles are easier to use and can be discarded if they get clogged, whereas larger sizes are preferred for storing product.

RESEALABLE PLASTIC BAGS: Ideal for storing hardware and small parts.

TIN CANS, TIN CONTAINERS, AND TIN JAR LIDS: I'm especially fond of recycled tuna cans, which are small and chemically resistant and have a wide, shallow shape that's ideal for mixing small amounts of product. They are also easy to carry around and don't spill.

GLUE

Hide glue: granules and mixed

RABBIT-HIDE GLUE: Also called *skin glue*, *animal glue*, or *hide glue*. Traditional adhesives used to construct furniture are made from animal by-products such as rabbit hide and fish bones. These natural ingredients are elastic, allowing the glue to move with the wood as it expands and contracts. The glues are also reversible—they can be dissolved with denatured alcohol—making them ideal for historical restorations. The adhesive bond can even be reactivated—just wet and warm the dried glue with a hair dryer.

Rabbit-hide glue is sold as granules that you mix with water (about ¼ cup granules per ⅔ cup water). Soak the hard granules for 10 minutes to soften them into a gel, watch them swell, and then melt in a double boiler to achieve a smooth, syrupy consistency. Store in a tightly closed glass jar. Rewarm if needed, adding water if the glue gets too thick. Keep up to one week, and then discard in the garbage (not the sink).

White glue, wood glue, and commercial hide glue

WOOD GLUE OR WHITE GLUE: Let's not be more royalist than the king, as we say in France: Wood glue and white glue are acceptable . . . except on top-end antiques. (Interestingly, even Elmer's used to be made with hide glue!) These glues can be dissolved with white vinegar (i.e., acetic acid).

GOLD LEAF INGREDIENTS AND TOOLS

Most techniques in this book require common tools and materials that you may already have on hand, even if you're not (yet) a refinishing enthusiast: linseed oil, sandpaper, plastic scrapers, old cotton T-shirts, etc. But gold leafing is a specialized technique, involving a number of tools and ingredients specific to the gilder.

Agate burnishers

AGATE BURNISHER: Used to polish the gold leaf to a high shine once dry, agate-topped burnishing tools come in myriad shapes to fit various details and crevices. (You can also use these to polish waxed details.) Professional gilders keep many types in their studio, but you can get away with just a few: one pointy, one flat, and one curved.

Carving tools

CARVING TOOLS: Available in different profiles, these are used to sculpt gesso and to re-create existing moldings and carvings.

CHAMOIS CUSHION: Prior to applying gold leaf, gilders place it on a cushion, sometimes one that's sheltered on three sides to protect it from drafts. The cushion is made of suede, which is rough enough to catch the leaf yet smooth enough to release it easily. I advise placing one leaf at a time on your cushion, but professional gilders often empty an entire booklet at once.

CLAY BOLE: Used for water gilding, this second prep coat is applied on top of gesso to create a supersmooth undercoat for gold leaf, enabling subsequent burnishing. Bole is made of Armenian clay, binder, rabbit-hide glue, and water, mixed with a pigment: classic red, yellow, blue, black, or green. I also use it as a colored base coat for custom lacquer jobs. Read more about bole on page 99.

GESSO: A special plaster that's applied to wood as a preparation coat for gilding and decorative painting, gesso creates a hard, flawless, flat base. (The material was also used as is—i.e., left exposed—on 18th-century English carved furniture.) Professional gilders still make their own gesso—a mix of chalk, water, and rabbit-hide glue—adjusting the recipe to the particular piece they're working on. But ready-made ones available at gilding- or art-supply stores are just fine for most applications. Read more about gesso on page 99.

Gilder's knife

GILDER'S KNIFE: Use the flat side of this spatula-like tool—akin to a butter knife—to remove the gold leaf from the booklet and place it on the cushion. The knife edge can be used to slice the leaf into smaller squares.

90-PROOF ALCOHOL: Always use fine 90-proof alcohol when gilding, not the rubbing alcohol you find in pharmacies or denatured alcohol from hardware stores. (You can also use 40-proof vodka in a pinch—just double the dose when mixing with water.)

SIZING: The glue used to adhere gold leaf when oil gilding. Initially, linseed oil was used—hence the term *oil gilding*—but today, most are made of faster-drying acrylic. (For large jobs like ceilings, you can find sizing that stays open for more than 24 hours.) Since the sizing coat remains between the gold leaf and the underlying bole, you can't burnish the gilding afterward, as you can do with water gilding, but you can do wonderful wax and patina finishes on top. Read more on page 97.

Squirrel-hair brush and chamois cushion

SQUIRREL- OR BADGER-HAIR BRUSH: Never touch gold leaf with your fingers. Instead, pick it up with a gilding comb, a wide, flat paper-handle brush made of squirrel or badger hair. The trick: Pass it across your forehead first to get the bristles just oily enough to grasp the leaf. (You can also pass it lightly over a bit of Vaseline dabbed on the back of your hand.) Other regular fine artists' brushes can help press on and smooth down the gold leaf.

PIGMENTS

The basic colors to keep handy for furniture use: black, white, sienna, burnt sienna, umber, and burnt umber. Buy them in any form you choose, but in the same medium (oil, water, or acrylic) so you can mix and match to create custom hues.

Powdered pigments

ARTIST COLORS: Available in oil and acrylic versions. Mix the former with linseed oil to create a stain with a long drying or "open" time. (Just add a few drops of japan drier—never more than 10 percent—to ensure it dries in a timely fashion, i.e., overnight.) Perfect for color matching and work requiring touch-ups and nuancing. The acrylic versions are water-based, so they set and dry fast— ideal for spot touch-ups followed by wax or any oil coating.

JAPAN COLORS: These colors can be used as is or diluted in linseed oil or pure gum turpentine, depending on the use you have in mind. Great for glazing, staining, and other applications. They are composed of pigments, linseed oil, and a drying agent (specifically japan drier, hence the name). Mixed, they keep forever in their tin cans; add a few drops of gum turpentine on top after each use.

JAPAN DRIER: Used for oil finishes and paints, this drying agent (aka siccative) is so named because it was used to cure glossy varnishes and paints that imitated japanning, or Oriental lacquerwork.

UNIVERSAL TINTING: These concentrated pigments come in many versions. Be sure to use the one compatible with your medium; some mix only with acrylics. The pigments are of passable quality so should be reserved for big pieces requiring large quantities of color and a stable reference (wide cerused surfaces, glazing).

PROTECTIVE GEAR

Protective gear

AIR MASK (RESPIRATOR): Don one whenever you're working with a product that emits fumes. Safety first!

APRON: Tie one on to protect your clothes (but note that you'll stain them anyway).

DUST MASK: Use when sanding and rubbing with steel wool—especially when working with wood that's been bleached. Dust masks (and goggles and gloves) are an annoyance to work with, but once you get accustomed to them you will never be able to do without.

GLOVES: Keep several pairs of disposable latex and heavier-duty nitrile gloves on hand. It's imperative to wear chemical-resistant gloves when stripping.

GOGGLES: I use them *always*. Store them next to a bottle of contact-lens saline solution: If you accidentally splash toxic solution or particles get in your eye, squeeze the bottle to flush your eye.

ORANGE SOAP AND HAND CREAM: Wash your hands with a natural soap. Scrub if necessary with a product that contains pumice, like orange soap. If some stains remain on your hands or skin, dampen a rag with alcohol and rub your skin for a few seconds; chemicals will get under your skin! Then wash again with water and soap. Hand cream or moisturizer is a necessity after this treatment.

SCRAPERS

METAL SCRAPERS: For professionals only: They require meticulous sharpening and have to be handled appropriately to avoid damaging the wood. Sold in sets of different thicknesses.

METAL SPATULAS: Almost as deadly as power tools! Use with caution, if at all: The sharp edges can damage just-loosened wood fibers. Best for professionals.

OLD CREDIT CARDS: My favorite? Expired Starbucks cards. Use as you would a plastic scraper. They're lightweight and versatile, with rounded edges that won't scratch the wood surface. Perfect for furnishings with lots of carvings and details: Cut the card to match the profile you are scraping.

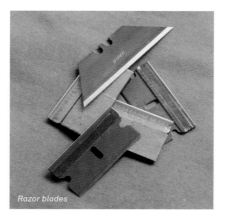

Razor blades

RAZOR BLADES: A perfect tool to smooth veneer, which cannot be sanded with sandpaper. Also use razor blades to slice off little specks or to scrape a pesky stain off raw wood. Just be careful with the sharp edges.

SCRUBBERS AND BRUSHES

Glue brushes

COARSE-HAIR GLUE BRUSHES: Their thick plastic fibers deposit just the right dose of glue onto furniture. The brushes are disposable, so do not reuse them.

NATURAL-BRISTLE BRUSHES: From paintbrushes to the finest artists' brushes, these natural-bristle tools are superior for applying alcohol- and oil-based products. Clean carefully after use with a petroleum distillate or, better yet, citrus oil, followed by a soak in warm water and dish soap. Rinse well, reshape with your fingers, and then dry them head down.

PLASTIC SCRUB BRUSHES: An array of used toothbrushes and dish scrubbers comes in handy for dewaxing. But be careful: Even plastic fibers can scratch wood.

SANDPAPER AND SANDING SPONGES: Read more about their use and applications—including how to fold sandpaper and choose the appropriate grit—on page 116.

Plastic scrapers

PLASTIC SCRAPERS: Cheap, safe, disposable, and versatile, too—they have so many uses. Keep a few varieties at the ready, some flexible and some stiff.

BRUSHES

Splurging on high-quality brushes—a practical indulgence—will save you time and add significant artistry to your work. Peruse discount racks at art stores and ask if they have periodic sales or end-of-stock items. Never buy cheap sets from supermarkets or convenience stores—they'll shed more than your cat!

- Coarser brushes are usually pig or boar silk; finest grades are badger or squirrel hair. To assess the quality of a brush before buying it, run the dry bristles along a flat surface. The hair should not separate too much and should spring back to the initial shape when lifted.

- Before using brushes for the first time, soak for 24 hours in linseed oil (for natural-hair bristles) or in water (for synthetic) to coat and condition the hair. Then wash carefully in natural soap and warm water, and reshape.

- Before each use, dip your brush in turpentine (if using oil), alcohol (if using shellac), or water (if using acrylic) and pat dry.

- After use, clean with the proper solvent and then wash with warm water and soap. Reshape them and then dry head-down.

Following these steps will assure longevity; your brushes will grow accustomed to your hand and how you use them. Once they've become too worn for their intended purpose, give them a second life by using them for rougher jobs like cleaning.

Synthetic-bristle brushes

SYNTHETIC-BRISTLE BRUSHES: Big ones are ideal for applying stripper, bleach, and other corrosive chemicals. Use artist's brushes with synthetic bristles for water-based stains and products, as they don't gorge themselves on water and thus cake.

Wallpaper brush

WALLPAPER BRUSHES: I use a long, skinny, high-quality natural-bristle wallpaper brush for the first buffing after applying a coat of wax. (Cut the hair if it's too long: 1 to 2 inches is ideal.) It removes all the loose wax, shimmies easily into corners and molding details, and hardens the surface. Enhance the shine by hand-rubbing with a wool or felt rag afterward.

"WHATEVER" BRUSHES: Old, used, half-caked brushes, hair eaten almost down to the handle . . . these serve as rescue and cleaning tools, as removal devices, to create decorative effects, etc. Give them one last task before throwing them in the trash, and then toss with gratitude.

Wire brushes

WIRE BRUSHES: These have no use in fine refinishing except to open the wood grain when cerusing or to create special effects like weathering. Some artisans prefer copper wire, which will not leave behind any rust particles on the wood.

SOAP

BAR SOAP: Great for lubricating stuck drawer slides. Any kind will do, but ideally pick a natural variety.

CASTILE SOAP AND MARSEILLE SOAP: Before using any chemical-based product to clean or remove stains, try Castile or Marseille soap. Made with olive oil, sea-salt water, soda ash, and lye, these all-natural soaps are as eco-friendly as can be. They are safe for cleaning furniture—and everything else in your house, too. My grandmother, who was from Marseille, used Marseille soap for bathing and shampooing, washing dishes, and cleaning her floors and furniture—and my grandfather always stole it to wash his beloved Peugeot!

STEEL WOOL

Use steel wool to clean dirt off the wood surface, to aid stripping, as a tool to create a special decorative effect such as ceruse, to abrade surfaces to faux age, to re-create wood grain when dragged in a glaze, and much more. But proceed with caution, as it scratches the wood. Steel wool removes wood fiber from the grooves to emphasize the up-and-down texture of the grain and burnishes the wood, making it inappropriate to use before staining. It's also *not* for smoothing or prepping wood: Too many people think sandpaper and steel wool have the same use—they don't!

Steel wool comes in various degrees of coarseness. Use grades 1 (medium) to 4 (extra coarse) only for rough stripping, on rustic pieces, or to create special effects. Use grades 0 (medium fine) to 0000 (superfine) to remove impurities between coats, to scuff-sand, or for spot treatments. And always clean furniture with an alcohol-dampened rag or tack cloth after rubbing it down with steel wool; any steel fibers remaining on the wood will corrode, and overlooked particles will damage your finish.

Steel Wool Grades

GRADE	DESCRIPTION	USE
0000	Finest grade	For buffing and cleaning, and for light scuff-sanding between coats. Use with wax or oil for a final, scratch-free sanding. Dip in paint thinner to clean light rust from steel, including old hardware and locks.
000	Very fine grade	You can still buff and polish, but only oiled and wax finishes; do not use with fine polishes and glossy surfaces. Use around a toothpick as a sort of Q-tip to remove stains and spots on wood or leather, but do so carefully.
00	Fine grade	For "cutting" between coats—i.e., smoothing between coats that need more than just a light scuff-sanding. This will give a nice grip for the next coat. Use with alcohol to remove shellac finishes, and with turpentine to remove wax finishes—as always, carefully.
0	Medium-fine grade	Do not use on finished wood. Use to clean loose rust (dip in kerosene or oil first), but only on rustic pieces. Can be used to intentionally create worn, faux-aged finishes.
1	Medium grade	For antiquing, creating patinas, and special aging effects. Use with paint or varnish removers to strip, but with a light hand.
2	Medium coarse	From this grade on, there is no reason to use on fine furniture except to create worn surfaces and finishes.
3	Coarse	Dip in oil glaze and drag onto a wood surface to re-create a dirty, speckled appearance.
4	Very coarse	Can be used instead of, or to help, wire-brushing to open the grain for cerusing. Also creates a worn, burnished look on hardwood species.

RECIPES

I want to make it easy, fun, and nonthreatening for you to take care of your furniture, which involves some traditional, time-tested recipes used for various techniques—from cleaning and prepping to finishing and maintenance.

Old Varnish Recipe

- Grind DAMAR crystals
  into a fine powder

- Mix with pure Gum Turpentine
  or oil of Turpentine

- adjust Thickness to your purpose

MAKING YOUR OWN

wax

Beeswax—my favored medium—is a solid material that has to be mollified with a solvent, gum turpentine, for use. Carnauba, a hard, brittle wax, is added to give strength and shine intensity to the mix. This combination makes the ideal polish: The beeswax moisturizes and nurtures the wood, giving it a mellow composition, while the carnauba creates a hard shine, and offers added protection.

White virgin wax beads

Carnauba wax flakes

Pure, natural beeswax block

Pure yellow beeswax beads

Types of Wax

BEESWAX: It's sold as 1- to 10-pound loaves, which you have to shred before melting, or beads, which are easier to measure and quicker to liquefy. There are two hues of beeswax at your disposal: *Yellow* is pure, unadulterated beeswax, straight from the dried honeycomb; *white virgin* is a bleached beeswax that creates an absolutely clear finish, without a tinge of yellow film—perfect for very light woods, metals, stone, or white marble.

CARNAUBA WAX: This is derived from a tropical plant native to Brazil. Commonly used for polishing cars, carnauba creates a shiny, tough finish. The drawback is that it's brittle and difficult to work with. It also takes a bit longer to melt. For our purposes, it's used only to give the beeswax more body.

Solvent

PURE GUM TURPENTINE: My solvent of choice is pure gum turpentine, derived from pinesap. It's a bit gummier than regular turpentine, giving it a tacky aspect that hardens to become part of the wood. The sap also makes gum turpentine very elastic, like rubber, so it really feeds and moves with the wood as it expands and contracts, and also nourishes it at the same time.

Honeybee

WHAT YOU'LL NEED

- ¼ pound carnauba*
- 1 pound beeswax
- 1 quart gum turpentine

* If you are mixing a smaller amount, use 2 tablespoons of carnauba for every 4 ounces of beeswax— no more or it will get too hard!

1   **MELT THE CARNAUBA.** Using a burner or hot plate, melt the carnauba in a double boiler (I use a professional plug-in model, as shown here) over low heat, as if you were simmering soup. The carnauba is melted first because it takes longer. It also helps regulate the temperature for the beeswax.

2   **ADD THE BEESWAX.** When the carnauba is fully melted, add the beeswax and heat until it softens—but no longer. Avoid cooking or burning the wax; keep the heat low, never more than 180 degrees.

3   **STIR IN THE TURPENTINE.** Once the waxes are melted, remove them from the heat and stir in the gum turpentine. If you are using any enhancements (see opposite), add them during this step.

4   **TRANSFER TO A CONTAINER.** Use a shallow tin or glass container with a wide mouth, so the paste wax will be easier to remove with a soft cloth; a tin jar lid is perfect. Do not use a plastic container, which may react with the gum turpentine and soften with the heat. Let the wax cool and solidify at room temperature (not in the fridge).

5   **VOILÀ.** You should have a rich, honey-colored paste.

6   **STORAGE.** Wax has a shelf life of many years if stored properly; screw the lid on tightly. Tin containers are best, since they block out any light and help prevent dryness. Add a few drops of turpentine before sealing the container if you won't be using the wax for some time.

TO COLOR THE WAX

Use oil-soluble pigments or universal tints (the ones mixable with oil, not acrylic). To make a colored mother batch, add the pigment after pouring in the turpentine; mix it with a little medium first. When calibrating your hue, bear in mind that it will lighten a bit as it cools. Be generous with your pigment to achieve a dark color.

Variations

Consistency

The more solvent used, the softer the wax becomes—and the lesser the shine. In general, I use the absolute minimum amount of solvent to make the wax malleable. But professional restorers typically mix batches of varying consistency to suit different applications. Here's what happens if you vary the amount of turpentine:

Less turpentine = harder wax. Use on small pieces of furniture or when you're finishing a piece for the very first time; you want to give it your best with a hard shine! Beware—lots of elbow grease is required.

A little more turpentine = a firm-bodied paste that's easier to spread, creating a more even result. Use this for larger surfaces, such as big tabletops, floors, and boiserie. This softer version is also ideal for pigmenting the wax to make a patina or glaze, because it's more workable and easier to mix the color. (Hard wax can give a streaky result.)

Lots of turpentine = a very soft paste, which the French call *encaustique.* Use this for maintenance waxing, i.e., to rewax old pieces. This is the best consistency when adding pigment— it creates a dark, richly colored wax that's easy to spread, saturating the wood with color. This is the ideal consistency for treating dried-up pieces to several feeding coats, for the first finishing coat of a new wood floor, and for applying to large surfaces like boiserie.

Additives

You can add a variety of enhancements during the initial melting process. But it's better to make a "mother" batch and then reheat a little bit of it in a double boiler to stir in the additive.

Add 4F pumice stone to create a fine abrasive paste, ideal for fixing scratches, blemishes, or the dreaded white ring from moisture damage!

Some people scent their wax; use only a few drops of essence. If you're scenting the mother batch, add it right after you mix in the turpentine, before the wax cools. Don't cook the essential oil.

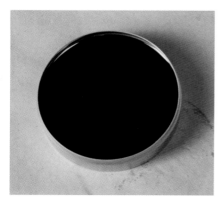

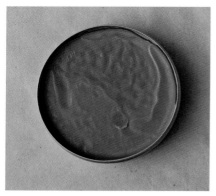

MAKING YOUR OWN
shellac

This recipe makes what's called a *medium cut* (or *2-pound cut*), which is the concentration used for French polish and other common applications. Professional refinishers make different cuts of shellac solution for various uses, but you can just dilute this medium cut with alcohol for general use. If you find yourself working with shellac frequently, consider taking a cue from the pros and keep a 1-pound cut (1 pound shellac + 1 gallon alcohol) at the ready, adding more alcohol for use as a sealer. Or set aside a little jar of medium cut, open the lid, and let the alcohol evaporate for a few days to create a thicker syrup that's perfect for brushing on spot repairs.

Shellac comes in three colors:

RUBY (OR GARNET), which imparts the nicest glow and gives wood a sense of depth. This is the preferred color for treating antiques.

AMBER, which has an orange coloration I find rather unappealing. Use it to seal wood before a darker finish or prior to oil painting in order to prevent wood knots from seeping through, or apply it to the back of furniture or drawer interiors.

BLONDE, which owes its pale-yellow cast to a bleaching process; this makes it perishable within just a few months. If you want a colorless finish, this will be the least intrusive option.

WHAT YOU'LL NEED

- ½ gallon pure, denatured alcohol (Russians use vodka— no kidding! French polish can be an expensive hobby.)
- 1-gallon jar
- 1 pound shellac flakes
- Wood or plastic stirrer
- Cheesecloth (optional)

1   **POUR ALL THE ALCOHOL INTO A GLASS JAR.**

2   **POUR THE SHELLAC FLAKES INTO THE ALCOHOL.** Don't reverse these steps! Submerging the flakes in the alcohol coats them so they don't clump.

3   **MIX WITH A WOOD OR PLASTIC STIRRER.** If you use high-quality product, the flakes should practically dissolve by themselves, without clumping.

4   **SHAKE OR STIR THE SOLUTION LIGHTLY EVERY FEW HOURS.** Wait overnight before use. You can filter the solution through cheesecloth to remove any impurities from the flakes, although I rarely do so because the quality of shellac today is very high.

5   **CHECK BEFORE USING.** The resulting solution should look like a light but rich syrup and feel a little tacky between your fingers.

6   **STORAGE.** Once mixed, shellac keeps for a few months if stored in a cool, dark place. You'll know the solution is past its prime when it goes on gooey and won't dry—this is especially common with blonde shellac, which has a very short shelf life. (In that case, don't freak out: Mix a new batch of shellac, apply, and you'll clean up the old, gloppy shellac while laying down the new coat.)

fillers

Fillers serve different purposes: to fill up the wood grain for a smooth finish, to patch a hole or a crack, or to rebuild a missing or broken element. Each application demands a slightly different ratio of water, alcohol, and oil, creating products with varying consistencies. Indeed, there are no hard-and-fast recipes; all measurements that follow are approximate. If a product feels too wet, add more sawdust. If it feels too dry, add a touch more water. Warning: Every time a filler product starts to set, stop using it. Discard it and use a fresh amount or make a fresh batch. For the same reason, don't bother storing your homemade fillers; mix a new batch each time. (Commercial fillers, however, have a longer shelf life, which can be further extended by spreading the product flat in its container after use and adding a few drops of the same medium, be it oil, water, or alcohol.)

WHAT YOU'LL NEED
- *Glass jar with tight-fitting lid*
- *Wood or plastic stirrer*
- *Tung oil*
- *Naphtha*
- *High-quality marine oil varnish*
- *Rottenstone or 4F pumice stone*

Oil-Based Grain Filler

1   **MIX THE FILLER.** In a container, mix equal parts tung oil, naphtha, and varnish to make a smooth slurry. See below for guidelines on adjusting consistency.

2   **ADD ABOUT ¼ TEASPOON OF ROTTENSTONE OR PUMICE.** Use enough to give the mix the consistency of thickened maple syrup. I prefer rottenstone, which darkens the mix so it disappears in the grain.

3   **SHELF LIFE.** The product keeps for months, stored in a jar with a tight-fitting lid. Before storing and after each use, add a few drops of naphtha to the top of the solution, but do not mix. The naphtha will increase the open time of the product, which helps preserve it. (Helpful hint: This tip applies to any oil-based product, including paint.)

The blanket term "filler" applies to three products of varying consistencies. Adjust the above and following recipes according to your needs.

LIQUID ← ────────────────────────────────→ THICK

For Grain Filling

Commercial grain fillers can be pretty toxic and are not well suited to period restoration. So I prefer making my own, which are usually more forgiving. The water-based filler (see page 249) is fume-free and nontoxic but is only usable for small surfaces, as it dries too quickly and doesn't give you adequate time to work it. The oil-based filler above has a longer open time.

For Patching

A more dough-like consistency is required to fill holes and cracks. You can adjust the water-based recipe to a cream cheese consistency; add more glue to create a more pliable product, etc. But I use good commercial alcohol- and water-based wood fillers regularly: they dry fast, clean nicely, and take stain perfectly.

For Rebuilding

To rebuild missing elements or to fill holes and cracks, you need product with a more putty-like consistency. Use the water-based method described on page 249, but use about half the amount of glue, creating a thicker paste that you can shape as desired and force into cracks or holes. No toxic product on your hands, and if you use a child-safe craft glue, your kids can join in the process!

WHAT YOU'LL NEED

- *Fine sawdust (you can buy this at craft stores— or salvage from a local cabinetmaker, who will be relieved to unload wood dust from his shop)*

- *Flat knife or spatula for mixing*
- *Cotton rag*
- *Carpenter's glue (white glue, such as Elmer's, is also sufficient)*

Water-Based Putty Filler

1   **MAKE A PASTE.** Mix 1 tablespoon of sawdust and 2 tablespoons of water to make a doughy paste. (Note that measurements are somewhat approximate. Be sure to add enough water to fully saturate the sawdust so you don't have any dried clumps.)

2   **EXTRACT THE MOISTURE.** Put the paste in the center of a cotton rag and twist it closed carefully. Squeeze out as much water as possible, to the point that the sawdust is almost dry again. Return the paste to the mixing container.

3   **ADD THE GLUE.** Mix with a dash of white glue—about ¼ teaspoon. The previous wetting prevents lumps and creates a perfectly smooth batter, the consistency of dough.

4   **APPLY AS NEEDED**. Be careful because it dries a lot faster than oil-based fillers.

Tips for Fillers

Some advise staining wood before filling the grain, which is easier; others recommend staining after, for more accurate coloration. I recommend staining before filling your grain; afterward, execute the appropriate sanding and readjust the color if needed.

All fillers shrink a bit. So apply lightly, which gives the product a better chance to bond and dry. And then reapply as needed.

Fill holes before the sanding step of refinishing when possible. This will create a more even surface (and save you from having to sand again).

Clean excess filler as you apply, using a cloth dampened with the medium of your filler. Even if sanded off later,

filler left to dry around the wound creates a halo, as stain will take differently there.

Avoid creating a surface depression when you sand the filled spot. You will not see the problem right away, but it will be obvious on the finished surface later. To avoid that problem: Do not apply over much product (which you'll just have to remove) and clean carefully around the wound when the product is still wet, waiting a bit for it to set but before drying fully. Then sand with a light hand all around the wood—not just where it was filled.

Finally, stain takes better and more evenly on freshly sanded filler. Avoid waiting too long before staining.

french polish pads

Executing a French polish requires a special pad, composed of a cotton or linen outer layer wrapped around an absorbent filler, generally cheesecloth. The pad should be a bit smaller than your fist, a size that gives you the best control. You apply the shellac solution to the inside of the pad—the filler—which helps disperse the product evenly to the outside fabric layer, and thus to your furniture.

WHAT YOU'LL NEED
- *Outer fabric (linen or cotton)*
- *Filler (wick, wool, or cheesecloth)*

For the filler, choose one of the following:

CHEESECLOTH: This is the cheapest and most readily available of the three. The loose, gauzy type is preferable, since it forms a nice fluffy ball when scrunched.

WICK: Made of the same loose cotton that's braided to make candlewicks, the material absorbs product well and releases it evenly. You'll find it in woodworking specialty stores.

WOOL: Ideally from an unraveled sweater that has been used and washed—the more worn the better. Don't use virgin wool.

1 **START WITH THE OUTER LAYER.** Lay an 8-inch square of linen or cotton flat on a table. If you prefer, you can use a larger rectangular piece of fabric and fold it in half to get two layers.

2 **PLACE THE FILLER ON TOP.** Smush your chosen filler (here, cheesecloth) into a soft ball and place on top. Many refinishers have a very specific way they do it, but do not obsess over technique, since you'll be reopening the pad often to recharge it.

3 **FOLD AND TIE.** Fold the four corners of your fabric square over the filler, twist, and fix with a rubber band to create a small pouf. Or fold in two opposite corners first, and then tie the other two together, tucking in the ends. Make sure the face of the pad is smooth and devoid of lines or creases. Flatten the pad a bit by pressing it onto the palm or back of your hand.

You'll use at least three pads to execute a French polish:

A COARSE-LINEN-WRAPPED PAD to rub the pumice into the wood at the beginning of the process. You want a linen weave that's a bit rough and sturdy, akin to canvas.

ONE OR TWO COTTON-WRAPPED PADS to build up the finish. Use a fine, white 100 percent cotton T-shirt—one that's been used and washed a number of times so it's soft and devoid of lint.

A FRESH, NEW COTTON-WRAPPED PAD to "spirit off"—i.e., to remove the lubricating oil to dry the freshly polished wood and give it a crisp gloss. You should always use a new, clean pad for "finishing the finish."

Making, Charging, and Storing a French Polish Pad

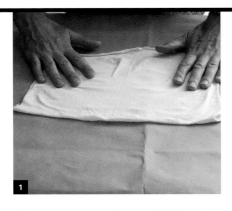

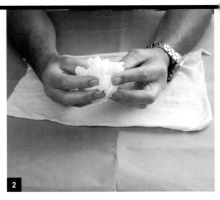

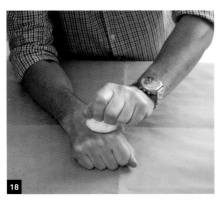

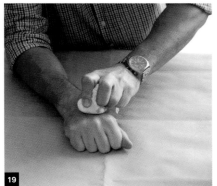

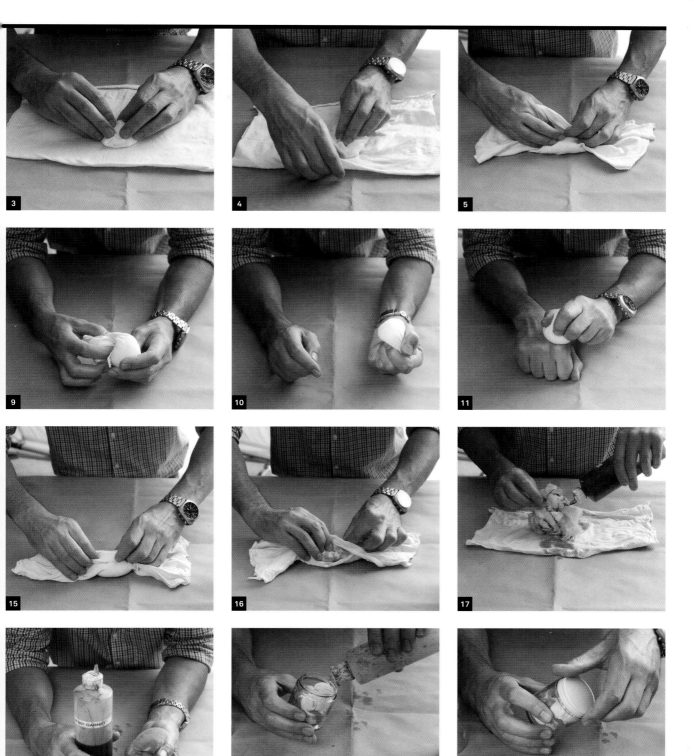

glaze

Although commercial glazes are readily available at art stores and from fine-woodworking catalogs, crafting a bespoke mix allows you to precisely customize your color or the duration of open time.

WHAT YOU'LL NEED

■ *2 parts good-quality oil varnish*

■ *1 part turpentine or naphtha*

■ *Dash of japan drier (never more than 1 part drier to 10 parts mixture), which compensates for the long open time of the oil solvent*

■ *Pigment for oils*

1   **MIX THE FILLER.** Combine all the ingredients and stir until the mixture has the consistency of a light syrup. You will be able to apply this easily and it will stay open for at least 20 minutes—ample work time.

2   **TEST FIRST.** From there, test the application on a safe part of the piece of furniture and adjust accordingly: If it's too sticky and not workable, add solvent. If it's too light or dark, adjust the color.

The Art of Improvisation

Glazing is a technique that demands nuance and a light hand. It involves playing with the existing wood, enhancing it, aging it, or helping it catch the light better. Too much drastic change or fancy layering and you end up with overly decorative faux painting—a fine art, but not our goal. On-the-fly adjustments to the texture and color of your product is part of every glazing job, no two being alike. Do not set your mind on an a priori recipe; finessing will inevitably be required. This is why I recommend oil glaze, a versatile product that has a long open time. Oil-based glazes allow you to sample copiously, directly on your piece of furniture. Don't like the effect? Wipe it off, correct the color or texture, and start anew.

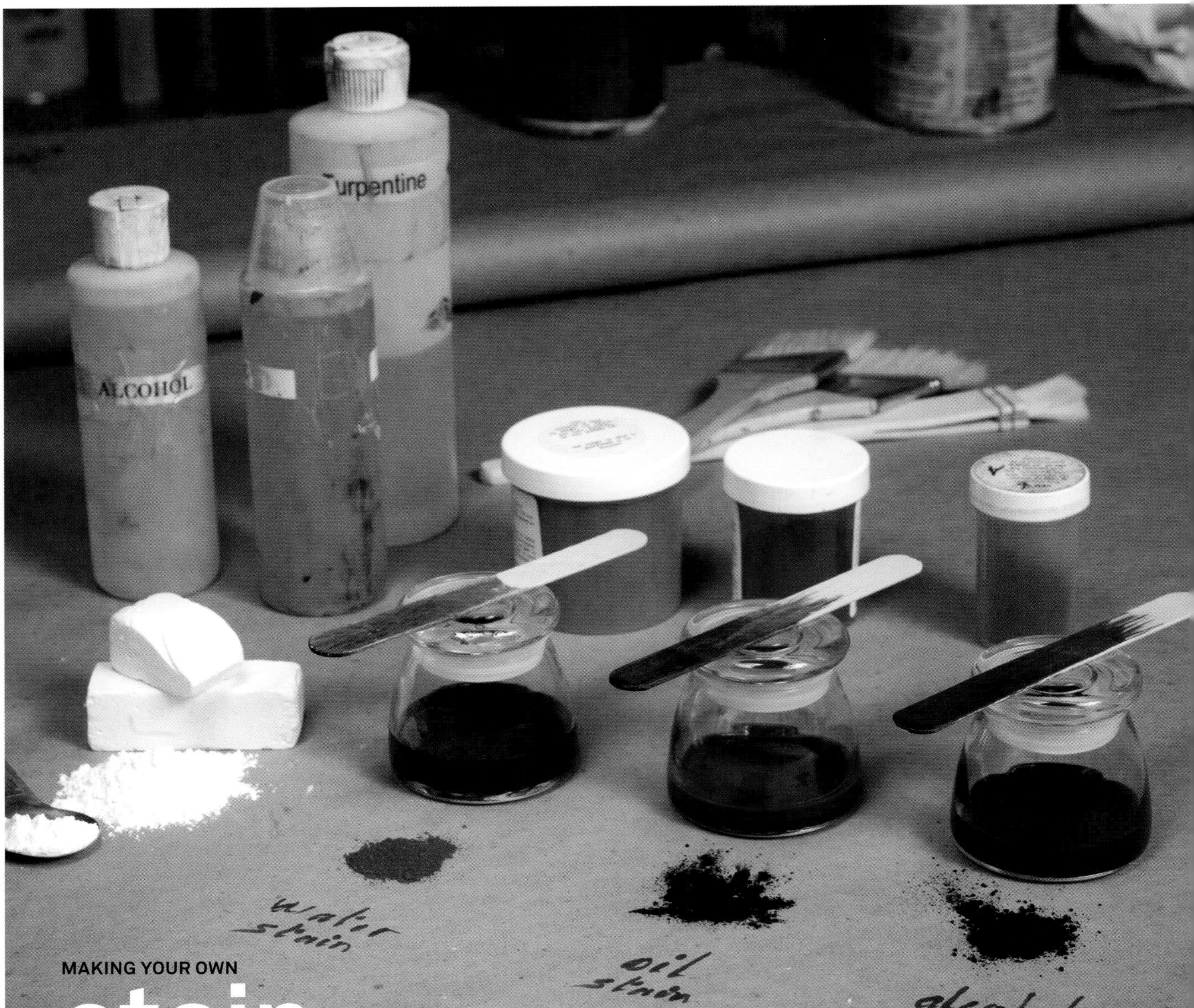

Turpentine

ALCOHOL

water
stain

oil
stain

alcohol
stain

MAKING YOUR OWN
stain

There are three types of stains: oil-, water-, and alcohol-based. For the recipes opposite, use pigment that's appropriate for the medium (each one is processed differently).

You can also add pigments directly to finishes like tung oil, creating a product that stains, seals, and finishes simultaneously (multitasking products are not a modern invention!). You can add pigments to varnish, although add only a small amount—just enough to give a highlight or subtle hue. Any more would look weird, and the result would be difficult to predict.

WHAT YOU'LL NEED

- *Glass container*
- *Pigment*
- *Medium appropriate to that pigment (e.g., oil for oil pigment)*
- *Wood or plastic stirrer*
- *Powdered whiting or powdered chalk (optional)*

Oil-based Stain

You can make oil-based stains with a good-quality gum turpentine or naphtha if you want a longer open time, which comes in handy when staining larger surfaces and avoiding lap marks.

1   **MIX PIGMENT WITH THE APPROPRIATE MEDIUM.** Start with 1 ounce or less of pigment per 1 quart of solvent. Add more pigment if desired; the exact amount will depend on how deep or intense you want the color to be. Stir and wait overnight.

2   **ADJUST THE TRANSPARENCY.** You may also add powdered whiting or powdered chalk to create a more opaque or semitransparent stain. While I don't recommend hiding the beauty of the wood, a higher degree of opacity can come in handy for darker species like ebony or Jacobean oak, or if your piece is quite a disaster (see page 169 for such an example).

3   **STAINS FROM THE SAME MEDIUM CAN BE MIXED.** This can help you adjust not only the lightness or darkness but also the color itself.

Water-based Stain

Even though water-based stain dries to the touch very quickly, it's important that after you apply the stain, you let the piece of furniture sit overnight before finishing.

1   **MIX THE STAIN.** Boil water. Add 1 ounce of powdered pigment per quart of water, adding more pigment as desired. Remove the stain from the heat and stir regularly. Transfer the stain to a container.

2   **LET THE STAIN COOL OVERNIGHT.**

3   **SHAKE THE CONTAINER TO STIR.** The stain is now ready to use.

4   **SHELF LIFE:** This stain has a long shelf life if stored away from light.

Tips

There are many natural-earth pigments: lime, walnut-hull powder, etc. Or search the Internet for custom pigment makers and mixers. The quality of their material is unparalleled and their preparation flawless!

Before mixing, take time to observe the wood you're staining and the color you want to achieve. I always tell people that wood has no color—it has *colors*. Look closely; the hue changes fiber by fiber, layer by layer. Look from another angle, in a different light, and the tone changes again. There's no right or wrong, only choices! It's up to you.

Alcohol-based Stain

Alcohol stain dries almost instantly, so you can apply the subsequent finish right away. For techniques during which you'll add stain to shellac, use this.

1   **MIX THE STAIN.** Use 1 ounce or less of pigment per quart of alcohol and adjust as desired. Add pigments to methanol (not regular denatured wood alcohol) and stir regularly for 1 hour. Better yet, put it in a bottle with a safe cap (so the medium doesn't evaporate) and shake it regularly.

2   **IT'S READY TO USE.** You don't even have to wait for the product to set.

3   **SHELF LIFE:** If stored tightly and away from light, alcohol-based stain keeps almost indefinitely. Mark the level with a marker to be sure the mix is constant.

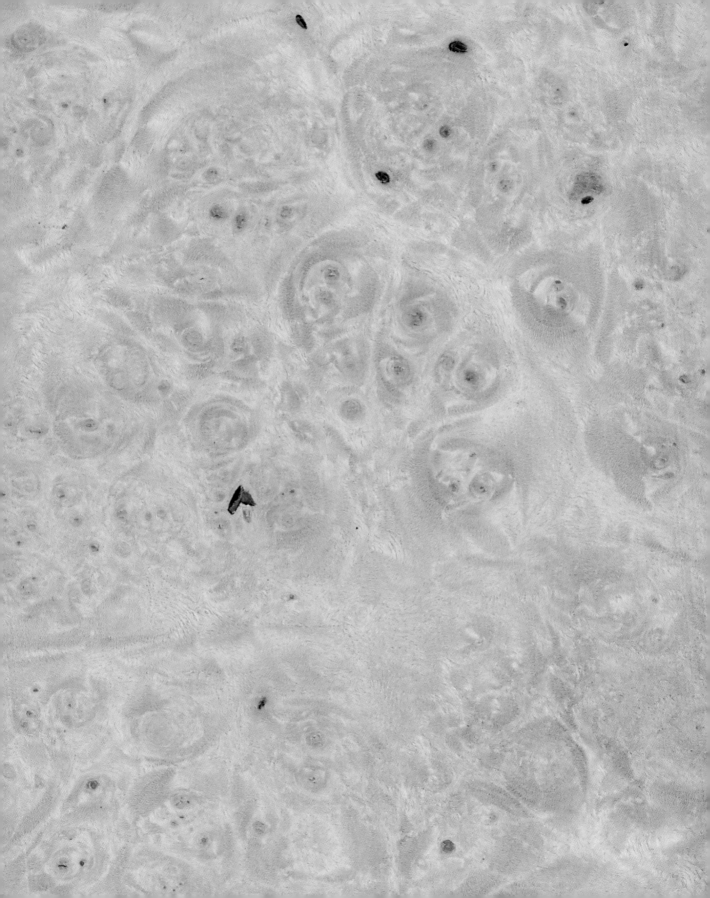

PART 6

THE CARE AND FEEDING OF YOUR FURNITURE

Whether you've just given your Victorian side table a new lease on life or are curious about how to maintain your midcentury-modern dining set in pristine condition, you'll want to follow a few guidelines to ensure the longevity of your possessions. This section outlines practical maintenance tips, advice on moving (since transport is a major cause of damage to furniture), and solutions for other common problems—from water rings and wormholes to broken hinges and dingy ormolu. I've even included sections on caring for marble-topped pieces and outdoor furniture. Take care!

Wormholes

Worms

Furniture beetles love laying eggs in antiques. They gravitate to dead wood and dampness (an argument for keeping your pieces in temperate conditions). As the larvae grow, they feed on and burrow into the wood, causing it to become porous and dry—and thus more fragile and susceptible to moisture. It can take years for the beetles to fully develop, at which point they exit via a neat, freshly drilled hole. And then—you guessed it—they find a husband, go back in, lay eggs . . . and repeat, ad nauseam. To break this vicious circle, keep furniture in as dry a spot as possible and inspect for new holes periodically.

Most antiques have old, dormant wormholes, but small piles of dust on the floor below are a telltale sign of new, active ones. To fix, apply a furniture-worm insecticide. Available in hardware stores, these products are quite toxic. Use them outside while wearing goggles and a mask.

1   **INSTEAD OF SPRAYING THE PIECE,** which leaves toxic residue and can damage the finish, pour the product into a thin-needled syringe and squirt just a little into the holes. You don't need to squirt into every single hole; one every 10 inches or so will suffice.

2   **LEAVE THE PIECE OUTSIDE OVERNIGHT** and keep kids and pets away from it for a day or two.

3   **AFTERWARD, INSPECT REGULARLY FOR NEW HOLES,** and use your syringe accordingly.

4   **PERFORM STEPS 1 THROUGH 3 ONCE OR TWICE A YEAR (OR AS NEEDED);** this safer method can eventually be done inside, on a spot-by-spot basis.

5   **PLACE CEDAR BLOCKS INSIDE THE PIECE TO PREVENT NEW INFESTATIONS;** you can also spray the interior with a 1:5 ratio of cedarwood essential oil and wheat-germ oil (or another neutral oil).

Insect Damage

Other than wood-beetle worms, the only other insect you need to worry about is termites. And if your furniture has termites, that's the least of your troubles—because it means your house does, too!

Wood beetle laying eggs

Wood beetle

Termite

Moisture Damage

Standing liquids can cause the dreaded ring or a stain. Take precautions to avoid this situation, but if there is any moisture damage, it's important to treat it pronto.

Dry spills caused by water, alcohol, oil, or any other liquid as soon as possible. Sprinkle the spot with 4F pumice powder or baby powder and leave it on for a few hours to draw out the moisture. Then evaluate the damage and proceed accordingly, following these guidelines.

Before

SUPERFICIAL SPOTS

For superficial damage and light-colored stains, the first line of defense is to let the piece dry thoroughly, as above—a hair dryer can help. This quick action may result in there being no permanent stain. Next, place a double-layered fabric on the spot. Top it with a warm, dry iron, checking often to assess improvement. If the mark is still visible, treat it by rubbing the surface with a good wood polish or wax.

After

DARK SPOTS

If you have a dark spot or stain, or if you've left the water mark untreated for some time, the damage is more serious.

1   **TRY SOLVENTS LIKE PAINT THINNER OR ALCOHOL.** (Test the product first on the underside of the piece.) Rub lightly with a damp rag and let dry.

2   **IF SOLVENTS DON'T WORK, TRY RUBBING THE MARK WITH SUPERFINE (0000) STEEL WOOL,** saturated with wax to avoid scratching the piece. Let dry.

3   **APPLY POLISH OR WAX TO PROTECT YOUR PIECE** once the stain has been removed.

SEVERE SPOTS

For more serious marks or stains that have penetrated the finish and harmed the wood itself, including damage from flooding, the repair will probably be more complicated. I recommend that you consult a professional—especially if the piece in question is a tabletop or centerpiece or has a high-gloss surface. The finish will have to be removed mechanically (by sanding or scraping it down) or chemically (with stripper). Depending on your level of experience, you may want to attempt the repair yourself if the stain is on a small surface, or if the piece has a wax finish. Removal will be fast, refinishing easier and more innocuous. Follow these steps:

1   **STRIP AND SAND THE SPOT;** this alone may remove the stain. Using a razor blade—with surgical precision—could do the trick as well.

2   **IF NOT, TRY A SOLVENT;** lemon or bleach works well for ink or dark stains.

3   **REPAIR THE FINISH** on the stripped section.

4   **STAIN THE FINISH** to blend with the rest of the piece, and then seal.

DOORS

Stuck Door

One of the most common problems encountered on antiques is a stuck or hard-to-open door, but the good news is that it's an easy fix. The usual culprit is excess humidity—either from the room in which it currently resides or from wherever it lived before. Stuck doors frequently plague pieces that have been stored for some time: The wood expands, and the door no longer fits. Here's what to do:

- **CHECK THAT THE PIECE IS LEVEL ON THE GROUND.** One foot higher than the others is sometimes enough to cause an imbalance and twist the joinery.

- **A FEW WEEKS IN A DRY, TEMPERATE ROOM** is often enough to solve the problem. Try this before sanding or shaving off any wood (see next point), which can result in the opposite problem: a door too small for its frame.

- **FOR MINOR ISSUES, SAND THE UNDERSIDE OF THE DOOR** to reduce friction. If there's slight friction, 220 grit should do the trick; try coarser 100 if the door is unable to close. Use a wood file or a hand plane if necessary to remove more material. But take off just a little; that's as far as you should go before calling a professional.

- **TO FIGURE OUT EXACTLY WHERE THE DOOR IS RUBBING,** sprinkle baby powder in the general area. Open and close the door a few times; the problem is where the powder rubs off.

- **MORE SERIOUS CAUSES INCLUDE A BROKEN HINGE OR A BROKEN DOOR PART.** See the next section for more tips, or hire a restorer; this is generally not a DIY fix.

Broken Hinge

A broken hinge may require professional services. But even if you do not intend to fix or replace the hinge yourself, regular assessment will prevent further damage, so be vigilant. The main culprits are usually faulty equipment, including newer replacement hinges and screws that do not fit the piece perfectly. For instance:

- **SCREWS THAT HAVE BEEN CHANGED** many times and are loose in their holes.

- **ILL-FITTING SCREWS THAT EXTEND PAST THE HINGE** surface to prevent the door from closing.

- **HINGES REPLACED WITH IMPROPER ONES**—too big, preventing the door from closing properly, or too shallow, pulling them off the wood they're screwed into.

- **ONE MISMATCHED HINGE.** They should all match, as should screws and nails. Replace as needed.

Possible solutions that will take care of problems and prevent further damage:

- **REPLACE THE HINGES** with more suitable ones.

- **REPLACE THE SCREWS** with more suitable ones.

- **REBUILD THE WOOD** to which the hinges are affixed, ensuring proper support.

- **SAND OR PLANE** any excess, swollen wood.

Split Panels

A split is a wound that cannot be reversed; the scar is there to stay. Treat the split as well as possible and then hide it, always using reversible methods and products (animal glues, homemade fillers) to allow future re-opening of the wound.

If the split panel is veneered, a professional will need to unframe the panel, unglue and lift the veneer, repair and patch the panel substrate, and reapply the veneer over the closed-up wound. He'll then file unmatched edges, stain, color patch, and refinish the panel to perfect the results. (You can see why this is a job for professionals only!)

Solid-wood panels are constructed to allow expansion and retraction within the surrounding frame, precisely to avoid splitting. If the mortise-and-tenon joinery is adhered via wood pegs, you can dismantle the frame to clean any dirt that's accumulated in the groove holding the panel. Treat the repair as instructed below and then reframe the panel, ensuring it can move freely. Chances are, the panel will never split again.

If you cannot unframe the panel, or if the panel is not split along its whole length, you can still follow the process below to get decent results.

1   **CLEAN THE WOUND** of any old glue or dirt.

2   **ASSESS THE PANEL.** If it's still set in its frame, then jump to Step 3. If the panel is free and split in two, apply glue to both sides and clamp together (see page 266). Let the panel dry for a few days, and then reset the frame. Skip to Step 7.

3   **ENLARGE THE WOUND** by pulling apart the two pieces a bit, just enough to insert a wood patch that will keep the surrounding panels tight in the frame.

4   **PATCH THE RESULTING GAP** by inserting a flat piece of wood—a stirrer, a tongue depressor, a shim trimmed to the thickness of the panel—inside the wound. Brush glue on both sides before insertion.

5   **USING 320- OR 400-GRIT SANDPAPER,** sand flush with the rest of the panel, add filler where needed, and finish to match.

6   **IF THE WOUND IS TOO SHALLOW OR TOO THIN** for this insertion technique, force in wood filler (see page 246 to learn how to make your own). Dab in just a little bit at a time; clean up excess as you go, and don't spread it around sloppily or you'll have to sand off too much, which could create a little depression around the split.

7   **SAND ANY EXCESS VERY CAREFULLY** with 320- or 400-grit sandpaper.

8   **HIDE YOUR HANDIWORK.** Patch, sand the surface clean and flush, and then color match to blend with the surrounding wood (see page 274).

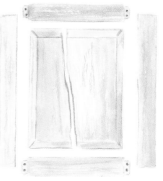

Split frame, dismantled

A wound

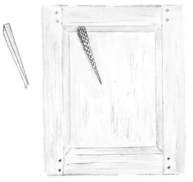

Split panel patching

Touch-up blending

DRAWERS AND SLIDES

Drawer Maintenance

First, regularly empty your drawers in order to check them for damage. Second, do not overload them! Weight will destroy the drawer bottoms and place stress on the sliding movement. Stacks of paper and books are no-nos. Go check your drawers right now; probably half of them are too full.

Keep the knobs or pulls tightly secured; loose hardware will affect sound operation. And open drawers properly. If a drawer has two knobs, it's because you need to pull evenly with both hands!

Stuck Drawers

Planing or sanding the undersides of the drawer box will often solve the problem. Then rub dry beeswax or soap on those parts as well as on the glides to achieve lubrication.

Loose Drawers

If the drawers push in too far or not far enough, or are not level, the inside wood glides are the culprit—usually because they're worn out or have come unglued. Assess the slides and the drawer box to determine the proper course of action. (Refer to "Drawer-Slide Repair," below, for more details.)

Split Drawer Bottom

A fissure in this location is impractical and can further compromise the drawer's structural stability, especially if the drawer is heavily loaded. Treat as you would a split panel: Tap the parts back together and glue. To avoid further separation, take a cue from old-school artisans and follow these steps:

1   **CUT A PIECE OF CANVAS OR COARSE LINEN** a few inches wide and the length of the split panel.

2   **APPLY A THICK COAT OF GLUE TO BOTH SIDES OF THE SPLIT,** along the underside of the drawer. Use hide glue or wood glue; both will retract a bit and ensure stability.

3   **APPLY THE FABRIC OVER THE WOUND.** Brush more glue onto the canvas.

4   **LET THE PIECE DRY OVERNIGHT.** Preserve your handiwork by not overfilling your drawers.

Split drawer bottom repair

Drawer-Slide Repair

Sticky, broken, or unglued slides—the small wood "tracks" that support the drawers—are common in furniture ranging from desks and dressers to side tables. Their sound operation is required to keep drawers aligned, so they can glide smoothly and evenly without tilting or catching. Rehabbing or even replacing slides is a pretty quick fix that shouldn't intimidate you.

WHAT YOU'LL NEED

- *Bar soap*
- *Paint thinner*
- *Animal glue*
- *Scrap pine (optional)*
- *Saw (optional)*
- *150- or 220-grit sandpaper*
- *Paste wax or a bar of wax*

1   **TRY BAR SOAP.** If the slides are not overly worn but the drawers are sticking, rubbing them with soap may be enough.

2   **REMOVE SLIDES.** If that doesn't work, remove the slides. They're usually affixed to the inside of furniture with glue, so it shouldn't be necessary to remove any screws or nails. Pour warm water over the slide and let gravity do its work; capillary action pulls the water down into the crevice and deactivates the existing glue—assuming it was a natural adhesive, like hide glue. If this technique doesn't work, repeat the process with paint thinner, which will dissolve other reversible wood glues.

3   **WAIT FOR THE WATER OR PAINT THINNER TO DO ITS WORK AND GENTLY TUG OFF THE SLIDES.** Wipe up excess water or paint thinner with a rag.

4   **IF THE SLIDES ARE IN SOUND SHAPE, TRY FLIPPING THEM UPSIDE DOWN,** so that the unworn bottom surface is now on top. Or put the left-side slide on the right side, so that the end closer to the back is now in front.

5   **IF THE SLIDE IS DAMAGED OR SEEMS OVERLY WORN, REPLACE IT.** And if you have to replace one, then replace both for evenness. Cut a piece of wood—preferably pine, which is smooth and not too hard—to the exact same size. Always use rough, unfinished wood; a good options is 1- or ¾-inch sticks from the lumberyard. Sand the top to a smooth finish with 320- or 400-grit sandpaper, skim with paste wax or a block of wax to lubricate, and attach to the original location with hide or wood glue.

6   **WAIT A COUPLE OF DAYS FOR THE GLUE TO CURE** before putting the drawers back in.

Drawer Troubleshooting

IF SLIDES ARE UNGLUED	Clean old glue residue off the glides and reglue them in their original location. Always glue them back into place—never use nails or screws: The frame will no longer be able to expand and contract, and you may go through the sides of the furniture.
IF SLIDES ARE LIGHTLY WORN	Instead of replacing the glides, try flipping them upside down or swapping their positions, putting the left one on the right-hand side and vice versa. You may have to do some adjustment, but it's worth trying.
IF SLIDES ARE TOO WORN	Try gluing a thin piece of flat wood or veneer or a shim to the top of the slide, restoring its height to the correct level.
IF THE DRAWER STICKS OUT	Plane or sand the drawer's back side.
IF THE DRAWER GOES TOO FAR IN	Glue a small piece of wood to the inside back of the furniture carcass or the back of the drawer, creating a stop. Or glue two smaller stops at the end of the glides.

GENERAL REPAIRS

Old Restorations

Good restorations or bad restorations, reversible or irreversible, visible or hidden . . . it is very important to detect them all, since they will affect new restorations, repairs, and refinishing. A historical restoration, done correctly, can add charm if exposed. It should be left untouched. As a rule of thumb, restoring up to 30 percent of the piece is acceptable on an antique. The degree of restoration will affect the value, but the piece will still bear the label of a legitimate antique. Any more than 30 percent seriously undermines the value, and an expert could be very severe on assessment. (This only applies to serious, pedigreed antiques. Unsure if yours qualifies? Take a few snapshots and send them to a dealer or an auction house.)

Some restorations are just bad repairs. You have to address them and proceed carefully. Faulty nails and screws can and should be removed, but irreversible glues cannot. At the first tug of resistance, or if you are unsure or unclear about what's happening during a particular process, consult a professional—if you proceed any further on your own, it's possible you'll execute another bad repair. A piece of furniture can only take so many before crying "Uncle!"

As a rule:

- **NEVER PUT SCREWS** or nails where there were none.

- **NEVER USE MODERN GLUES.** Trust me on this one: I witness the damage modern glues do on a daily basis.

- **KEEP AS MANY OLD PIECES,** parts, old restorations, and even old finishes as intact as possible.

- **LEAVE OLD RESTORATIONS ALONE IF THEY STILL HOLD,** especially on period restorations—even visible ones. Also leave new restorations exposed if they are in unseen parts. Think of future restorers.

- **DO NOT REMOVE OLD LABELS,** pencil marks, and the like. Feel free to add your own reversible ones.

- **TAKE ADVICE:** Artisans will always be flattered by your interest and respect.

Broken Leg

Especially on chair frames and inherently less-stable tripod table bases, a broken leg is very common. In fact, on table bases, one often gets the double-whammy of loose joinery at the base of the pedestal column and a broken leg below (see example and tutorial on pages 208–213). To fix a broken leg, follow these steps:

1   **FULLY SEPARATE THE TWO PARTS;** this is a must for a proper job. If it is impossible to do so safely, consult a professional. A superficial job will last only so long, and—worse—will further damage the piece.

2   **CLEAN THE BREAK CAREFULLY.**

3   **USE WOOD GLUE OR HIDE GLUE,** which are less potent than newer glues but which have the advantage of being reversible.

4   **DRILL A HOLE** that extends through both sides of the break, perpendicular to the wound.

5   **INSERT A WOOD PEG TO KEEP THE BREAK STURDY.** Never use a metal rod, screw, or nail, which will eventually tear apart the wood. Be sure the edges of the wound fit together perfectly, and clamp firmly—without oversqueezing the glue or letting parts shift from their ideal spot. Wait overnight.

6   **SAND, PATCH, AND MATCH** to the surrounding finish.

Before

After

Casters

The little swiveling devices at the bottom of furniture legs receive a lot of abuse, so check them regularly to see if they're torn or their wheels are worn. Casters are primarily designed to bear the weight of the piece, not you, so don't roll across the room while seated on an old armchair—this is not modern office furniture we're talking about!

To fix, flip the furniture upside down and unscrew the casters. The screws are usually there only to keep the unit in place. The main armature is a metal rod that inserts into the leg, augmented by smaller tacks or screws that fit under the leg bottom. A second type of caster attaches via a cylindrical brass cup, which slips over the end of the leg to prevent tearing the surrounding wood. All those parts have a meaning; if any are missing or damaged, replace all the casters with a new set—evenness is key. They should be easy to remove and replace: There are only a few standard models, and you can find nice reproductions in hardware catalogs.

Casters

Broken Drop-Leaf

The main cause of broken leaves is a loose or broken hinge. Replacing them will usually fix matters. Remove the old hinges, refill the old screw holes, and install good-quality new ones. (The proper screws are very often provided with quality reproduction hardware. If they're not, ask which ones are correct.) In fact, changing all of the hinges for a proper new set is a good idea; keep the old ones if you are a purist. A bit of judicious sanding here and there will help set the new hardware perfectly in place and keep running smoothly.

WOODWORK

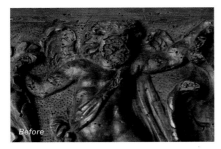
Before

Filled parts

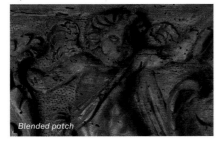
Blended patch

Missing Parts

Small missing wood parts like torn corners, slivers of molding, and holes can be addressed by filling them properly (see "Making Your Own Fillers," page 246). If the part is too big, a new piece of wood will have to be grafted onto the furniture to restore its integrity. This repair should be left to a professional; the support will have to be carved to a regular shape to receive the new piece of wood, which will be made flush after attachment (think hip replacement surgery or prosthetic limbs). Here are some guidelines on what to do:

PROBLEM	SOLUTION
Missing wood part	General replacement and repair
Missing molding	Replacement and reconstruction
Missing carving or ornament	Recasting
Holes and divots	Refill, shape, and patch; finish to match.

Bubbling Veneer

Bubbling is generally the result of excess humidity or glue failure. You can reactivate the glue relatively easily by warming it slightly: Here's how:

1   **PLACE A FEW LAYERS OF WHITE TISSUE PAPER** on the wood for protection.

2   **GO OVER THE TISSUE PAPER** with a slightly warm iron (plugged in and set to low heat) for a minute or so.

3   **PRESS THE VENEER ONTO THE WOOD BACKING.** Maintain pressure with a finger for a few minutes or use veneer tape.

Unglued or Peeling Veneer

If the veneer is peeling or has become unglued, first try to fix it as you would bubbling. If that fails, or if the unglued section of veneer is too big, then follow these steps:

Torn and missing veneer

1   **CUT OPEN THE VENEER WITH AN X-ACTO KNIFE OR A RAZOR BLADE,** slicing in the direction of the wood grain.

2   **INJECT HIDE GLUE UNDER BOTH SIDES OF THE WOUND** with a thin stick or a syringe.

3   **APPLY PRESSURE ON BOTH SIDES,** pushing toward the wound to squeeze out excess glue.

4   **CLEAN EXCESS GLUE** with a damp cloth.

5   **WAIT UNTIL THE GLUE HAS SET,** about 10 minutes. Then place a few layers of tissue paper on top and apply a slightly warm, unplugged iron; rest it on top until cool.

6   **THE WARMTH AND WEIGHT OF THE IRON** will ensure a perfect repair.

7   **YOU MAY NOT HAVE TO REFINISH THE SURFACE AFTERWARD;** just blend it by applying more of a matching finish.

Lifting and unglued veneer

Depressed Veneer

Veneer can also be pockmarked with a hollow depression, probably resulting from the wood surface being hit. Relevel the spot with a steam iron placed atop a cotton cloth. (Or use a damp cloth and a dry iron.) Adjusting the heat to a level that won't damage the wood is critical; start on low heat/steam, and turn up little by little until the veneer lifts.

Missing Veneer

Missing veneer sections can be patched with wood filler, but only if the wound is small and insignificant. Otherwise, patching will require new veneer.

You can buy wood-veneer samples in packs of 20 or 40 on eBay or from fine-woodworking catalogs. (These also make wonderful references for identifying wood species, and are large enough for making numerous repairs.) Note that modern veneers are thinner than old ones, so patching may require gluing together two layers in order to achieve a surface that's flush with the surrounding veneer. If so, choose pine, poplar, or maple for the under-layer, and glue with the grain perpendicular to the top veneer piece.

1   **USING AN X-ACTO KNIFE, CLEAN THE WOUND OF DIRT AND RESIDUAL GLUE.** A perfectly clean wound is essential! Scrape carefully and avoid sanding, lest you go over the edges of the wound to form an invisible crater. Next, trim the perimeter to create straight edges and a regular shape that's easier to fill.

2   **CLEAN THE WOUND THOROUGHLY** with an alcohol-dampened rag.

3   **MATCH THE VENEER** with a piece in the same (or a similar) wood and thickness if possible. If the veneer is too thin, you may need to layer the wood, alternating the direction of the grain.

4   **PLACE A PIECE OF PAPER OVER THE WOUND** and trace its exact outline.

5   **CUT YOUR PIECE A TAD LARGER THAN YOUR TEMPLATE.** Adjust the size by placing the patch over the wound and sanding the edges at a 90-degree angle until you've achieved a perfect match. (Do not trim with a razor blade, as you will invariably end up with a too-small patch.)

6   **USING A GLUE BRUSH, APPLY HIDE GLUE** on the wound.

7   **PLACE THE PATCH ON TOP.** Apply pressure from the center to the edges to squeeze out any excess glue. Once the contact is even, stop.

8   **USING A BURNISHER OR A SMOOTH, HARD BLOCK OF WOOD, APPLY CONSTANT, EVEN PRESSURE FOR A FEW MINUTES.** *Even* is the operative word, and a couple of passes should be plenty. Do not crush the wood fibers; it is better for the veneer to be thicker than the surrounding surface than the opposite. Once the glue has dried, you can scrape off any excess to make a flawless, invisible line. Affix a piece of veneer tape on top and let the patch dry overnight.

9   **REMOVE THE TAPE AND PAPER TEMPLATE CAREFULLY** with a damp rag, a razor blade, and/or sandpaper.

10   **SCRAPE WITH A CLEAN RAZOR BLADE.** Use a light hand and a number of passes (versus chipping away a thick layer).

11   **STAIN AS NEEDED** to match the existing veneer.

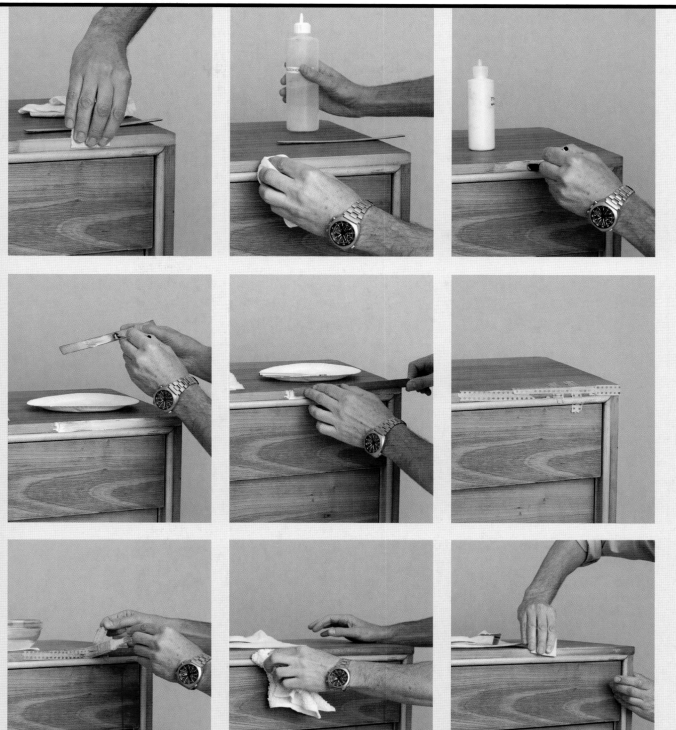

Blending Repairs

This process is a work of patience, trials, and errors. Channel your inner plastic surgeon! There's an array of products to help obscure a repair. For small and fast touch-up, consider felt pens, wax sticks, or crayons. You will find professional versions of these tools at fine-woodworking suppliers, but Crayola crayons are also perfectly acceptable, as are standard stationary felt pens (especially the calligraphy ones, with their long brush-like tips). In addition, you can mix various products—powder pigments, stains, wood-toned paints—so long as they share the same medium.

The main colors needed for wood repairs are always the same: lamp black, titanium white, yellow ochre, burnt ochre, sienna, burnt sienna, cadmium red, and Van Dyke brown. Start with this palette, and add as many other hues as desired.

1   **SAND FIRST.** Color takes best right after sanding.

2   **TRY DYES.** Start with products that will dye the wood or filler in depth, such as alcohol- or water-based stain. Saturate the wood until you achieve an acceptable tone. Let dry.

3   **NEXT, SWITCH TO THICKER PRODUCTS** like oil stains or colors, mixing and layering.

4   **ASSESS YOUR WORK,** but don't overthink it. Wood has no one color; it has thousands of ever changing layers, like a prism. Avoid spending too much time finding the perfect hue. Color, correct, let dry, seal (if needed), find another tone in the surrounding wood, apply, and repeat.

5   **ASK FOR AN HONEST OPINION.** Do not be the judge of your work. As good as your repair may be, *you* will always see it. Ask somebody if they can tell where the repair is located. If not, then you're done.

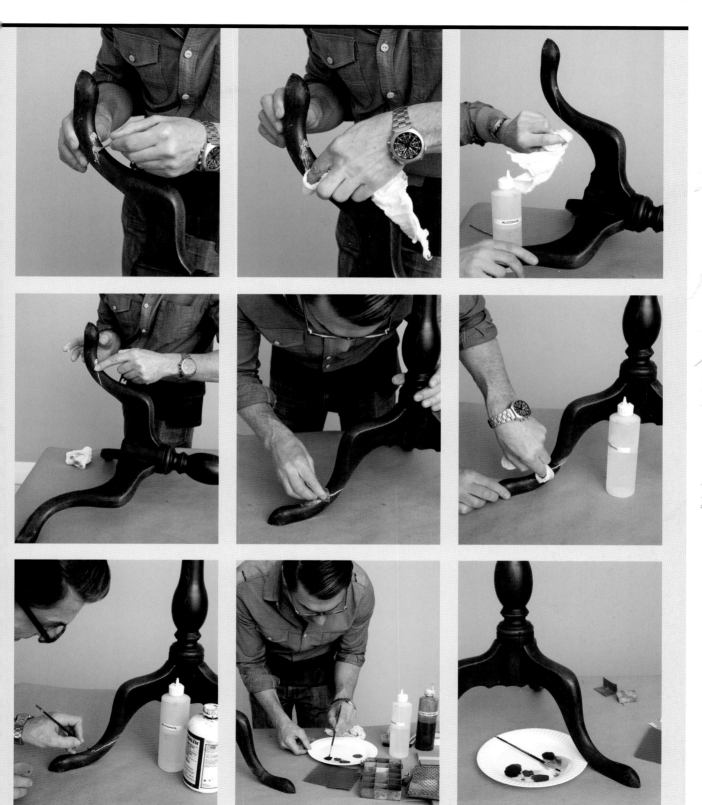

HARDWARE

General Tips

Abuse, breaks, lost parts, and shoddy replacements have likely taken a toll on your hardware. Here are some tips that apply to all genres:

- **REMOVE HARDWARE** before cleaning or fixing it.

- **AFTER REMOVAL,** clean the wood to which it was affixed.

- **FILL UP THE EXISTING HOLES** using filler or a toothpick, broken flush so new screws can get a strong hold.

- **REPAIR TORN WOOD** around or underneath hardware by refilling or regluing open wounds. Clamping may be required.

- **REPLACE THE SCREWS.** Chances are, the screws have been badly replaced already, preventing proper function. Swap them for new ones appropriate to the piece: correct material (brass or steel) and size, and always flat head (no Phillips). They all have to be similar.

- **DON'T BE TOO MUCH OF A PURIST.** It's acceptable, and even preferable in many cases, to replace old hardware. (Although save the original hardware just in case.)

Lifted Inlay

Metal inlay, usually brass, often framed drawers or tops on Victorian and 19th-century French pieces. You'll frequently encounter a lifted section, the result of a too-dry environment. Resist the temptation to Krazy-Glue it back into place, which is irreversible, or to drill nails through the inlay, which will further damage the brass and the underlying wood. Consider hiring a professional, who will fix the problem thusly:

1   **LIFT THE ENTIRE PIECE OF INLAY.**

2   **WHILE WARMING THE METAL WITH A TORCH OR THE OPEN FLAME** of a stove (see, this is why you need a professional!), flatten and straighten the inlay with a rubber or wood mallet.

3   **CLEAN ANY RESIDUAL GLUE** from the brass and the wood surface.

4   **SCRAPE THE SIDE** of the previously glued inlay with a file, giving the brass a bit of texture to grip the new glue.

5   **DEGREASE THE METAL SURFACE CAREFULLY WITH ALCOHOL;** some artisans then rub garlic on the underside for more bite.

6   **LIGHTLY WARM THE BRASS WITH A TORCH,** and then apply a new coat of wood or rabbit-hide glue.

7   **FORCE THE INLAY BACK INTO PLACE** with a rubber mallet and a small block of hardwood, moving from one end to the other to squeeze out the glue. Wipe up any excess glue. The inlay should fit perfectly and not require any clamping, although it might need a heavy weight.

Hinges

For issues involving hinges, replacement with a similar new one will likely solve the problem. Don't try to replace just one little screw, and if you have to change one hinge, change all of them. The mix-and-match approach looks bad and could compromise the structural integrity of the piece. In fact, an inferior repair is often what caused the problem you are trying to remedy. The replacement hinges should be stylistically similar to the original. When replacing, remember to repair holes and torn wood; when gluing, clamp both sides of the door or furniture frame and wait overnight.

Locks and Keys

Such complex, sophisticated mechanicals as locks have to be treated with care. These simple actions will solve most problems, and should be done every few years for maintenance:

Antique lock

1   **CLEAN DIRTY OR STUCK LOCKS WITH PETROLEUM SOLVENT,** such as naphtha or paint thinner.

2   **SOAK OVERNIGHT** to loosen up caked rust and dirt.

3   **SCRUB WITH A SOFT BRUSH,** like a toothbrush, and go deep inside the lock with a bendable tool like a bottle cleaner.

MAINTENANCE AND USE TIPS (AND NO-NOS)
Never force locks, introduce sharp objects to unlock them, or attempt to use a different key.
Never sand locks to clean them! You will impair their function.
Never use oil as a lubricant: It attracts dust and dirt that can damage the lock. Instead, funnel graphite powder into the mechanism.
Never try to open the lock box, which is often riveted; you won't be able to put it back together, plus you'll unsettle the mechanism.

WHEN TO CALL A PRO
To open the lock box and replace any broken pieces.
For a new key, which will need to be finessed by what the French call an *ajusteur*.
To replace locks and keys, which is almost always the best solution because a repair will never have the ease of movement of the initial setting and will eventually damage the furniture.

Baroque escutcheons and keys

Handles, Knobs, and Escutcheons

It was standard practice to change these elements frequently, either to follow fashion or to upgrade a set featuring several broken or lost parts. You'll often see that the holes of the previous set were filled and new ones created. If you strip or refinish the piece of furniture, survey the inside of the drawers to find the original location. Revert to the initial setting or stick to the present one—it's your choice. Follow the usual routes for evaluation, repair, and care, and always avoid sandpaper, steel wool, and metal brushes, which can scratch the finish.

Specialty Hardware

Sound function is your priority here—not aesthetics. Proper operation is a must, even for more decorative elements. Replace, don't repair, the following:

- **PIANO LIDS** that open improperly or that slam shut

- **HINGES** on a drop-front desk

- **CASTERS** on mobile pieces

Removal is critical. The aforementioned are usually associated with torn or split wood, metal being harder than wood fiber. You may have to clamp or reinforce the wood surface before removing the hardware, so as not to further shred it.

Hardware Makeover

You can give any piece a quick makeover with new hardware: drawer pulls, knobs, handles, escutcheons. You'll routinely see antiques with the original hardware in bad shape, or refitted with new, more style-conscious hardware.

- **HOW TO CHOOSE:** When picking a style, consider the color, finish, and period-appropriateness as well as the scale vis-à-vis the overall piece. The best way to figure out what you like and what works is to buy a few varieties from a good hardware source and test them out by holding them up against your piece. Then just exchange what doesn't work for more of what does. My favorite resource, though, is hardware catalogs, like Whitechapel Ltd. (my go-to for historically accurate period reproductions). Not only do they sell myriad items, but also the catalogs *themselves* are ideal for "trying on" styles and sizes: Cut out the templates and hold them up to your piece to judge if they are too big or too small. You can even use a photocopy machine to scale up the image.

- **SPACING:** Knobs and pulls should be neither too close nor too far away from each other. A rule of thumb is to divide the full width of the piece (or the width of the individual drawer) by six; position the hardware at roughly ⅙ and ⅚. Defer to your eye rather than the tape measure—this is not an exact science.

- **CENTERING:** For single knobs, again use your eye instead of a tape measure; the center of a panel or drawer may not be at the best location, depending on whether the hardware is at eye level or lower. You may drill the holes in the center, but the length or shape of the piece will make it look too high or too low. Place pieces of light-tack painter's tape as mock hardware, and step back. How does it look?

- **HOLES:** You may have to patch existing holes and drill new ones to accommodate hardware that's differently sized or configured than the original.

Finally, do not buy cheap hardware. Hardware is like jewelry for your furniture!

Cleaning Hardware

Solid bronze or brass can be cleaned with ammonia and then treated with brass polish, while plated metal (also called *gilt metal*) needs to be revived with soap and water only, lest you damage the finish. And in no case should abrasives like wire brushes or steel wool ever be used.

GILT METAL

Only soap cleaning with a soft toothbrush will do for gilt (i.e., plated) bronze. And embrace the patina: It's a sign of quality to have slightly dull gilt ormolu. Do not try to revive it with brass polish, lest you remove additional plating. In the same vein, avoid replating (too intense!) unless done by a professional with experience in antique ormolu hardware who's capable of re-creating an aged effect. The appearance of worn metal is much nicer than fresh replating.

IRON

Iron rusts. Either clean the rust or stabilize it to save the existing patina. When cleaned and sealed, rusted iron won't corrode any further, at least as long as the coating still works.

1   **SOAK THE PIECE OVERNIGHT** (or longer) in paint thinner to loosen the rust and dirt. Rinse well.

2   **RUB THE SURFACE WITH STEEL WOOL TO REMOVE ANY LOOSE RUST,** using a very fine grade (0000) to ensure you don't scratch the surface. The grade you choose—and the degree to which you remove the rust—depends on your aesthetic. Stop where desired.

3   **AVOID SANDING DOWN TO THE RAW METAL,** an inappropriate aesthetic for antiques that will diminish their value. (A cleaner look is fine for 20th-century modern pieces.) Resist the temptation to go to coarser grits; yes, you'll see faster results, but you'll scratch the metal—forcing you to go in reverse, to finer and finer grits, to erase the abrasions.

4   **IF YOU WANT TO CLEAN FURTHER,** use coarser steel wool or sandpaper (ideally, 400 grit or higher) until you achieve the level you like. Then progress to a finer-grit steel wool to polish any scratches made with coarser grits.

5   **DRY THE METAL WITH A HAIR DRYER OR A RAG,** and then apply brown or black wax (or even shoe polish) and buff to a shine. The wax will thwart further corrosion and preserve the deep, rusty patina. Boost the protective benefit of the wax by heating the metal lightly over an open flame or torch; you will see humidity evaporating. Applying the wax *à chaud* (on a hot surface) creates a longer-lasting bond. The patina and shine will also be so much richer!

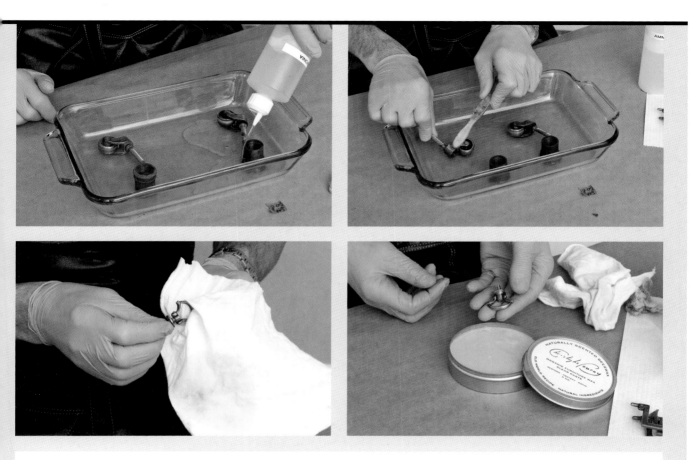

SOLID BRONZE AND BRASS

1   **PLACE THE HARDWARE IN A GLASS DISH FILLED WITH AMMONIA.** Let it sit for 5 minutes.

2   **SCRUB CLEAN WITH A TOOTHBRUSH.** Don't attempt to remove gunk with a steel-wool pad, which will scratch and damage the metal.

3   **ONCE HARDWARE IS FREE OF GUNK, YOU CAN SAFELY POLISH IT TO A NICE SHINE** with a soft, clean cotton rag or an application of good brass polish, in paste or liquid form.

4   **REMOVE THE POLISH BY SCRUBBING IT** with a worn toothbrush or other soft-bristle brush under running water—an especially important step for intricate pieces. (Follow the same protocol with silverware to remove toxic chemicals left behind by polishing cream.) Dry carefully with a clean rag, followed by a hair dryer (even if it feels completely dry); the metal should be warm when done.

5   **LEFT UNTREATED, BRASS WILL GET A NICE DULL SHINE OR AN AGED SOFT PATINA** You can also chemically patinate your hardware (see following page). Whether or not you added a patina, protect your handiwork by treating the hardware to a light coat of amber-colored paste wax, which keeps it clean longer. I prefer waxing to spray lacquering, which is chemical-based and creates an overly shiny look. While chemical lacquers seal in the look for eternity, waxed hardware will age nicely over time.

Giving Hardware a Patina

1   **DEGREASE THE HARDWARE.** Use an acetone-dampened rag.

2   **PLACE THE HARDWARE IN A GLASS DISH.**

3   **PREPARE THE PATINA BATH.** Premade patinas in various colors—Flemish gray, black iron, verdigris, dark bronze, etc.—are available in craft shops. Here, I used acid to create a pewter-y tone, which related nicely to the woodwork of the piece it was going on. (Pewter was also a period plating finish, found mainly on iron hardware to prevent rusting.) Pour the solution over the hardware.

4   **SOAK UNTIL EVENLY COATED**—5 minutes or so. If some parts do not take, remove the hardware, discard the acid, pour a fresh batch, and repeat.

5   **REMOVE AND DRY.** Using tongs or a wood stick (not bare hands), remove the hardware elements from the bath. Dry thoroughly with a clean rag.

6   **USE 000 OR 0000 STEEL WOOL TO CREATE HIGHLIGHTS IF DESIRED.**

7   **APPLY PASTE WAX TO PROTECT THE FINISH.**

LEATHER CLEANING

Desktops and other leather surfaces you find on vintage or antique furnishings have typically been treated to a finish. Not an applied topcoat per se, but a wax that's been rubbed in and then buffed, or a fine padding of shellac that penetrates the top layers of the skin. Accordingly, when cleaning them, avoid mechanical tools (scrapers, brushes, steel wool), which remove the finish along with the dirt. Instead, use a cleaning agent such as rubbing alcohol or a soft, clear all-natural soap like Castile, diluted in water. These products will banish crud and water rings without damaging or altering the finish.

Leather Care and Maintenance

IF THE LEATHER IS . . .	. . . DO THIS
In need of general cleaning and maintenance	Dampen a very soft rag made of a white (not colored!) cotton T-shirt, wring out as much water as possible, and wipe the surface energetically.
Dirty	First, clean as above. Then, using a clean rag, apply a tiny bit of wax-based saddle soap and wipe off; buff to a shine (do not rinse).
Stained	Always test in a hidden place. Clean as in maintenance. Then, rub a clean cloth, dampened with rubbing alcohol, in a circular motion. Next, recondition the leather with cream or wax. Cover oil stains with talcum powder to drain out the oil.
Wet	Like wood, leather abhors dampness, so never store in a humid area. Pat any dampness dry with a cloth, let dry fully, and then treat as you would dirty and/or stained leather.
Dry	Follow directions for cleaning/maintenance, and then use saddle soap. Next, apply a moisturizing leather cream and buff to a shine. Makeup remover applied with a clean cotton cloth, rubbed in a circular motion, will also clean and moisturize.
Cracked	Whether the protective skin of the leather is peeling or has fully blossomed into a wound, the process is the same: Clean with a dry cloth only, then apply a leather-oil treatment—but only on medium to dark leather, since the product will darken it.
Mildewed	Clean with a soft cotton rag dampened with a 1:1 solution of water and white vinegar.
Suede	Use a pristine white pencil eraser to clean any stains, then revive the nap with a very fine wire brush (found in fine woodworking or art supply stores).
In need of a shine	Not appropriate for sofas and seating. For other furnishings, condition first and then buff to a light glow. Use colored shoe shine on desktops only, and in the appropriate hue.

1   **DAMPEN A RAG WITH RUBBING ALCOHOL** and rub the leather in a circular motion. Repeat until your rag comes away clean, and then let the piece dry for about 15 minutes. (If your leather is missing its "skin," or finishing coating, you will not be able to clean it; it will peel. See "Troubleshooting.")

2   **PROTECT YOUR CLEAN LEATHER** with a finishing coat of wax in a matching hue. This step is not unlike polishing your loafers—although furniture wax is much harder and more protective than shoe polish. Avoid applying it to any gilding and/or tooling, such as the border detailing here, unless you use clear wax.

3   **LET THE WAX DRY FOR A BIT,** then brush off any excess.

4   **USING A WOOL RAG, BUFF TO A HARD SHINE—** almost like patent leather. Be patient; this step takes time! But afterward, your leather surface is practically impervious; water will bead right off.

Troubleshooting

If your leather is peeling, cracked, or otherwise shredding small particles, you need to replace the leather or, at the very least, halt further damage by stabilizing and sealing the surface.

1   **FIRST MOISTURIZE WITH TACK, SADDLE, OR MINK OIL,** which use animal by-products, or—even better—linseed or tung oil, which have a drying agent and won't leave behind a greasy film. Oil will darken the wound and might hide the problem nicely on its own.

2   **LET THE OIL DRY THOROUGHLY,** and then pad the surface lightly with shellac—just as you would for a French polish. Carefully brush the shellac inside any cracks. This re-creates the original "skin" of the leather. When you have achieved a nice coating, let the piece dry overnight.

3   **NOW THAT YOUR LEATHER IS PROTECTED,** you can wax it and buff it to a shine.

MARBLE

The term *marble* actually describes a category, as a variety of stones—Carrara, Calacatta, Siena—fall under this denomination. (On the other hand, granite, slate, and soapstone are specific stones.) Featuring vivid color and figuration, marble is mainly found topping dressers, nightstands, and side tables, as well as kitchen countertops in contemporary applications.

Cleaning

Although you should avoid cleaning with strong detergent and solvents, including white vinegar, a natural soap such as Castile or Marseille is perfectly safe. Use warm water and a soft scrub brush. You'll be surprised at the amount of grime this removes: Your white Carrara tabletop will get back its alabaster sheen!

Protection

Old marble tops were usually hand-polished to a lower grade of shine than they are today. That honed aspect, though beautiful, leaves them vulnerable to damage; many stones are inherently porous and fragile.

- **PROTECTIVE SOLUTIONS** can be applied only to clean, thoroughly degreased marble; otherwise, you may wind up pushing any dirt into the surface of the stone. I actually like modern sealers, but only those purchased from stone specialists. Mention what variety stone you are sealing and that you require only light protection—nothing that will coat.

- **A BETTER OPTION IS TO USE CLEAR** (not amber or colored) beeswax made from bleached, virgin wax. Rub in a small amount, section by section, with a clean cloth. Wait an hour and buff to a light shine—just like waxing wood furniture!

- **BREAKS IN MARBLE TOPS ARE OFTEN CAUSED BY IMPROPER TRANSPORT.** The safest way to move and store marble is on its side (see "Transporting," page 294). Once placed back on top the piece, the slab must be perfectly flat; correct any tilting with shims. Never lean on a marble top, and avoid placing heavy objects on it; marble can actually bend over time.

Repair

Because marble tends to be very figured, repairs can often be hidden in the patterning of the veins. You can fix breaks and fissures with glue and various translucent and colored fillers—there are many specialized marble-repair products available—but it's really a job for the pros. (The exception: a small chip, and only if the marble has a low shine.) The filling, color matching, and repolishing execution have to be perfect for invisible results. And superstrong glues will ensure a longer life for your precious piece; this is one of the few cases in which I recommend using modern epoxy-based glues and very stable techniques.

Stains

- **OIL AND GREASE:** Mix plaster of Paris and water (about a 1:1 ratio) into a paste-like consistency and apply it to the stain. Let it dry for fifteen minutes. Then pour a little acetone or trichloroethylene onto the mixture, just enough to rewet it into a paste, and let it dry for a few hours. Remove the hardened paste with a wood or plastic spatula, so as not to scratch the stone, and rinse with water. Alternatively, make a paste by mixing Comet or a similar powdered cleaning agent with a small amount of water—just enough to keep the dough together. Apply the paste to the stain and cover it with plastic wrap, taping down the edges to lock in the moisture. Wait overnight and then wipe clean.

- **WINE, INK, AND OTHER COLORED STAINS:** Old stains are hard to erase but can often be lightened. Mix plaster of Paris with just enough bleach to create a paste, apply it to the stain, and let it sit overnight. Rinse the paste off with water and let the piece air-dry.

- **RUST AND WOOD TANNIN:** This is the only time you're permitted to use acid on stone! Wearing gloves, rub oxalic acid on the stain with a cotton swab. The spot will lighten. Rinse with water, then let the piece dry. Repeat the process as needed until the stain disappears.

TEAK

Teak director's chair

It's funny how furniture designed to withstand the elements for a season is often treated as no-maintenance furniture. The truth is that outdoor pieces, especially those made of teak or wicker, do require yearly maintenance for longevity. Teak's naturally oily composition gives it built-in protection from the elements, but sun and water can still combine to burn through its outer layer, resulting in a grayish cast. Although a desirable look to some, this patina is actually a sign of decay. Fortunately, it's reversible. If the wood surface, the joints, and the overall structure are sturdy and sound, the piece can be revived via a combination of cleaning and sanding to remove the sunburned superficial fibers. Note: This is an outdoor job and is best done in the shade.

WHAT YOU'LL NEED

- *Bucket*
- *Bleach*
- *Plastic scrub brush*
- *220- or 320-grit sandpaper*
- *100 percent cotton rags*
- *Wood alcohol*
- *Teak oil or tung oil*

Cleaning

1   **GIVE THE PIECE A THOROUGH WASH** with kitchen cleanser or water infused with bleach (1:1). Scrub carefully and rinse well. You will be amazed at the amount of grime you remove!

2   **DRY OVERNIGHT IN THE SHADE.**

3   **SAND CAREFULLY** with 220- or 320-grit sandpaper.

4   **WIPE THE WOOD CLEAN** with alcohol and a rag.

5   **APPLY A LIBERAL COAT OF TEAK OIL OR TUNG OIL.** Let it sink in and reapply where the wood is thirsty. Dry overnight.

6   **APPLY ONE MORE COAT OF OIL THE NEXT DAY** if you are a neurotic New Yorker like I am.

7   **STORE NEATLY** in a dry indoor spot until next season.

Maintenance

For yearly maintenance, wash and oil as above. Sanding will not be necessary every time if you maintain your teak furniture nicely. Such pieces will really last a lifetime. (To wit: Teak furniture from turn-of-the-century cruise liners can still be found at antiques shops.)

WICKER

Wicker is another popular material for vintage outdoor or porch furniture. The wicker category encompasses a number of woven organic materials: cane, rattan, willow, reed, rush, grasses, splints, etc. Give your wicker a good scrub every year. Aging does not result in a nice patina on wicker, so don't feel guilty about giving pieces a makeover! However, avoid varnishes or paint if possible, as wicker expands and contracts a lot, eventually cracking or peeling any hard finish. Before any new paint or varnish job, stripping will be necessary—and a nightmare to execute.

WHAT YOU'LL NEED

- *Castile or Marseille soap*
- *Scrub brush*
- *Linseed oil or liquefied paste wax*
- *100 percent cotton rags*

Cleaning

1 **WASH THOROUGHLY** with soapy water and let dry fully.

2 **TREAT TO A LIGHT SLICK OF LINSEED OIL OR A COAT OF WAX.** (Add a bit of turpentine to paste wax to make it more syrupy.) Let dry and buff to a pleasant shine. You may need to use a scrub brush to remove any excess wax lingering in the crevices of the weave.

WHAT YOU'LL NEED

- *Wood glue*
- *Thin brass nails*
- *Splint material*
- *X-Acto knife, razor blade, or sharp scissors*
- *220- to 320-grit sandpaper*
- *Oil-based stain*
- *Linseed oil*
- *100 percent cotton rags*

Maintenance

Wicker restoration is a long and painstaking process best left to professionals—especially for ornate and elaborate Victorian pieces. But if only small parts are damaged or missing, give it a try. Splint material can be purchased via fine-woodworking catalogs.

1 **REMOVE ANY BROKEN STRANDS** in their entirety.

2 **IF NEEDED, RESTORE THE FRAME STRUCTURALLY,** gluing and nailing it back together.

3 **SOAK THE SPLINT MATERIAL IN WATER** for about 30 minutes so it becomes pliable and workable.

4 **WEAVE IN THE REPLACEMENT PIECE,** and then glue and nail into place. Let dry.

5 **CUT AND ADJUST THE REPLACEMENT PIECE TO SIZE** using an X-Acto knife or sharp scissors.

6 **SAND THE REPAIRED AREA,** since the new splints' fibers get raised during the soak. Use 220- or 320-grit sandpaper.

7 **USE AN OIL-BASED STAIN OR GLAZE** to color the new splints to match the surrounding wicker.

8 **FINISH WITH A COAT OF TUNG OIL.** New fiber may suck up a lot before it says, "Enough!"

MAINTAINING YOUR ANTIQUES

Keeping your wood furniture in superior shape requires regular maintenance, mostly to clean and revive the finish. At the same time, you can check for any damage that has occurred. Most tasks are done on a monthly or yearly basis, but there are also daily precautions you can take to ensure sound condition. Among them is following proper transportation protocols; thus I've included tips on how to wrap and move your pieces.

PROTECTING YOUR PIECES

In addition to periodic cleaning, there are many precautions you can take to mitigate damage:

- **MAINTAIN A TEMPERATE CLIMATE IN YOUR HOME,** ensuring consistency from day to night and from season to season. Use humidifiers and dehumidifiers if needed.

- **SAVE THE MOISTURE CAPSULES AND PACKETS** found in new products and appliances, and place them inside drawers and cabinets.

- **KEEP FURNITURE AWAY FROM DIRECT SUNLIGHT,** which bleaches exposed surfaces and can crack or peel the finish, create a white haze, or otherwise damage the wood. Shut window treatments during the day or when you're away.

- **AVOID PLACING FURNITURE NEXT TO RADIATORS** and other heat sources.

- **USE FURNITURE FOR ITS INTENDED PURPOSE ONLY.** Don't use chairs as footstools or ladders, or tables as ironing boards!

- **AVOID DAMP OR WET SPOTS.**

- **DON'T STORE FURNITURE** in the attic (too dry) or in the basement (too wet).

THE PERFECT COASTER

Always use coasters when placing drinks, plants, or flower vases on wood surfaces. Otherwise, moisture can seep into the finish and penetrate the wood itself, creating a water ring or a ghostly haze. (The finishing coat is still fine; the damage is actually underneath.)

Not just any coaster will do—plastic and cork can mark the wood, and fabrics don't block moisture. However, combining those three materials creates a superior safeguard, so I suggest you make your own coasters. Assemble three layers with white glue in this order:

TOP: Plastic, metal, or glass water barrier. I often make special coasters for clients, featuring a decorative treatment like silver leaf as the waterproof top layer.

MIDDLE: Cork for cushioning

BOTTOM: Felt (its smooth surface will not leave a mark)

DAILY

Unless your house is egregiously dirty or exposed to the elements—or you're an obsessive neat freak—daily maintenance of your wood furniture is not required. Simple dusting is enough, as needed. Avoid using over-the-counter products like sprays, which serve no purpose and can create a greasy buildup—which, ironically, attracts *more* dirt. A feather duster is preferable, since even a dusting cloth used daily increases the chance of damaging furniture.

MONTHLY

Wipe the piece with a soft, clean rag—preferably felt or used cotton, which minimizes lint dispersion. Use a light hand to avoid snagging on any splinters or lifted parts in the wood. The monthly cleaning is also a good time to assess the condition of the piece, noting and addressing any wormholes or dust piles, water or sun damage, loose parts, etc.

Inspect furniture from every angle by moving it around and/or away from the wall. When you live with a piece, it's easy to overlook changes, and degradation becomes routine.

YEARLY

Whatever type of furniture and finish you have, I do not recommend using products (wax, oil) on it more than once or twice a year. The exception: kitchen tables and other utilitarian pieces subject to abundant wear and tear.

Dust the piece carefully before using any polish, wax, or cleaner so you don't push dirt particles into the finish.

PACKING

You need to pack furniture every time you move it—yes, *every* time! By which I mean not just when relocating to a new house, but also when carrying it from room to room. Protection is key, as is properly wrapping the piece. In addition, the wrapping materials should be safe and not damage your piece or its finish. To wit:

- **NEVER USE BUBBLE WRAP** directly on wood—doing so could ruin a finish!

- **ALWAYS WRAP DELICATE PIECES** in glassine or tissue paper before using moving blankets, which are quite heavy and can rub off corners or details. Upholstered pieces should be wrapped first in a special type of plastic bag reserved for this purpose (see Resources, page 296).

- **NEVER USE TAPE DIRECTLY ON THE WOOD** or any part of the furniture.

- **AS ALWAYS, DON'T CHEAT OR SKIMP**—or you'll be sorry!

WHAT YOU'LL NEED

- *Clean blankets (multiple)*
- *Box cutter or scissors (for cutting tissue and tape)*
- *Glassine or tissue paper*
- *Packing tape (no masking tape)*
- *Shrink wrap (optional)*

Wrapping Furniture

1   **PLACE SHIMS IN DRAWERS TO KEEP THEM SHUT TIGHT,** and protect feet with cardboard.

2   **HAVE TWO PEOPLE LIFT** and move the piece.

3   **CENTER THE PIECE** on a blanket.

4   **WRAP IN GLASSINE** or tissue paper (see Resources, page 296).

5   **FOLD UP THE CORNERS** and sides of the blanket.

6   **WRAP TAPE AROUND SEVERAL TIMES,** pulling tight.

7   **CENTER A NEW BLANKET** on the piece.

8   **FOLD DOWN THE SIDES AND CORNERS;** they should extend over the lower blanket.

9   **AGAIN, WRAP TAPE AROUND SEVERAL TIMES,** pulling tight.

10   **WRAP THE BLANKETED PIECE WITH SHRINK WRAP** for extra reinforcement.

11   **TIME TO MOVE!**

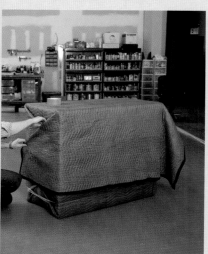

TRANSPORTING

Moving—whether from room to room or home to home—is one of the most common causes of damage to your furniture. Avoid many mistakes by following a few simple rules and abiding by common sense:

- **NEVER SLIDE A PIECE OF FURNITURE FROM ONE SPOT TO ANOTHER.** It will damage the legs or feet (especially turned and curved designs), destabilize the joinery, and unsettle the construction—not to mention scratch and dent your floor.

- **ALWAYS LIFT THE PIECE,** which may require two people.

- **LIFT FROM THE BOTTOM OR THE SIDES,** never from the top.

- **NEVER HOLD A PIECE OF FURNITURE BY ITS HARDWARE.**

- **REMOVE ALL LOOSE SHELVES BEFORE HANDLING** and lock all drawers and doors, which could swing open. Same with moving or loose parts like crown molding and finials.

- **REMOVE MARBLE TOPS AND STORE THEM ON THEIR SIDE,** never flat. Same for moving: always on their side.

- **KEYS ARE EASILY MISPLACED OR LOST DURING MOVES.** Rather than place them in your pocket, tape keys inside one drawer of the piece (locking as many others as you can), and close it tight with a little paper shim before wrapping and packing.

- **PACK AND WRAP THE PIECE OF FURNITURE WHERE IT IS**—even if moving from one room to another. This is the best way to avoid banging it into doorways, handrails, and other furniture—the most frequent cause of damage.

- **SIMILARLY, TELL PROFESSIONAL MOVERS TO WRAP THE PIECE IN FRONT OF YOU.** If they say, "We'll wrap it in the truck," you have two responses: (1) "No!" or (2) "Write down on the receipt that you packed it outside." I guarantee they'll come back very quickly with a couple of blankets.

- **NEVER TRANSPORT A PIECE OF FURNITURE ON TOP OF A CAR, PERIOD!** Save that for your bikes and skis. Don't be tempted; professionals don't do it, so why would you? (Although, remind me to tell you about the time my father was transporting two tables on his truck; he approached a bridge . . .)

- **DO NOT MOVE ON RAINY DAYS;** humidity is bad for furniture and you risk water damage.

- **IN THE CAR OR TRUCK, LAY PIECES PERFECTLY FLAT ON THEIR BACK SIDE** and settle with rags and blankets. Secure with pads and blankets.

- **USE STRAPS, NEVER ROPES,** which are round and could cut into the wood.

- **FINALLY, DO NOT TEXT WHILE YOU DRIVE!**

RESOURCES

A&H ABRASIVES
800-831-6066
Sanding supplies.

ALLIED PIANOS
www.alliedpianos.com
Piano and furniture restoration
and fine-refinishing supplies.

BEHLEN'S PRODUCTS
This U.K.-based company makes
a comprehensive and reliable
line of fine-refinishing products
retailed by all wood-product
catalogs and websites.

THE BROOM BROTHERS
www.thebroombrothers.com
Great handmade brushes and brooms;
makers of the wax-burnishing tool
featured in the dry-wax rub technique
on page 204.

CHEAP JOE'S ART STUFF
www.cheapjoes.com
Paints, pigments, papers, brushes,
and more—with frequent sales
and discounts.

CONSOLIDATED PLASTICS
www.consolidatedplastics.com
Nice source of bottles and containers
for storing products and mixes.

DECORATOR'S SUPPLY
www.decoratorssupply.com
Has manufactured and supplied classic
architectural detailing—including
composition moldings for furniture and
mantelpieces—since the 1880s. Also a
great reference for period ornaments.

DIRECT SAFETY
www.directsafety.com
Go here for eye protection, masks,
and gloves.

ETSY
www.etsy.com
Need a hand-turned finial, organic
cleaning product, or one-of-a-kind some
such? Try Etsy! I do, and I get lucky most
of the time.

GAMBLIN
Quality line of classic solvents, resins,
varnishes, and gums used in period
finishes. Found in all art-supply stores.

GARRETT WADE
www.garrettwade.com
Comprehensive and stylish retailer of
quality hand tools and finishing supplies.
I've used their goods since I first moved
to New York. (It's in Garret Wade's
Spring Street showroom that I learned
the English translations of my French
restoration-trade vocabulary!)

GRACIOUS HOME
www.gracioushome.com
Much more than hardware, it's a full
housewares resource—one of the first
to carry exotic and specialty products,
including great furniture-care items.

HIGHLAND WOODWORKING
www.highlandwoodworking.com
Source for quality hand tools and
project supplies.

LEE VALLEY & VERITAS
www.leevalley.com
Mail-order and retail supplier of
woodworking and gardening tools
as well as cabinet hardware.

LIBERON PRODUCTS
Great line of traditional wood-finishing products made in the U.K. and retailed via myriad suppliers and websites.

LIE-NIELSEN TOOL WORKS
www.lie-nielsen.com
Offers a range of high-quality hand tools for woodworking. Ideal resource for your first block plane!

MASTERPAK
www.masterpak-usa.com
A catalog of unique and archival materials for the packaging, shipping, storing, and displaying of fine art, artifacts, and antiques.

MOHAWK FINISHING PRODUCTS
www.mohawk-finishing.com
Touch-up and repair products for wood and leather.

NORTHERN SAFETY AND INDUSTRIAL
www.northernsafety.com
Safety and protection supplier.

PERGAMENA
www.pergamena.net
Great supplier of leather, parchment, etc. Even if you never need to use those materials, the site is super informative and the Meyers family will always take your calls and answer questions about leather.

SENNELIER
A high-quality line of classic art items—especially fine paints, colors, and pigments—found in all fine art-supply stores.

SEPP LEAF
www.seppleaf.com
Offers genuine gold and metal leaf, gilding tools, and supplies, as well as products from the aforementioned Liberon line.

SUTHERLAND WELLES
www.sutherlandwelles.com
Makers of the best tung-oil finish, plus all other wood-finishing needs, from nontoxic food-safe finishes to waterproof marine spar varnish. Nicest people to order from. (For years, you'd pay only after receiving your products!)

SWARMBUSTIN' HONEY
www.swarmbustinhoney.com
Based in Chester County, Pennsylvania, Walt Broughton makes the best honey! Also fab: pure beeswax for mixing your own furniture polish and finishing products.

TALAS
www.talasonline.com
Great source of conservation, preservation, and restoration supplies—as well as information and advice.

ULINE
www.uline.com
Boxes, shelves, containers, cleaning products . . . everything you need to start converting a spot in your garage (or anywhere else) into a wood-finishing studio.

VAN DYKE'S RESTORERS
www.vandykes.com
Although this resource used to carry more woodworking and finishing supplies, it now focuses on period furniture and house-fixture hardware.

WATERLOX
www.waterlox.com
Great tung-oil-based products for interior and exterior applications. Purchase via their website or other retailers.

WHITECHAPEL LTD.
www.whitechapel-ltd.com
The place for perfect, high-end historic reproduction hardware. Every style, every period—iron or brass! I use the brand's products for everything that I don't order custom from France. That says it all!

WOODWORKER'S SUPPLY
www.woodworker.com
An extensive catalog for tools and products: wood, metal, leather restoration, caning, and much more.

FURTHER READING

These are not technical finishing books but tomes (and a periodical) that can help enrich your knowledge of furniture and decorative arts history via the quality and expertise of the artisans and experts who wrote them. This reading list will help you discover past worlds that remain present through the artisans who carry on their crafts.

THE ANTIQUE COLLECTOR'S CLUB
Publisher of art-reference books on antique furniture—by period or country.

ASSOULINE
This publisher has a great series of books on 20th-century designers and decorators—from Jean-Michel Frank to Eileen Gray—who used many of the techniques highlighted in this book in the context of modern interiors.

L'ART DU MENUISIER (THE ART OF THE JOINER), BY ANDRÉ J. ROUBO
This is the first systematic historic compilation of traditional, 18th-century cabinetmaking, written by an old master. Reeditions and online copies are easily found. Offers an incredible sum of knowledge and beautiful etched illustrations.

AUTHENTIC DECOR: THE DOMESTIC INTERIOR 1620–1920, BY PETER THORNTON (CRESCENT BOOKS)
An exhaustive way to set pieces of furniture back in their period rooms. You can learn a lot about furniture by looking at the way it was set. A classic!

CLASSICAL FURNITURE, BY DAVID LINLEY (HARRY N. ABRAMS)
Classicism in European furniture by a fine furniture maker and designer.

CLASSIC WOOD FINISHING, BY GEORGE FRANK (STERLING PUBLISHING)
A classic by an old master of traditional techniques and a great innovator in wood decorative finishes, always with an artisanal twist and plenty of anecdotes.

COMPENDIUM OF INTERIOR STYLES, BY FRANÇOIS BAUDOT (ASSOULINE)
A comprehensive and easy chronological overview of classic historical styles.

DORURE ET POLYCHROMIE SUR BOIS, BY GILLES PERRAULT (ÉDITIONS FATON)
Classic gilding techniques—from water to oil—as well as traditional paints, written by a restorer of the Château de Versailles.

FINE WOODWORKING
This trade magazine highlights cabinetry projects with a traditional twist, and every issue includes an editorial about finishes.

LIBRAIRIE DU CAMÉE
www.librairieducamee.com
This small shop in Paris's Saint-Germain-des-Prés neighborhood has every book you could want about furniture styles, gilding, ceramics, crafts, and decorative arts, both old and new.

LA MARQUETERIE DE PAILLE, BY LISON DE CAUNES AND CATHERINE BAUMGARTNER (ÉDITIONS VIAL)
A book about straw marquetry penned by the French high priestess of the trade: the granddaughter of famed Art Deco cabinetmaker André Groult.

A MARQUETRY ODYSSEY: HISTORICAL OBJECTS AND PERSONAL WORK, BY SILAS KOPF (CHAMELEON BOOKS)
Learn from a reputed master why marquetry was called "painting in wood." This book intertwines historic knowledge with personal creative work.

PERIOD FINISHES AND EFFECTS, BY JUDITH AND MARTIN MILLER (RIZZOLI)
A classic book on wood techniques and decorative painting, with an emphasis on aged finishes. One of the first and only books to contextualize these techniques in a decorative setting.

SAVOIR REFAIRE SES SIÈGES SOI-MÊME, BY RAPHAËL-DIDIER DE L'HOMMEL (OUEST FRANCE)
Classic upholstery with step-by-step before-and-after photos and great settings to inspire.

UNDERSTANDING WOOD: A CRAFTSMAN'S GUIDE TO WOOD TECHNOLOGY, BY R. BRUCE HOADLEY (THE TAUNTON PRESS)
Read all about the fascinating universe of wood to determine what you can do with the material and finishes.

VENEERING SIMPLIFIED, BY HARRY JASON HOBBS (ALBERT CONSTANTINE AND SON, INC.)
A small book about the history and progression of veneer techniques that reads like a novel.

ACKNOWLEDGMENTS

Many thanks to Martha Stewart for her continual support and inspiration, and to Kevin Sharkey.

To Suzanne Williams and Jerry Howard, who put everything in motion.

To my agents, Jennifer Griffin and Sharon Bowles, for their great work.

To Lia Ronnen, Jessica Bloom, Michelle Ishay-Cohen, Sibylle Kazeroid, Kara Strubel, and Nancy Murray for the talent, drive, and ambition they put into this project.

To Jen Renzi and James Wade for their talent, artistry, and patience.

To all my New York City; Sharon, Connecticut; and overseas friends, family, and clients who gave so much support and material to these pages.

To my father, Christian Pourny, and my uncle, Pierre Madel, for introducing me to the magic of antiques.

To the artisans in my studio, especially Khristian Guilcatanda.

To John Saladino, who gave me my first big break in this country.

To David Kleinberg and Associates, for their passion for artisans.

To longtime supporter *Elle Decor*, the first magazine to publish my work, and Wendy Goodman.

To Garrett Wade and Whitechapel Ltd. for graciously providing tools and hardware, respectively.

To Jason Jobson, partner in life and in crime, as we say in French.

INDEX

Fig. 8

Fig. 7

Fig. 3

Fig. 5

Fig. 4

Fig. 6

Fig. 2

Fig. 1